Bequest of
Father Stephen Lee
Member of
Theology Faculty

1968 – 1995

Buddhist and Taoist Studies I

Buddhist and Taoist Studies 1

定　價：新臺幣　　　　元

David W. Chappell
Michael Saso

編著者：

發行所：南　天　書　局　有　限　公　司

登記證字號：行政院新聞局局版臺業字第一四三六號

出版者：南　天　書　局　有　限　公　司

臺北市虎林街一○八巷一○二號
電　話：七六七一四二六○
臺北市郵政信箱三六一二三號

印刷者：太　一　彩　色　印　刷　公　司
台北市重慶北路三段233巷14號

中華民國六十七年二月景印

SOUTHERN MATERIALS CENTER, INC.

P. O. Box 36-22 Taipei, Republic of China.

Asian Studies at Hawaii, No. 18

Buddhist and Taoist Studies I

Edited by Michael Saso
and David W. Chappell

ASIAN STUDIES PROGRAM
UNIVERSITY OF HAWAII
THE UNIVERSITY PRESS OF HAWAII

Copyright © 1977 by The University Press of Hawaii
Manufactured in the United States of America

Library of Congress Cataloging in Publication Data
Main entry under title:

Buddhist and Taoist studies.

  (Asian studies at Hawaii ; no. 18)
  Bibliography: p.
  Includes index.
  1. Buddhism—Addresses, essays, lectures.
2. Taoism—Addresses, essays, lectures. I. Saso,
Michael R. II. Chappell, David W., 1940–
III. Series.
DS3.A2A82 no. 18 [BQ4055] 950'.08s [294.3]
ISBN 0-8248-0420-1   77-21729

Figures 4.1, 4.2, 4.3, and 5.1—photographs courtesy of Michael Saso.

Figures 1.1, 3.1, 3.2, 3.3, 5.2, 5.3, 5.4, and 5.5—line art executed by the University of Hawaii Instructional Resources Services Center for the Department of Religion, University of Hawaii.

Contents

Figures

Preface

The essays presented in the following pages were selected from papers delivered near or on the occasion of the Asian Studies on the Pacific Coast annual conference, held at the Manoa campus of the University of Hawaii from June 19 through June 21, 1975. The volume is entitled *Buddhist and Taoist Studies I* because other volumes are planned for the series of dialogues which are initiated here in the public forum. The methodologies used by Buddhist and Taoist scholars are similar enough to be included in a single volume as a sort of collaborative effort beneficial to both disciplines. The topics are, however, different enough to merit an introductory note of explanation. Thus, the state of Buddhist studies is highly advanced, the sources in the Buddhist Canon safely dated, and the scholarly articles on refined topics many. The state of Taoist studies on the other hand is almost the reverse of that of Buddhist studies. The texts of the Taoist Canon are for the most part not critically dated, Taoist studies have become popular almost within the last decade, and articles on religious Taoism can still be counted in a simple bibliography.

The present work, comprising five essays and an extended bibliography, mainly emphasizes Taoist studies, though the chapter by Professor David Chappell is wholly concerned with the Pure Land tradition of Chinese Buddhism. The underlying theme of the book, however, is neither Buddhism nor Taoism, but the manifestation of these two religious movements in China. Buddhism and Taoism are essential ingredients of that third entity which often goes unnamed, the religious beliefs of the men and women of traditional China. Whether called "folk religion" or "Chinese popular religion" or simply the belief system of the Chinese people, the basic structure of Chinese religious thought must be sought in neither the Pure Lands of Buddhism nor the esoterica of Taoism, but in the popular yin-yang five element cosmology of the masses. It is this latter world view which acts as the basic background for the Chinese view of the cosmos, and which occurs over and over in the essays by Thomas Boehmer, John Keupers, Duane Pang, and myself. The threefold division of the Chinese cosmos into Heaven, the realm of pure yang; Earth, the visible world of yin and yang in combination; and the Underworld, the stygian darkness dominated by yin, informs both the imported notions of the Buddhist Pure Land heavens and the underground stages of Taoist hells, described in the second and the fifth chapters below.

Collaborative studies of Buddhism and Taoism, as is true of many topics in Chinese studies, have been pioneered by the great Japanese sinologists, whose works appear in the extensive bibliography at the end of the volume. Among these the most noted scholar is Professor Kubo Noritada, director emeritus of the Tōyō Bunka Kenkyū Jō, of Tokyo University and publisher of a number of major works on religious Taoism, some of which appear in the bibliography. Professors Fukui Kōjun, Yoshioka Yoshitoyo, Ōbuchi Ninji, and Kamata Shigeo, all practicing Buddhist monks, have also contributed major works concerning the dating of texts in the Taoist Canon, the influence of Buddhist texts on religious Taoism, and other related topics. Professor Kamata has pointed out many passages in the Taoist Canon which contain the documents of Mādhyamika, Yogācāra, Fa-hsiang, and other major schools of Buddhism. Though remarkable for a sense of doctrinal unity in the explanation of the teachings of religious Taoism, the Taoist Canon was also used as a repository for Buddhist texts in China. Thus Buddhist and Taoist alike have benefited from the collaborative study of the two disciplines.

The first chapter of this volume, my essay on Buddhist and Taoist notions of transcendence, owes much for its inspiration to the teachings of the Mao Shan Shang-ch'ing sect of Taoist meditation, as taught in present-day Taiwan. The Taoist master Chuang-ch'en Teng-yün, whose library collection has been partially published in the *Chuang-lin Hsü Tao-tsang* (Taipei: Ch'eng-wen Press, 1975) represents the orthodox Mao Shan tradition of meditative alchemy as transmitted for some thirty-six generations, that is circa late T'ang, and preserved in the clan archives since that period. It is interesting to note that the text of the *Tao-te Ching* and the *Chuang-tzu Nei-p'ien* play an important role in the teachings of this sect, as do the cryptic writings of the *Yellow Court Canon,* quoted in the text. In the traditions of the orthodox Mao Shan order of Taoists, ritual is but a visible manifestation of the meditations of internal alchemy, performed by the priest during the grand liturgies of renewal.

In the second essay, David Chappell, Assistant Professor of Buddhism in the Department of Religion at the University of Hawaii, presents a careful and clear analysis of Pure Land Buddhism as it influenced four great thinkers of the early middle ages, that is, fifth- to seventh-century Buddhism in China. Seng Chao (A.D. 375–414), Hui-yüan (523–592), Chih-i (538–597) and Tao-ch'o (562–645) were deeply influenced by the notions of the Pure Land tradition. A common stock of Pure Land ideas was used by many Buddhist masters of fifth- and sixth-century sects. Professor Chappell concludes that in emphasizing the notion of a Pure Land, the degree of confidence which the devotee had concerning his own salvation was more important than the doctrines or philosophies of opposing schools.

In the third chapter graduate student Thomas Boehmer, a major in Asian religions at the University of Hawaii, analyzes the symbols of Chinese alchemy from the viewpoint of internal or meditative alchemy. Much of the inspiration for Boehmer's article came from the monumental work of Dr. Joseph Needham, *Science and Civilisation in China,* especially the second part of volume V, *Alchemy and Chemistry*. The article represents a clear and concise effort to analyze the symbols of the little-known meditative aspects of internal alchemy.

The fourth chapter represents a first attempt in English to describe the intricate rituals of the Lü Shan "Red Head" order of popular Taoist exorcists. This is far more than a simple description of a Chinese exorcism, however, since the roots of popular ritual, as opposed to the classical orthodox liturgies of renewal, are clearly delineated in John Keupers' well-written essay. Keupers, who earned a doctorate in religious studies from the University of Louvain, has spent many years in Taiwan doing research into Taoist ritual in both north and south areas of the island. From his rich experience both the casual reader and the fieldworker are given the necessary tools for distinguishing the "orthodox" from the popular, the alchemical meditative from the popular exorcist tradition. The origin of Red Head exorcism is traced to the Sung dynasty charlatan Lin Ling-su, a Taoist from Fukien province, who ingratiated himself with the Hui Tsung emperor.

In the fifth chapter Duane Pang, also a graduate student in Asian religions at the University of Hawaii, presents a finely drawn analysis of a complete Taoist *P'u-tu* ritual for freeing the souls in a general amnesty from the stygian depths of the underworld. Pang's essay also is a timely "first" effort in the study of religious Taoism in western languages, since it deals with a rite which is obviously inspired by Buddhism, but with a peculiarly Taoist purpose; that is to say, the souls in the underworld are freed from torments not to be recycled into Buddhist *saṁsāra,* but to be wafted to the heavens in the floating of lanterns set adrift in the sea. The article owes a great debt to the Taoist masters Li Han and Albert Ch'en, both Wu-tang Shan experts practicing in the Chinese community of Honolulu. Duane Pang himself has performed as *Fu-chiang* or assistant cantor in the ritual which he describes, and is destined to become a Taoist ritual expert for the Honolulu community after spending the next few years in Taiwan in pursuit of further Taoist lore and legerdemain.

The dialogue begun in *Buddhist and Taoist Studies I* is to be continued in a second volume now in manuscript. In this forthcoming work the emphasis shifts to Buddhist topics, balancing the Taoist preponderance here. The ecumenical research invoked by the common study of Buddhism and Taoism has a far-reaching purpose, which goes beyond the convening of a handful of scholars and the presentation of seminar research. It is in a spirit of sharing a global heritage, of understanding the Asian mind in the humanistic as well as the sociological sense and making that heritage known, that the present small volume of essays is presented. It is hoped that the dialogue can be continued and expanded.

Michael Saso
University of Hawaii at Manoa

Buddhist and Taoist Studies I

1 Buddhist and Taoist Ideas of Transcendence: A Study in Philosophical Contrast

MICHAEL SASO

Chinese religion is basically secular. That is to say, it is concerned mainly with offering prayers of petition for good things, prayers of atonement to avoid evil, and prayers of thanks for material benefits received. Though the prayer of mystical union with the transcendent ultimate power of nature is not missing in the acts of worship or adoration of the common man, religious experience is normally associated with prayers or rituals aimed at attaining blessing of some sort. In offering acts of ritual worship, the Chinese layman and laywoman can call upon either of two classes of religious mediators, the Buddhist or the Taoist priest. To the layperson, these two distinct types of religious functionaries are theoretically different in their approaches to the transcendent, though the choice of Taoist or Buddhist most often depends on which is the nearest or most accessible at the time of ritual need. Thus the Chinese perceive the roles of Buddhist and Taoist as complementary: the former is more concerned with the afterlife and holds a monistic view of the cosmos (only the world of union is real, the present material world is illusory), while the latter is basically dualistic and believes in the reality and relative goodness of the visible world while seeking union with the transcendent through mystic prayer.[1]

That the notions of transcendence held by the Taoist and the Buddhist priest are indeed different is the subject of the following pages. More specifically I shall try to show that the religious Taoist (as opposed to the philosophical Taoist) differs basically from his Buddhist counterpart in explaining the cosmos and in seeking union with the transcendent originator of nature. Buddhism, on the other hand, in the form which became popular in China, emphasized the importance of the next life.[2]

Though the real Buddha may have taught a different doctrine, to the Chinese believers the Buddha himself came to be thought of as a transcendent being. The doctrine of the bodhisattva, who denies himself ultimate Nirvāna until all sentient beings are enlightened, and the doctrine of the Pure Land, where ultimate salvation is worked out after death, gradually dominated the minds of the believers in devotional or popular forms of religious Buddhism.

The Mahāyāna school of Buddhist teachings emphasizes the ideas of transcendence and an afterlife on the philosophical as well as on the devotional level. The original rejection of metaphysical speculation by the Buddha was reversed by both Indian and Chinese scholars. For the scholar-monk in China, philosophical discourse became a particularly effective way to win the hearts of the intellectual literati and, therefore, the approval of the reluctant mandarin class for the foreign doctrines from India. Whether seen from the one philosophical extreme of the Mādhyamika *(San-lun),* which denied the epistemological possibility of conceiving the absolute, or the other extreme of the Yogācāra, which identified the enlightened mind with the transcendent Buddha nature, all of the Mahāyāna schools had ultimately to admit the inexpressible reality of the transcendent while denying the substantiality of the phenomenal aspects of nature. Whether understood by logic or intuition, the transcendent aspects of the Buddha and the illusory aspects of phenomenal existents were essential doctrines of Buddhism in China.

Though the Buddhist metaphysicians in China saw little in religious Taoism that was in any way acceptable or similar to their own beliefs, they did find the writings of certain early Taoist philosophers, specifically the *Lao-tzu* and the *Chuang-tzu,* particularly useful for the interpretation of certain Buddhist ideas and sometimes for the translation of Buddhist terminology into Chinese. Just as the emperors legitimized their reigns by appealing to the texts of classical antiquity (whether these texts were of Confucian or Taoist origin depended on the politics of the time), so too the Buddhists found it helpful to cite both Confucian and Taoist classics as a means of winning both popular and official approval. In this regard the highly difficult and esoteric texts of the *Chuang-tzu* and the more politically oriented work of the *Lao-tzu* were among the more important books for the interpretation of such basic notions as transcendence, *wu;* and void, *k'ung* or *hsü (śūnya).*

Taoist texts seem to have been used more commonly during the earlier years of the North-South period (ca. A.D. 265–281). The coming of Kumārajīva, the famous monk from central Asia, occasioned a turning point in the use of Taoist texts in a Buddhist context.[3] Kumārajīva disagreed with two of his supporters, Hui-yüan and Seng-chao, over the proper interpretation of the term *śūnya,* or *k'ung,* in the philosophy of the Mādhyamika. The commentaries of Seng-chao and more especially of Hui-yüan are filled with quotes from the *Chuang-tzu.* So, too, later Ch'an or Zen masters delighted in pointing to such passages in the *Chuang-tzu* as that where the Tao is likened to the pile of dung by the gate as inspirations for Buddhist notions of sudden enlightenment. By stamping on the ground or holding up a simple writing brush, the master teaches the disciple that "there, but for the illusory aspects, is the Buddha, true substance, *tathatā,* the transcendent, *wu.*"

Whatever the meaning of the Mādhyamika as interpreted by Kumārajīva and Hui-yüan, or of the intuitive insights of later Zen masters, the reaction of the Taoists to an appropriation of the *Chuang-tzu* was hostile. To the followers of the religious Taoist persuasion the identification of Brahman with Ātman, or self with the Tao, was certainly repugnant if not downright mistaken. The external world was illusory only as an object misrepresented to the senses as final cause; that is, as being worthy of pursuit by the grasping will or as a means of satisfying the external senses. Men and women, in running after the pleasures of the external world or in joining in its conflicts, are wasteful of breath and vital essence and thus are brought to quick death from overweening self-seeking and desire. In the Taoist view of the microcosmic process, the loss of breath and vital essence leads ultimately to exhaustion and the departure of spirit. The loss of the three life-principles brings death. Even though the Tao of Transcendence is everywhere generating, both within the microcosm of man as well as in the dung by the gate, it certainly is not identical with the object generated. Transcendent dualism came to typify the early philosophy of religious Taoism.

The philosophy of religious Taoism is, therefore, basically dualistic. The forty-second chapter of the *Lao-tzu* indicates that the Tao of Transcendence was seen to be five steps removed from the world of phenomenal existence:

The Tao gave birth to the One;
The One gave birth to the Two;
The Two gave birth to the Three;
The Three gave birth to the myriad [visible] creatures.[4]

The doctrine expressed in the opening chapters of the *Lao-tzu* indicates that the world is divided between the realms of the transcendent, *wu,* and the generated, *yu.* Expressed in the words of the *Chuang-tzu,* the state of the Tao is one of permanence, *i,* while that of the world "within the four seas" is one of relativity, impermanence or change, *hua.* There was in fact no denial of the reality of the visible world, nor initially was there a definition of its actuality as leading away from the Tao. The philosophy of the *Lao-tzu* and *Chuang-tzu,* then, was not properly understood by the Buddhists.

If the two philosophies were so divergent, one might well ask why that of the Taoist never found a vocal champion. How, indeed, was it possible that the informed literati did not contradict the textually incorrect interpretations of the Buddhists? The answer is far more complex than a simple drawing of intellectual boundaries and a choosing of philosophical sides would indicate. There is sufficient reason to believe, on the one hand, that the Confucian historians did not care about the doctrines of religious Taoism, and, on the other hand, that the Taoists were successful enough in preserving their secrets as to make no noticeable impact on the writers of dynastic histories.[5] The answer therefore probably lies within the nature of esoteric religion itself. The very strength and enduring qualities of religious Taoism were preserved in the transmission of its own traditions and doctrines quite apart from the world of Confucianism or Buddhism. It was in its popular and colorful liturgy of renewal that religious Taoism survived among the people and in the courts of the emperors. Perhaps one can see both commoner and emperor allied in a sort of common-sense lack of interest in the Buddhist and Confucian intellectual tradition. Just as the common man or woman of China rejected the philosophies of the Mādhyamika and the Yogācāra for the pleasures of the western heavens, so too ruler and ruled alike supported the colorful *Ling-pao* liturgies of the religious Taoist, which expressed in visible, concrete, and dramatic form the doctrines of the yin-yang five element cosmology.[6]

Whatever the attitude of the people and the court to the splendors of Taoist festive ritual, an examination of the earliest Taoist Canon clearly shows that the philosophical aspects of transcendent dualism were not neglected. The explanations of religious philosophy were, rather, esoteric, and thus were not made public or championed before the Confucian or the plagiarizing Buddhist. The highest social circles of the Six Kingdoms period did seek avidly for such esoteric Taoist texts as the *Yellow Court Canon.* But this difficult text was almost unintelligible without the oral interpretations, or *k'ou-chüeh,* of a master. The esoteric texts of religious Taoism were transmitted as a part of the rite of investiture or ordination of a new Taoist. The ordinandus was made to write out the text of the master and then to compare it meticulously with the original to avoid copyist error. The philosophy of transcendental dualism was, therefore, a part of the esoteric transmission; whereas to the external world of the ritual-loving masses, the elite mandarins, and the imperial court, the Taoists taught the cosmological doctrines of the yin-yang five-element theory. Thus, the philosophy of religious Taoism was transmitted as an esoteric, canonical tradition, not doctrinally divergent from the yin-yang five-element theory. The esoteric doctrines were taught only after initiation into a specific Taoist order.[7]

Whereas Buddhism in China, at least during the North-South period and through the Sui and T'ang dynasties, was noted for its wealth of schools and divergent philosophical traditions, the Taoist movements during the same period were noted for their strong sense of doctrinal ecumenism. From the time of Lu Hsiu-ching (d. A.D. 477) and the formation of the first canon, the three earliest Taoist movements were united into a textual *sarvayāna,* or "all in one," vehicle of doctrinal transmission.[8] The three sources of Taoist unity were the earliest Heavenly Master, or *Meng-wei,* tradition; the *Ling-pao* court ritual tradition; and the meditative *Shang-ch'ing* sect founded atop Mao Shan, or Mount Mao, in central China. By the sixth century these three groups were united into a single, classical tradition, undisturbed by factionalism or doctrinal divergence until the meddling of the Hui-tsung emperor and the approval of the heterodox *Shen-hsiao* order of Lin Ling-su in A.D. 1118; that is to say, the philosophy of transcendent dualism united the various Taoist movements into a canonical ecumenism until well into the Sung period.[9]

The Taoist Canon clearly shows that the three earliest religious Taoist movements were separated more by spatial than by doctrinal differences. The development of religious Taoist movements began during the later Han period and reached a zenith by A.D. 370 in the early part of the North-South period. The oldest of the traditions, the Heavenly Master tradition, developed in the kingdom of Shu, or modern-day Szechuan. It was typified by a highly literate hierarchy that used Han dynasty administrative terms to found a new spiritual administration throughout parts of Szechuan and the southern part of Shensi province. Imitating the visible court system of the earlier Han empire, members of this hierarchy sent documents, memorials, and rescripts through the spiritual bureaucracies of the heavens, earth, and underworld. The golden age of China's past was reconstructed in the spiritual order. Two special rituals called *ch'u-kuan* and *fa-lu,* in which the spirits within the microcosm were "exteriorized" or sent out, emptied the center of man for the encounter with the eternal Tao of Transcendence.[10] Only after the spirits had been sent out could the Taoist initiate ritual ceremony and address documents and petitions to the spirits of the highest heavenly courts. The *Meng-wei* tradition developed the doctrine of the Three Pure Ones, *San-ch'ing,* who were symbolic personifications of the three life-principles of breath, *ch'i;* vital essence, *ching;* and spirit, *shen.*

The second of the early Taoist movements, the *Ling-pao* tradition, developed in the southern and eastern provinces of the Three Kingdoms and the North-South period in China. Somehow related to the *T'ai-p'ing* movement, the Yellow Turban rebels, as well as to the *Book of the Great Peace* of Yü Chi, the *Ling-pao* movement made use of the apocryphal *Ch'an-wei* texts to construct a magnificent ritual of renewal known as *chin-lu chiao* and a burial liturgy called *huang-lu chai* modeled on the court ritual described in the *Yüeh-ling* chapter of the *Book of Rites*. The famous *Ling-pao Five Talismans,* which are foreshadowed in the *Ho-t'u* chapter of the Apocryphal texts, became the basic esoteric document of *Ling-pao* liturgy.[11] At a very early date, probably by the time of Lu Hsiu-ching, in the mid fourth century, the *Ling-pao* rites of renewal (Gold Register *chiao* festival) and burial (Yellow Register *chai* burial) adapted the *fa-lu* ritual of exteriorizing the spirits and the sending off of documents to the three realms as an essential part of its public liturgy.[12] Thus the two early Taoist movements were unified in ritual practice before the completion of the *Wu-shang Pi-yao,* A.D. 577.

The third early Taoist movement was established between A.D. 366 and 370 on Mao Shan near Nanking in central China.[13] The sect took for its name the *Shang-ch'ing,* or Highest Pure order. Whereas the *Meng-wei* and *Ling-pao* orders were ritual-oriented, the *Shang-ch'ing* order was meditative in its approaches to the transcendent Tao. The inspiration for the new order was taken from a lady Taoist "wine libationer," Wei Hua-ts'un, of the *Meng-wei* sect. Fleeing from north to south China because of the barbarian invasions, she came to Mao Shan and in a vision received from various spirits of the past the basic meditative books of the order. These books were summarized in the *Yellow Court Canon,* or *Huang-t'ing Ching,* which gives a new list of esoteric spirits' names, *nei-ching,* and directions for meditation, *wai-ching,* deriving from the early *Ts'an-t'ung-ch'i.* Legend says that Lady Wei died in A.D. 334, leaving her books and methods with one of her sons. The son gave the books in turn to Yang Hsi, a court official of the southern Chin dynasty. Between A.D. 366 and 370, the books of Lady Wei became the subject of a series of nocturnal visions seen by Yang Hsi. While in a near-trance state atop Mao Shan, Yang had visions of Lady Wei and a whole court of heavenly spirits.[14] Two friends, Hsü Hui and Hsü Mi, acted as secretaries for Yang, and these two men soon became visionaries themselves. Between A.D. 366 and 370, they wrote out in beautiful calligraphy the doctrines of the new order as "dictated" by the spirit of the lady wine-libationer. The writings were pieced together a century and a half later by T'ao Hung-ching in the *Chen-kao* (*TT* 637-640). The new doctrines of the *Shang-ch'ing* sect taught that the method of exteriorizing the spirits and preparing the center of the microcosm—that is, the Yellow Court—for the presence of the indwelling Tao of Transcendence involves meditation rather than ritual, as practiced by the two earlier orders. Thus, all three early orders sought to exteriorize the spirits from the cosmos, and, by emptying the center of man, to prepare him for the immortalizing encounter with transcendence.

The earliest Taoist movements had three distinct features in common. The first was a list, or *lu,* of the spirits' names and descriptions. The second was a special canonical text, *ching,* which typified the meditative and philosophical means of attaining unity with the Tao of Transcendence. The third was the *k'o-i* ritual, or meditation itself, which led to union. All three of these early Taoist orders sought the same end result, that is, union with the transcendent Tao. The three methods were united by Lu Hsiu-ching into a single *sarvayāna,* or doctrinal and canonical unity, by A.D. 471, and were further refined and discussed by T'ao Hung-ching before A.D. 536. Because the various rituals were easily interchanged and mutually learned, Taoists had become aware of the unifying texts by the time of Lu Hsiu-ching and adhered to the doctrine of transcendental duality.

An understanding of the three notions of *lu* register, *ching* canon, and *k'o-i* meditative ritual is essential if one is to understand the philosophical unity of the doctrines of religious Taoism. The *lu* register of spirits' names is a term deriving from the feudal states of late Chou China and from the apocryphal *Ch'an-wei* texts of the early Han period. The *lu* was the list of vassals, feudal territory, and paraphernalia under the control of the lord or king. To the Taoist, the *lu* is a list of spirits' names and descriptions, the *chih,* or spiritual jurisdiction, under which they are classified, and the means by which they may be summoned and commanded.[15] In order to swear in the lords, dukes, and barons of feudal China, a talisman, *fu,* or contract, *ch'i,* was drawn up. In the ritual of investiture, the talisman was cut in half, one part being given to the king, the other to the vassal. At the time of the winter solstice, lord and subject came together again, and the right to command was proven by rejoining the two halves of the *fu.* In the same manner, the Taoist adept was given a spiritual *chih,* or territory, and all of the spirits therein were put under his jurisdiction. During the ritual of ordination or investiture, a contract was made with the spirits, and *fu* talismans were burned in order to "swear in" the legion of spiritual vassals under the Taoist's command. Thus, for the early *Meng-wei* order, there were twenty-four *lu,* or registers, early versions of which can be found in the Taoist Canon. By the use of esoteric insignia, talismans, and conjurations the Taoist was given the power of command over a spiritual *lu.* The earliest *fa-lu* rite of the *Meng-wei* Taoists was used to command the spirits to leave the body in order to prepare the individual for encounter with the transcendent Tao or to present petitions before the throne of the heavenly rulers. The *lu* of the *Meng-wei* sect became the common property of all three orders. It was used as a prelude to the *Ling-pao* rites of renewal and burial, and is found at the beginning of all *k'o-i* rituals in the canon. (The *k'o-i* ritual is discussed later in this chapter.)

The *ching,* or canonical texts, of the three early movements were (1) the *Lao-tzu Tao-te Ching* for the *Meng-wei* order; (2) the *Tu-jen Ching*[16] for the *Ling-pao* order; and (3) *Chuang-tzu Nei-p'ien,* or the first seven chapters of the *Chuang-tzu,* for the *Shang-ch'ing* order. The first-mentioned book of the *Lao-tzu* was and still is passed on as a part of the rite of investiture of orthodox Taoism. The second *Tu-jen* Canon is named early in the nineteenth chapter of Ko Hung's *Pao-p'u-tzu,* thus indicating that the text was in use by the end of the third century and beginning of the fourth century A.D. A formal analysis of the *Tu-jen* Canon suggests that it has been influenced by the first, seventh, and twenty-first chapters of the Buddhist *Lotus Sūtra Fa-hua Ching.*[17] The text is used in all burial rituals as a means of applying the *Ling-pao* scriptures and their saving power to the souls in hell. Finally, the *Shang-ch'ing* order used the first seven chapters of the *Chuang-tzu* as the basic philosophical text for the meditation of union with the transcendent.

The three most important texts in religious Taoism of his day, T'ao Hung-ching (d. A.D. 536) tells us, are the *Chuang-tzu Nei-p'ien,* the *Lotus Sūtra,* and the *Yellow Court Canon.*[18] T'ao Hung-ching was writing at a time when the Mao Shan *Shang-ch'ing* sect was at the height of its power and the neighboring *T'ien-t'ai* sect with the *Lotus Sūtra* as a fundamental canon was reaching the peak of its popularity, so his citation of Buddhist and Taoist texts together does not seem surprising. This scholarly monk, who did not show any great liking for the noisy and vulgar *Ling-pao* rites,[19] correctly identified one source of Taoist salvational texts as being the Buddhist *Lotus Sūtra.* The doctrine of exteriorizing the spirits, which derives from the *Meng-wei fa-lu* ritual, is expanded and refined in the *Yellow Court Canon.* Finally, the philosophy of transcendence as enunciated by the first seven chapters of the *Chuang-tzu* is proper to his own *Shang-ch'ing* order. It is thus possible to summarize the teachings of *Shang-ch'ing* Taoism as (1) *Chuang-tzu Nei-p'ien,* doctrine of the absolute transcendent; (2) *Fa-hua Ching,* doctrine of salvation; and (3) *Huang-t'ing Ching,* doctrine of exteriorizing the spirits, leading to union with the transcendent.

Thus we see that the doctrine of transcendent duality is basic to the three early Taoist orders. According to the doctrine, the state of the transcendent absolute, that is the Tao of the *Wu-wei,* is essentially different from the Tao of Immanence, the Tao of the *Yu-wei.* The Tao of Permanence is the first in a series of generating causes, which in the act of generating is unmoved and unchanged.[20] From the generated state of chaos comes by movement the principle yang, and by quiescence the principle yin. In the esoteric explanation (as opposed to the commonly accepted doctrines of the yin-yang five element theory), yin is seen to contain within it a minute drop of yang, making the female principle the source of birth and new life. The three generated principles, that is, the first mover *T'ai-chi,* or *hun-tun,* the second mover yang, and the third mover yin, are seen to be principles of life and generation for the total cosmos.[21] By reversing the process of generation, that is, by proceeding backward from the myriad creatures and the myriad spirits, one can arrive at the state of simplicity, or *t'ai-chi (hun-tun).* It is at this point that the potency for standing before the Tao of Transcendence is made available. By emptying the Yellow Court, the potency for the absolute is clarified. The process is depicted in Figure 1.1.

It is interesting to note that the three methods for emptying the microcosm are, in fact, expressed in the *k'o-i* meditative ritual.[22] Thus the first *fa-lu* meditation of the *Meng-wei* order simply empties the microcosm by constructing the external mandala of the spirits, drawn forth from their residences within the microcosm. The second *Ling-pao* order empties and refines spirits in a lengthy series of meditative *k'o-i* rituals. Beginning with the *chin-t'an* rite, the microcosm is first purified of all earth and underworld spirits, and the eight entrances to the microcosm or the sacred area of ritual are sealed off. The *kuei-men,* identified with the trigram *ken* in the northeast, or the entrance of the demonic forces, is given special attention in the rite. Next, in the esoteric rite called *su-ch'i,* the many spirits are refined into the five primordial principles of motion. The *su-ch'i* renews a feudal treaty with the five elements, effected by use of the *Ling-pao Five Talismans.* The five elements are represented by the five spirits, who are enfiefed or commanded by the talismans, and these spirits restore the cosmos to primal vigor.[23] In the *k'o-i* ritual of *Meng-wei* Taoism, the wood of east (three) and the fire of south (two) are refined into the first five; that is, into primordial breath, or Primordial Heavenly Worthy. The earth of center is refined into the second five of life spirit, the *Ling-pao* Heavenly Worthy. The metal of west (four) and the water of north (one) are refined into the third five, or vital essence, the *Tao-te* Heavenly Worthy. Finally, in the last ritual meditation, the three fives are united into the One, *T'ai-chi* or *hun-tun,* the Tao of Immanence. It is at this point that the final document begging for blessings for all laymen and women is sent off to the heavens, at the same time

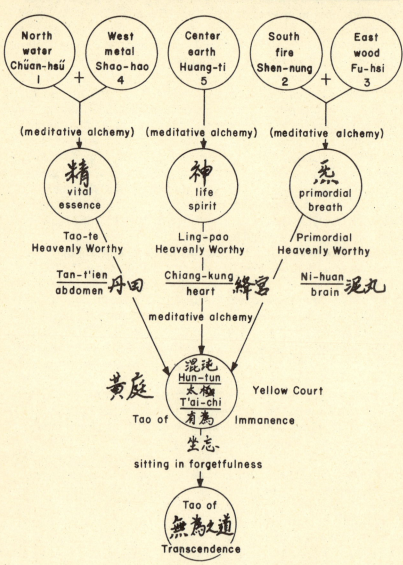

Figure 1.1   Transcendental Dualism.

gaining union with the Tao of Transcendence for the Taoist.[24] In the basic meaning of esoteric religion, it is the master (the Taoist) who attains immortality for himself, and he passes on the inwardly won blessings to the community by ritual.

The doctrines of the third order, the *Shang-ch'ing* sect, are contained in the *Yellow Court Canon*, which I shall attempt to summarize. The doctrines are in no way different from those of the *Meng-wei* or the *Ling-pao* sect. The method, rather, changes from one of ritual purifications to one of quiet meditation. The *Yellow Court Canon* itself is a very difficult text, almost impossible to understand or translate without the commentary of a master. The oral or written secrets which explain the esoteric terminology ordinarily are passed on to the adept at the time of investiture or ordination. As is often the case in the extant Ming dynasty Taoist Canon, the documents that reveal the esoteric teachings with regard to the Yellow Court are not included in the canon. According to oral tradition in modern Taiwan, there are three important sources of early (that is pre-Sung) commentaries on the *Yellow Court Cannon*.[25] The first is the original teachings of the *Shang-ch'ing* sect itself, before the popularization of the order that took place during the Sung period. The second is the archives and doctrines of the Hua Shan sect in Shensi province, which received the teachings of the *Shang-ch'ing* order in a direct transmission during the T'ang period. The third source is the holdings of the Taoists of Fukien province and of their descendants now practicing in Taiwan. These latter holdings were one of the main sources for compiling both the Sung and the Ming dynasty canons.[26]

A fourth, more modern source for studying the *Yellow Court Canon* is the manuscript holdings of the *Meng-wei* tradition kept by the Heavenly Master at Lung-hu Shan in Kiangsi province, southeast China. Since the Sung dynasty, Lung-hu Shan was one of three centers granted imperial approval to ordain clergy.[27] The holdings of the Heavenly Master were brought to Taiwan in 1888 by Lin Ju-mei and constitute an important source of the doctrines of orthodox Taoism as transmitted by the *Cheng-i (Meng-wei)* sect since its establishment at Lung-hu Shan.[28] From the three ancient sources and one more modern source, it is possible to establish that the esoteric teachings with regard to the *Yellow Court Canon* have not changed substantially since the fifth- and sixth-century collections of Lu Hsiu-ching and T'ao Hung-ching. The doctrine of transcendental dualism has been transmitted consistently, along with the *Chiao* of the *Ling-pao* sect and the *fa-lu* of the *Meng-wei* order, without significant change. The definition of "orthodoxy," *cheng* to the Taoist, is thus interpreted to mean an exact transmission of canonical, traditional texts and rubrical explanations without change from the time of classical Taoist antiquity.

The opening lines of the *Yellow Court Canon* assert the doctrine that the first step to prepare the body for immortality is the externalizing or casting out of the many spirits that dwell within the microcosm. The microcosm has three loci for assembling the spirits, the *ni-wan*[29] palace in the brain, the Red Palace, *ch'iang-kung,* in the heart, and the cinnabar field, *tan-t'ien,* in the belly. These three centers are foci for assembling the various microcosmic spirits, and they correspond to the three cosmological divisions of the macrocosm: heaven, earth, and watery underworld. When purified, these foci contain the three principles of life, that is, primordial breath *(ni-wan)*, spirit (heart), and vital essence *(tan-ti'en)*. The three principles, when joined or fused in the microcosmic center of man, the Yellow Court, form the basis of the "pill of immortality" or the "hierophant." The processes of breathing in and breathing out are to be interpreted in the purely spiritual sense; that is, they take place totally within the Yellow Court, which is a *hsü,* a void center which, though having no physical location within the microcosm, is a place from which the source of life works invisibly. It is by a process of alchemical meditation that the myriad spirits are expelled, while breath, spirit, and vital essence are brought into the Yellow Court and "hardened" or "congealed" there. By employing this process of meditation, one can win immortality.

In the initial statements of the *Yellow Court Canon,* esoteric terms so obscured the true meaning of the text that a variety of possible interpretations could be and were attributed to the work. It is essential to turn to early commentaries on the canon to understand how it was used and understood by the orthodox *Shang-ch'ing* tradition. In the first chapters of the *Chen-kao,* the lady Taoist Wei Hua-ts'un inveighs again and again against the use of a heterodox and vulgar sexual-hygiene interpretation of the *Yellow Court Canon.* The text is not to be taken in a physical or sensual sense. The doctrines of the *Interior Yellow Court Canon, Huang-t'ing Nei Ching,* list a register of spirits' names which are the new esoteric *lu* of the *Shang-ch'ing* sect. These are the spirits to be exteriorized, *chieh-t'o chu shen.*[30] Only the three principles of breath, spirit, and vital essence are to be retained.

It is evident from the text that the spirits and not physical principles are the objects of refinement or preservation within the void Yellow Court. The word *ching,* which means seminal essence or vital essence, could not be interpreted in the physical sense, since both men and women are told to preserve it, that is, to keep it from flowing outward. The principle of seminal or vital essence is something contained by all men and women equally, in the lower cinnabar field of the belly. It is, in anthropomorphic terms, the spirit of *Lao-tzu, Tao-te T'ien-tsun*. It is represented in art as a "flowing red pearl," a symbol of the immanent Tao *T'ai-chi*, generator of a drop of life-giving yang in nature. It is this drop which renews the cosmos at the winter solstice, causing winter to turn into spring in the annual cycle of nature. The drop of yang is not the eternal Tao *(Wu-chi)* but is the eternal product of the Tao *(T'ai-chi)* working in nature. Thus the transcendent Tao gives birth to the One, *T'ai-chi*. From the *T'ai-chi* (in motion) is generated yang, the principle of life which contains within itself an infinitesimal drop of yin as symbolized by cool jade. From the *T'ai-chi* (at rest) is next generated the principle of yin, inside of which is an infinitesimal drop of yang, symbolized by the red pearl.[31] The three principles, though generated from the Tao of Transcendence, are not identical with it.

Of the three loci for assembling or controlling the spirits, the Red Palace of the heart is the most important in the process of interior refinement.[32] It is the heart, according to the doctrine of the *Huai-nan-tzu*, which rules over the spirits of the body. In the doctrine of the Yellow Court, the red-coated spirit of the heart is lord over the spirits of the microcosm, keeping the will and the mind from flowing outward toward the desire of external things. Running after external desires causes breath, spirit, and vital essence to flow away and be lost. Death results from the exhaustion of the breath and vital essence, after which the spirit leaves the body. The two accesses to the Yellow Court, then, must be closed by the spirit of the heart. The two entrances are equated with the trigrams *ch'ien* and *k'un*, respectively.[33] It is specifically the heart which must effect the closing by turning man away from his outward pursuit of glory and riches, or pleasures of the visible world, and by directing him to the inward pursuit of immortality through the concentration of the spirit, breath, and vital essence in the Yellow Court. The doctrine of spiritual perfection in which man must forget the pursuits of the visible world and think of union with the transcendent Tao is, therefore, the basic esoteric teaching of the first chapters of the *Yellow Court Canon*. The text speaks of a spiritual fire,[34] which congeals and unifies the three principles, and prevents them from flowing outward and changing.[35]

The principle of life breath, *ch'i*, or primordial breath, is housed in the *ni-wan* palace of the brain. *Ni-wan* is an early Chinese transliteration of the Sanskrit word *nirvāṇa*. It has sometimes been translated as "muddy pill" in a Taoist context but, in fact, must be taken in the esoteric sense of the central palace of the brain which houses the spirit of primordial breath. Just as vital essence and spirit must be drawn from the two lower centers, so breath must be brought down into the Yellow Court for alchemical refining. The process of bringing the three principles into the void center is spoken of as "watering the root of spirit" and "forming the hierophant," both of which are technical terms for refining the three into One and bringing about the presence of the Tao of Immortality in the void center of the microcosm. "Primordial breath" can hardly be taken in the literal sense of breath, since it is housed in the brain rather than in the lungs. In the esoteric tradition, the holding of breath or the swallowing of breath (male principle) and saliva (female principle) are interpreted as techniques leading to concentration but not as the ultimate purpose of the meditation. Thus, three spiritual principles are to be congealed into the One in the void Yellow Court. The text is not to be interpreted in the literal sense.

In the next stage of the process described in the *Yellow Court Canon,* the three principles of life, that is, breath, spirit, and vital essence, are to be refined into the *T'ai-chi* or the *hun-tun* principle of the immanent Tao of Gestation, *Yu-wei Chih Tao.*[36] The process is the same as that described above for the *k'o-i* liturgy except that, in the case of the *Yellow Court Canon,* the refinement is accomplished by meditation. The purpose of the meditation is related in content to the *Ts'an-t'ung-ch'i* where the three fives (east's three and south's two; center's five; west's four and north's one) are reduced to One by alchemical refinement.[37] Similar to the enumeration of the *Ts'an-t'ung-ch'i,* the *Yellow Court Canon* proposes to refine the three fives, or the three life-principles, now interpreted as spirits, into the original state of *hun-tun* or primordial chaos. As in the ritual of the *Meng-wei* order and the *Ling-pao* traditions, breath (Primordial Heavenly Worthy), spirit (*Ling-pao* Heavenly Worthy), and vital essence (*Tao-te* Heavenly Worthy) are brought into the Yellow Court and congealed, *i,* into the state of *T'ai-chi,* the Tao of Immanence. It is in a process similar to that of the "sitting in forgetfulness," or the *tso-wang* of Chuang-tzu, that the meditation on the eternal Tao of Transcendence is initiated in the *Yellow Court Canon* tradition.[38]

The meditations of internal alchemy are thus seen to be a reversal of the process of gestation. From the myriad creatures the adept refines out all thoughts and all spirits until the Three remain. From the Three, the Taoist proceeds by meditative process to the Tao of Transcendence:

> The myriad things returning lead to the Three,
> The Three to the Two,
> The Two to the One,
> The One to the Tao of Transcendence.[39]

The process of refinement or reversal is followed ritually during the Taoist Chiao festival of renewal. In the morning audience *(tsao-ch'ao)* the Primordial Heavenly Worthy is brought into the Yellow Court. At noon *(wu-ch'ao)* the *Ling-pao* Heavenly Worthy is made present. At night *(wan-ch'ao)* Lao-tzu is summoned. Finally, in the *tao-ch'ang* ritual, the three spirits are reduced to the state of simplicity, *hun-tun.* The seventh chapter of the *Chuang-tzu* points to the principle whereby the process of gestation has begun.[40] Yin and Yang came to dwell inside Hun-tun, and were so happy within that they decided to give Hun-tun the two eyes, two nostrils, two ears, and mouth of all creatures. Thereupon they drilled seven holes, or apertures, one on each of seven days. On the seventh day, Hun-tun died. Now in the reverse process, the Taoist seals off the apertures, that is, the adept reverses the process of gestation, so as to stand before the Tao of Eternal Transcendence.

It is precisely at this point that the notion of transcendence as enunciated by the Mahāyāna Buddhist philosophers parts ways with the Tao of Transcendence. If the Tao is present in the dung by the gate, it is indwelling as a generating principle, distinct from the thing generated. The mode of existence of the generated is that of participating in being, *yu,* or "being received," as opposed to the state of being by transcendence, *wu.* The state of the former is one of change, *hua,* and outgoing, while that of the latter is one of permanence, *i* or *ch'ang.* The transcendent act is called *wu-wei,* while the immanent act is called *yu-wei.* It is not so much that beings by generation or participation do not exist, but that their existence (being as possessed or received, *yu*) depends on another being that is self-generating or eternally generated without outflowing act, *wu-wei.* Thus, transitory or changing things do exist but are not the cause of their own existence (not self-generating).[41]

If, by voiding the center of the microcosm, man can stand before the eternal transcendent Tao, the very cause of his existence, then there is no way of interpreting the transcendent to be a part of his compounded (generated) nature. The myriad creatures derive from yin and yang and they, in turn, from chaos. But chaos is, in turn, generated by the eternally unmoved generator, the Tao of Transcendence. If one predicates being of the generated, then the generator must be termed "nonbeing," not because it does not exist, but because its mode of being is entirely different (transcendent) from that of the thing generated. The process of generation is called *sheng,* the word used for life, birth, and generation. Such a meaning was certainly not intended by the Buddhist philosophers of either Mādhyamika, Yogācāra, or the later Zen schools. The states of *wu* and *yu* are both real and both existentially different. Thus, the doctrines of transcendence and duality typify the philosophy of religious Taoism.[42] The real world as empty or illusory, or the identity of consciousness with transcendent mind, both possible doctrines of Mahāyāna

Buddhism, are inadmissible to the religious Taoist. "Reversing" the order of nature is not so much acting against nature as it is acting with the path of the transcendent Tao.

The charge of metaphysical inconsistency, at this point of the philosophical argument, must indeed be avoided by the Taoist adept. Surely, if the Tao of the Transcendent *wu-wei* is absolute, the activity of the Tao of Change can in no way affect it. The Taoist can hardly "summon" the transcendent; that which is summoned must by its nature be nontranscendent.[43] The Taoist adept does not by his meditation seek to do the impossible, nor does he contradict the philosophy of transcendence. Instead, he interprets the doctrine of the void as taught in the third chapter of the *Chuang-tzu*. The Tao is present in the heart-mind, *hsin*, which is void. Thus void, *hsü*, is seen as a necessary condition for realizing the presence of the transcendental Tao. The heart-mind filled with the affairs of the senses, the worries of external things, "chasing after" sensual pleasure, cannot be aware of the presence of the infinite. "Only the Tao dwells in the void," *Chuang-tzu* teaches.[44] The purpose of *hsin-chai*, "fasting of the heart," therefore, is to void the heart-mind so that the Tao may dwell within, or, rather, so that the mind may become aware of the activity of the Tao in nature. Void, therefore, must be translated as "potency for the infinite."

By way of summation, it is interesting to note that all three of the early Taoist movements sought to purify the mind and to exteriorize the spirits as a necessary prelude to the encounter with the Tao of Transcendence. The earliest *Meng-wei* order created the *fa-lu* meditation for exteriorizing the spirits of the microcosm in an orderly sort of mandala. Later, the *Ling-pao* order ritually refined the myriad spirits into the Five, the Five into the Three, and finally the Three into the One Tao of Immanence. Lastly, the contemplative *Shang-ch'ing* school sought to purify the mind and empty the microcosm of spirits by the meditation of the *Yellow Court Canon*. In all three schools, the Tao of Transcendence was necessarily conceived of as being something different than the *T'ai-chi* or the Tao of Immanence. The generated world and the generator were distinguished by the terms *wu* and *yu* in the *Lao-tzu*, and by the words *i* and *hua* in the *Chuang-tzu*. The Buddhist doctrines of *Śūnyatā* and transcendence, were, therefore, worlds apart from the philosophical notions of transcendence taught by the masters of orthodox religious Taoism. Transcendence in the *Chuang-tzu* represented a contrast, not a corollary, to the teachings of the Mādhyamika and the Yogācāra.

In concluding this chapter, I would like to quote from two documents that probably date from the late T'ang or the early Sung period. The texts demonstrate the consistent and continuous line of transmission of the doctrine of transcendental dualism. The doctrine as I have propounded it here has come down in an unbroken line from the earliest masters of *Shang-ch'ing* Taoism to the adepts in modern Taiwan. If one can open the pages of the *Chen-kao* to find Wei Hua-ts'un condemning the physical interpretation of the *Yellow Court Canon,* and speak in conversation with modern Taiwan Taoists of the traditions of Hua Shan, Mao Shan, and Fukien Taoism, then one also can find in the T'ang and Sung dynasty canon spokesmen for the doctrines of transcendental dualism. I cite here two documents from the twenty-fourth volume of the canon, which are used as commentaries on the doctrines of the *Yellow Court Canon:*

BREATHING WITHIN THE WOMB[45]

The womb [of the microcosm, *hun-t'un*] is formed
By preserving primordial breath in the center.
Primordial breath is breathed inside the womb [*hun-t'un*].
Breath coming into the body is called life [birth];
Spirit leaving the bodily form is called death.
By knowing the spirit and breath, one can have eternal life.
Therefore life, breath, and spirit are nourished
By keeping them in the void, with nourishing transcendence.
When spirit goes forth, then breath goes forth too.
When spirit indwells, then breath indwells too.
If one desires long life,
Spirit and breath must not be moved by any thought;
There must be no coming or going,
No exit or entrance [of breath and spirit].
Let them be there of themselves, naturally.
By practicing this doctrine perfectly,
One will walk the path of the true Tao.

THE SEAL OF THE HEART CANON[46]

The highest alchemical drug has three components—
Spirit, breath, and vital essence.
Bright and sparkling, fragrant and mysterious!
Preserve their transcendence [*wu*]
Keep their immanence [*yu*].
By careful carving, they are perfected.
In the swirl of wind, chaos congealed.
In a hundred days of labor, spirit is formed,
And bows in respectful obeisance
To the emperor above.
The flight of ascent is a single stroke.[47]
The man who knows this is quickly enlightened;
He who neglects it will find the path hard to travel.

Dance on a heavenly ray of light,
Inhale and exhale nourishing purity.
The loss of the male source [breath] is death.
The coming of the female principle [vital essence] is life.
It is like a spinning thread that never ceases,
Like a deep-rooted flower eternally blooming.
In every man [and woman] there is vital essence.
Vital essence must be made one with spirit.
Spirit must be joined with primordial breath.
Breath must be joined with the realized Tao.
The man not joined to the Tao
Is strong in name only.
Spirit depends on external forms for birth;
Vital essence depends on breath to maintain its fullness.
Do not lose it! Do not let it diminish!
The pine and the cedar are always green.
The three components are one in principle.
A wondrous mystery that cannot be told!
Its possession is existence,
Its dissipation is annihilation [zero].
The seven sense apertures [eyes, nostrils, ears, mouth]
Must be joined in an inward union,
All filled with a brilliant light;
The light of holy Yin and holy Yang.
The light penetrates and fills the Yellow Court.
Once attained, eternally attained.
Of itself the body becomes light.
The Great Harmony fills it to overflowing.
The bones of mortality are scattered,
Like a jade bracelet shattered by the freezing cold.
He who attains the pill of immortality is spiritualized.
The pill is in the body's center.
It is neither "white" nor "green"!
Chant it a hundred-thousand times,
Its wondrous meaning is self-evident!

NOTES

Many modern writers identify the philosophy of Lao-tzu and Chuang-tzu with the doctrines of Ch'an or Zen Buddhism. Whatever exegetical arguments are used to establish the meaning of the two early Taoist texts, their interpretation according to the Taoist masters of the orthodox religious tradition as seen in the Taoist Canon, and in the following pages, is quite different. See Michael Saso, *The Teachings of Taoist Master Chuang* (New Haven: Yale University Press, 1977), chap. 1 for an extended historical treatment of the development of Taoist religious teachings.

2. A number of recent writers, imbued with the spirit of modern skepticism, have attempted to show from the earliest Pali and Chinese texts that the original teachings of the Buddha were almost agnostic in nature. The Buddha, according to this interpretation, rejected not only all metaphysical discussion concerning the transcendent and the hereafter, but may have considered the state of Nirvāṇa to have been a complete freeing, or cessation from being. Whatever the validity of arguing from the fragmentary Pali *Nikāyas* or Chinese *Āgamas* where closely placed fragments are often contradictory to one another, the Chinese found the Mahāyāna doctrines of salvation and the transcendental nature of the Buddha more appealing.

3. Richard H. Robinson, *Early Mādhyamika in India and China* (Madison: University of Wisconsin Press, 1967), pp. 104–105.

4. Lao-tzu, *Tao-te Ching*, chap. 42.

5. T'ao Hung-ching, *Chen-kao* (Taoist Canon, or *Tao-tsang*, hereafter cited as *TT*, vols. 637–640), chap. 19. The point of this passage is to show that the *Yellow Court Canon* and other *Shang-ch'ing* scriptures, though avidly sought by the fifth- and sixth-century elite, were successfully collected and hidden in the arcanum of Taoist esoterica.

6. Michael Saso, *Taoism and the Rite of Cosmic Renewal* (Pullman: Washington State University Press, 1972), chaps. 1, 3, 4.

7   The esoteric nature of religious Taoism is often misunderstood by the scholar unfamiliar with the rules for transmitting documents that were observed by the orthodox Taoists. Early works such as the *Wu-shang Pi-yao* (*TT* 768–779) chap. 35, p. 1b line 1 to 2b line 5, show the stages of perfection required of the Taoist novice before being allowed to receive the *Shang-ch'ing* scriptures.

8. See Ch'en Kuo-fu, *Tao-tsang Yüan-liu K'ao* [A Critical Study of the Origins of the Taoist Canon] (Shanghai: Commercial Press, 1949), pp. 39–45. Hereafter cited as *TTYLK*.

9. See Saso, *Teachings of Master Chuang*, chap. 1 for the history of *Shen-hsiao* Taoism.

10. Ibid., chap. 4, for a study of the *fa-lu* ritual.

11. *TT* 183, *T'ai-shang Ling-pao Wu-fu Hsü*, shang, pp. 6b–11b.

12. See Ch'en Kuo-fu, *TTYLK*, pp. 38–44. Lu Hsiu-ching (d. A.D. 471) edited the *Ling-pao* Canon which had been enlarged by the time of Ko Ch'ao-fu, end of the fourth century.

13. Ch'en Kuo-fu, *TTYLK*, pp. 31–39.

14. Ibid., pp. 32–34.

15. See *TT* 877, *T'ai-shang San-wu Cheng-i Meng-wei Lu*.

16. See *TT* 38–39, *Yüan-shih Wu-liang Tu-jen Shang-p'in Miao Ching Chu*.

17. The author's opinion, deriving from the Cheng-i Tz'u-t'an Taoists of Hsinchu city, north Taiwan. Note that T'ao Hung-ching substitutes the *Lotus Sūtra* for the *Tu-jen Ching* in the *Chen-kao*, chap. 19, line 2.

18. *TT* 640, *Chen-kao*, chap. 19, lines 1–3.

19. *Chen-kao*, chap. 11, p. 13b, lines 2–4.

20. *TT* 69, *Chou-i T'u*, p. 2a, lines 1–8.

21. Cf. Fung Yu-lan, *A History of Chinese Philosophy*, trans. Derk Bodde, 2 vols. (Princeton: Princeton University Press, 1953), vol. II, chap. 11, pp. 435–436.

22. Saso, *Teachings of Master Chuang*, chap. 4, enlarges upon the meditative ritual and its process of interior refinement.

23. The five talismans are inserted into five bushels of rice, arranged in an east-south-center-west-north mandala. The rite is described in a number of

places in the canon, for which see *TT* 281, *Wu-shang Huang-lu Ta-chai Li-ch'eng I,* chap. 16.

24.   Sung Yin-tzu, *Huang-t'ing Wai Ching, Yin-fu Ching Ho Chu* (Taipei: Tzu-yu Press, 1958), chap. 3, p. 6a, line 7. (Hereafter cited as *HTWC.*)

25.   The commentaries in the Taoist Canon on the *Yellow Court Canon* are found in *TT* 130–131, with the glosses of Liang Ch'iu-tzu (Pai Li-chung), a T'ang Taoist who lived ca. 722. The same commentator is found in *TT* 190. The Sung dynasty encyclopedia of Taoist lore, *Yun-chi Ch'i-ch'ien, TT* 677–702, chapters 11–12, contains a briefer commentary also ascribed to Liang Ch'iu-tzu. The *HTWC* cited in note 24 is a Ming dynasty work.

26.   See Ch'en Kuo-fu, *TTYLK,* pp. 171–190.

27.   Lung-hu Shan, Mao Shan, and Ko-tsao Shan were the three centers at which a Taoist license of ordination could be purchased. At present the 64th Generation Heavenly Master from Lung-hu Shan grants licenses from a government sponsored organization in Taipei, Taiwan. Since the arrival of the 63rd Generation Heavenly Master in Taiwan in the early 1950s, the traditional grades and orders have not been followed, licenses being sold without reference to the Taoist's knowledge of the classical registers.

28.   The history of Lin Ju-mei's journey to Lung-hu Shan in 1886 and his return to Hsinchu in 1888 is recounted in Saso, *Teachings of Master Chuang,* chap. 2.

29.   *HTWC,* chap. 1, p. 1a, lines 5–7; commentary, pp. 1b– 3b.

30.   *HTWC,* chap. 1, p. 1a, line 5.

31.   *HTWC,* chap. 2, p. 3b, gloss of Li Ming-ch'e.

32.   *HTWC,* chap. 1, p. 4a, lines 1–3.

33.   *HTWC,* chap. 1, pp. 4b–5a. The trigram *ch'ien* is identified with *hsüan,* the male or yang entrance to the Yellow Court, and *k'un* with *p'in,* the female or yin entrance.

34.   *HTWC,* chap. 1, p. 6b, lines 5–7.

35.   *HTWC,* chap. 1, p. 6b to 8b, gives an extensive commentary on the process of hardening the three principles and preserving them within.

36.   *HTWC,* chap. 2, p. 2b, line 1.

37.   *Ts'an-t'ung-ch'i* (*Shou-shan Ko Ts'ung-shu* edition, vol. 152), p. 21b, line 4.

38.   *Chuang-tzu* (*Chuang-tzu Yin-te,* Harvard-Yenching index series no. 20), chap. 6, 1. 92; chap. 6, 1. 93; Cf. chap. 3, *hsin-chai,* and chap. 4, 1. 26.

39.   *HTWC,* chap. 3, p. 7b, lines 6–7: *"Wo shih wo; yüan-shen hsien chien."* *HTWC,* chap. 2, p. 2b, line 2: *"San-wu ho ch'i, yao pen I." HTWC,* chap. 2, p. 3b, line 2: *"San-wu, Hou-t'ien chih ch'i."*

40.   *Chuang-tzu,* chap. 7, lines 33–35.

41.   *Chuang-tzu,* chap. 6, line 30.

42.   *HTWC,* chap. 2, p. 3b, line 2.

43.   *HTWC,* chap. 3, line 7: *Tao tzu ch'ih,* "The Tao comes and stays of its own accord."

44.   *Chuang-tzu,* chap. 4, line 28.

45.   *TT* 24, *Kao-shang Yü-huang T'ai-hsi Ching.*

46.   *TT* 24, *Kao-shang Yü-huang Hsin-yin Ching.*

47.   The passage has been interpreted to mean the uselessness of various lesser techniques, such as holding the breath or swallowing saliva, for meditating on the Tao of Transcendence. Such techniques are disciplinary, and are designed to teach concentration to the beginner. They are discarded by the adept, for whom sitting in forgetfulness and the encounter with the Transcendent is a single stroke.

2   Chinese Buddhist Interpretations of the Pure Lands[1]

DAVID W. CHAPPELL

THE CONCEPT OF A "PURE LAND"

The quest for a pure land or a promised land is a theme found in many cultures. It is a dream many people can relate to, either because they (or their acquaintances) also long for a better land, or because they so despair of finding fulfillment in the present that they feel compelled to place their faith in a better life after death. A major expression of this hope for a land which would transcend and free people from the pain of the present is the development of Pure Land devotionalism in East Asian Buddhism which centered on the Western Pure Land of Amitābha Buddha.

It is sometimes assumed that the hope for a better life in a heaven or paradise after death is the product of people who are simple-minded or of simple faith. However, the development of the concept of "pure lands" in the history of Buddhist thought is anything but simple, and the efforts of Buddhist thinkers to interpret this belief in the light of other Buddhist doctrines have generated rather intricate and complicated theories. This was especially true during those centuries when Pure Land devotionalism had developed into a separate school in China, but it also was true at other times and for thinkers not particularly associated with the Pure Land School of Chinese Buddhism.

Buddhism entered China during the first century A.D., but the major indigenous forms of Chinese Buddhism did not develop until the sixth to eighth centuries.[2] This clearly was the case for the imperially sponsored schools of Chinese Buddhism such as T'ien-t'ai, Fa-hsiang and Hua-yen, but it was also true for Pure Land and Ch'an, which evolved from popular practice. There is a vivid demonstration of this chronology among the sculptures of Lung-men. Tsukamoto Zenryū has calculated that between A.D. 495 and 535 there were carved 78 images of Śākyamuni and Maitreya (the Buddhas of the past and the future), whereas there were only 27 sculptures of Amitābha and Avalokiteśvara (the Buddha and principal bodhisattva of the Western Pure Land). However, the popularity of Pure Land devotionalism increased dramatically during the next century, so that from 650 to 704 there were only 20 sculptures made of Śākyamuni and Maitreya whereas there were 144 images of Amitābha and Avalokiteśvara.[3] This implies that countless Chinese looked forward to the Western Pure Land as the place where they would meet Amitābha and Avalokiteśvara. In the minds of many it had become their future homeland, a place of refuge and hope, another world to live in.

Devotion to the Pure Land finally evolved into a school[4] pioneered by such people as Tao-ch'o (562–645), whose lifetime fell between the sets of dates given by Tsukamoto. Tao-ch'o gave the title *An-lo-chi* ("A Collection of Passages Concerning [the Land of] Peace and Happiness") to the treatise that he wrote because *an-lo* was a phrase which had become almost exclusively identified with the name of Amitābha.[5] Originally, *an-lo* translated the Sanskrit word *sukhāvatī*, which described the state of bliss achieved in enlightenment. Thus, it was associated with nirvāṇa, an association which continued after it had been adopted as the name of the Land of Amitābha Buddha in the *Larger Sukhāvatīvyūha-sūtra*.[6] However, with its identification as a place (*an-lo-kuo* or *an-lo-t'u*, Skt. *sukhāvatīvyūha*, "the land of bliss") the concept of unlimited bliss became concrete, and was depicted in specific images which could capture the popular imagination.

Fujita Kotatsu has recently published the best study to date on the origins of Pure Land Buddhism. A number of the descriptions of *Sukhāvatīvyūha* he traced back (1) to Indian images of the universal king *(cakravartin)*, particularly those associated with King Mahasudassana's royal city of *Kusāvatī*, (2) to Indian mythology of the ideal world represented by the Northern Realm *(Uttarakuru)*, (3) to concepts of the heavenly realms *(devaloka)*, especially the heavens of *Brahman* and *Paranirmitavaśavartin*, and (4) to idealized models of a Buddhist *stūpa*.[7] However, in spite of the contributions these images made to the development of the concept, Fujita rejected the complete reduction of *Sukhāvatīvyūha* to these sources. He concludes that *Sukhāvatīvyūha* (1) is different from the capital of a *cakravartin* king because there is no king in the Pure Land, (2) is different from the Northern Realm because Mt. Sumeru does not exist in connection with the Pure Land, (3) cannot be a heaven because it is outside the cycle of birth and death, and (4) because the Western Pure

Land is ruled by the Buddha of Infinite Life (Amitāyus), is different from a *stūpa* which holds the relics of a deceased Buddha. In fact, because the Pure Land does not have a moon or stars, hills and hungry ghosts, male and female, it must be a realm of a totally different nature. Fujita therefore asserts that the only concept with which *Sukhāvatīvyūha* can be directly identified is the idea of a Buddha Land *(fo- ch'a, fo-kuo,* or *fo-t'u,* Skt. *buddha-kṣetra).*[8]

What is a Buddha Land? Teresina Rowell has demonstrated that a Buddha Land is the sphere of influence of an enlightened one, the area in which he exercises his power and knowledge, the sphere which receives his beneficent influence.[9] The idea of a Buddha Land is particularly associated with Mahāyāna Buddhism, however, because it teaches the coexistence of so many diverse Buddhas. Because of the doctrines of dependent co-origination and nonsubstantiality *(śūnyatā),* the divisions of space and time collapse in Mahāyāna.[10] This eliminates the problem found in Hīnayāna where only one Buddha was thought to exist at any one time, and even then there were gaps when there was no Buddha in the world (such as during our present age). By comparison, from the very beginning of Mahāyāna there have been profuse references to many different kinds of Buddhas and their Buddha Lands coexisting and interpenetrating.[11]

According to early Mahāyāna doctrines, any particular Buddha was but a temporary manifestation of the one realm of truth *(fa-chieh,* Skt. *dharmadhātu),* also called the true body of ultimate reality *(fa-chen* or *chen-shen,* Skt. *dharmakāya),* or the one eternal *tathāgata* Buddha. Thus, particular Buddhas such as Śākyamuni and Maitreya are seen as merely Apparitional Bodies *(hua-shen* or *ying-shen,* Skt. *nirmāṇakāya)* which emanate from the unchanging *dharmakāya.* Each Apparitional Buddha (such as Śākyamuni) also has an Apparitional Buddha Land (such as this present *sahā*-world or place of defilement and suffering). Since each Buddha Land was created in "response" to the needs of the beings who occupy it, it was called both an Apparitional Land *(hua-t'u)* and a Response Land *(ying-t'u).* Although the *dharmakāya* is synonymous with the one realm of truth *(dharmadhātu),* it is symbolically stated that the *dharmakāya* "has" a True Land *(chen-t'u,* roughly equivalent to the *fa-chieh* or *dharmadhātu)* from which the temporary Apparitional Lands emanate.[12]

An equally important doctrinal development in Mahāyāna Buddhism was the evolution of the bodhisattva ideal. A prime example of a bodhisattva is Dharmākara, who became Amitābha Buddha when he achieved full enlightenment. The forty-eight vows that he made in order to provide the best conditions for the salvation of beings reflect the compassionate activity of a bodhisattva in "purifying his land" (that is, helping beings in the area of his influence). Thus, when the bodhisattva achieves Buddhahood, his "purified land" becomes a Buddha Land or "Pure Land" *(ching-t'u)*.[13] In addition, the resplendent appearance that these heroic bodhisattvas achieve when they reach Buddhahood became known as a Reward Body *(pao-shen;* Sanskrit probably is *saṃbhoga-kāya)*. The concept of the Reward Body was a later development, however, and did not reach China until the fifth century with the arrival of the *Laṅkāvatāra-sūtra*.[14] Pure Land devotees argued that Amitābha Buddha was a Reward Body. Thus, they implicitly accepted the doctrine of the three bodies of the Buddha (the *trikāya* doctrine): namely, the *nirmāṇakāya, saṃbhogakāya,* and *dharmakāya,* each of which had its own "land." Nevertheless, as we shall see, the twofold scheme which appeared in early Mahāyāna and in early Chinese writings on the subject remained conceptually strong for those like Tao-ch'o who also used the *trikāya* doctrine to explain the Buddha Lands.

SENG-CHAO (375–414)

Two important facts inherent in Chinese Buddhism are (1) that major doctrinal efforts to understand and classify the Pure Lands were made by thinkers not included in the lineage of Pure Land devotionalism in China, and (2) that the main scriptural sources for those thinkers frequently were not the classical Pure Land texts: namely, the *O-mi-t'o-fo-ching (Amitābha-sūtra), Kuan-wu-liang-shou-ching,* and the *Wu-liang-shou-ching*.[15] A case in point is Seng-chao (375–414),[16] perhaps the earliest Chinese thinker whose analysis of the Pure Land survives. Interestingly, it was the *Vimalakīrtinirdeśa-sūtra* which evoked his analysis and which also served as the platform for the expression of the Pure Land doctrines of Chih-i.

The *Vimalakīrtinirdeśa-sūtra*[17] is among the earliest of the Mahāyāna sūtras. Set squarely within the "wisdom" tradition, it presents the classic insights of nonsubstantiality and nonduality. Nevertheless, its style is clearly different from the rather arid format of the Perfection of Wisdom literature, as its themes are woven within a vivid and entertaining narrative describing the compassionate activity of a lay bodhisattva named Vimalakīrti. Included within this framework are occasional references to the purifying activity of the bodhisattva in his "sphere of activity" or "land"; descriptions of different kinds of Buddha Lands; and, finally, the assertion of their mutual nonduality. Although these Pure Land ideas are found within the early third-century translation of Chih-Ch'ien, they become more explicit in the later translations of Kumārajīva and Hsüan-tsang.[18]

Although the sūtra contains many passages advocating bodhisattva practices that are meant to purify the Buddha Lands, the passages relevant to our discussion are those which describe the actual conditions of the lands to be purified. In particular, the last section of chapter 1 and a part of chapter 11 contain statements that have a bearing on the nature and interrelationships of the Buddha Lands.[19] We see from a reading of these two sections that the *Vimalakīrtinirdeśa-sūtra* assumes (1) that there are numerous Buddha Lands; (2) that these numerous Buddha Lands are manifested in order that other beings might be saved; (3) that these Buddha Lands are of differing qualities to meet the needs of beings with different capacities; (4) that these Buddha Lands also differ in their degree of superiority or inferiority, *sheng-lieh,* and in their degree of purity and impurity; and (5) that Buddhas of other lands wishing to convert inhabitants of our present world of suffering (this *sahā*-world) do not completely reveal to them their own pure lands. Nevertheless, (6) just as all Buddhas find their identity in the *dharmakāya,* so too there are no essential differences among the Buddha Lands; (7) ultimately the Buddha Lands are all nonsubstantial, *śūnya;* and (8) all Buddha Lands interpenetrate and mutually contain one another.

This is an impressive list of ideas concerning the nature and interrelationships of the Pure Lands, but it is neither the style nor the intent of the text to arrange these ideas in any systematic way. Seng-chao's *Chu-wei-mo-ch'i-ching,*[20] composed sometime between the Kumārajīva translation in 406 and Seng-chao's death in 414,[21] is the earliest Chinese commentary extant. The comments on the sūtra by Kumārajīva and Seng-chao, which are interspersed occasionally with opinions by Tao-sheng, Seng-jui, and Tao-jung, make it a fascinating document of early Chinese Buddhism.

In the *Chu-wei-mo-ch'i-ching* we find Seng-chao discussing the Pure Lands versus a falsely conceived duality.[22] He argued that since the distinctions between purity and impurity, this and that, exist only in response to the affections of beings, they are without any enduring essence. Just as these forms are without any enduring basis, how much more nonsubstantial is the Land of Reward, *pao-ying-t'u,*[23] which is devised in terms of the needs and illusions of such beings. Seng-chao concluded that

When the purity and impurity of a land is discussed in terms of the beings [who live there], the Reward Land is being referred to. This is not the Land of the *tathāgata* which is different from the particular place of Reward. Let me attempt to explain this. The Pure Land which the *tathāgata* cultivates takes "no particular place," *wu-fang,* as its essence. Therefore, it happens that sentient beings who have a diversity of practices gaze in the same direction but see different things, *t'ung-shih-i-chien*. Because they see different things [the distinctions of] purity and impurity arise. But by means of "no particular place" the True Land, *chen-t'u,* is formed. If someone wrongly holds to [the distinction of] purity and impurity, then this is the Reward of sentient beings [in accordance with their views]. The reality of the Buddha Land, however, is rooted in "no particular place."[24]

Later in the commentary Seng-chao discussed the idea that this world is defiled to all but those who have the "dharma-eye." He also raised the issue of two kinds of lands, common and saintly, *fan-sheng erh-t'u,* in terms of this idea of purity and defilement. However, these distinctions are to be transcended by nonduality. Thus, his basic point is that due to the nonduality of purity and defilements, "the Buddha does not have a particular place, but appears in response to beings," *fo wu-ting suo-ying wu erh hsien.*[25] Seng-chao seems to conclude that any apparent distinction between a Pure Land and a defiled land is based on illusion and disappears in the daylight of enlightenment.

Ching-ying Hui-yüan (523–592)

The next attempt to analyze and classify the Pure Lands was made by Ching-ying Hui-yüan, whose work is much more detailed than is Seng-chao's treatment. A namesake of Ching-ying Hui-yüan, viz., Lu-shan Hui-yüan (344–416), is much more famous in Pure Land Buddhism as the organizer of the White Lotus Society which was dedicated to rebirth in the Pure Land of O-mi-t'o-fo (Amitābha). However, Ching-ying Hui-yüan probably had a more direct, if unacknowledged, influence on the formation of Sui-T'ang Pure Land Buddhism than did Lu-shan Hui-yüan, who was elevated to the position of a Pure Land patriarch only in later times. Perhaps the reason why Pure Land devotees directly mentioned Ching-ying Hui-yüan so infrequently was that he himself did not wish to be reborn in the Pure Land. Rather, he was a follower of Maitreya and wished to be reborn in Tuṣita heaven,[26] the home of the future Buddha—a common wish among those who had been influenced by the Yogācāra tradition in China.[27]

Nevertheless, Ching-ying Hui-yüan discussed Pure Land doctrines in a number of his writings, and wrote two influential commentaries on Pure Land sūtras, the *Kuan-wu-liang-shou-ching i-shu* and the *Wu-liang-shou-ching i-shu.*[28] Although there may be some contradiction among his various works,[29] his clearest and most systematic treatment of the Pure Lands is found in his *Ta-ch'eng i-chang* [Encyclopaedia of Buddhism].[30] The main scriptural sources that he used in his chapter on the Pure Lands (chapter 207 according to the enumeration of the *Taishō Shinshū Daizōkyō*) are not of the Pure Land devotional type, but are the *Nirvāna-*

sūtra, the *Avatamsaka-sūtra,* and the *Vimalakīrtinirdeśa-sūtra.* Moreover, the three treatises from which he quoted are the *Ta-chih-tu-lun* attributed to Nāgārjuna; the *Shih-ti-ching-lun* of Vasubandhu; and the
Chu-wei-mo-ch'i-ching by Seng-chao and Kumārajīva.

Basically, Hui-yüan adopted two different but interpenetrating
schemes to classify the Pure Lands. In the first, he arranged the Pure
Lands from the point of view of the Buddhist follower who is attempting
to practice the precepts, gain a better rebirth, and seek enlightenment.
Such a follower experiences three kinds of Pure Lands, in ascending
order: (1) Lands of Worldly Purity, *shih-ching-t'u;* (2) Lands Pure in
Appearance, *hsiang-ching-t'u;* and (3) the Land of True Purity, *chen-
ching-t'u.* Hui-yüan's second scheme is also threefold and is based on the
trikāya doctrine. Accordingly, it is arranged in descending order from
the point of view of ultimate truth: (1) the Land of Dharma-nature, *Fa-
hsing-t'u;* (2) Lands of Real Reward, *Shih-pao-t'u;* and (3) Lands of
Perfect Response, *Yüan-ying-t'u.* The nature and interrelationships of
these two systems have been described in detail in the section on the Pure
Lands in the *Ta-ch'eng i-chang.* Accordingly, what follows is a summary
of a major portion of that chapter.[31]

In the first scheme, Lands of Worldly Purity are places where common
beings, *fan-fu,* live. They have won such lands by their pure actions, even
though these were performed with a defiled consciousness. This is a
realm of wordly purity insofar as it contains the adornments and treasures valued by those who live a life of illusion. Not only are the boundaries of such lands limited, but they are different for everyone. Because
the common beings who live there grasp onto specific forms in their
religious practice, all the adornments of these lands are also fixed. Lands
of Worldly Purity are basically of two kinds: (a) lands attained by those
who practice good deeds, seeking rebirth in a better station within this
worldly existence; thus, these beings are born within the various heavens
of the Realm of Desire and Realm of Form, and their deluded passions
continue to accumulate bad karma; some of them do escape from the
Three Realms (of Desire, Form and Formlessness), but only through the
influential power of a good spiritual guide, not through the influence of
these heavens; and (b) the lands attained by those who seek to transcend
the world. Examples of the latter are the Western Pure Land of Amitābha and the Fragrant Land discussed in chapter 10 of the *Vimalakīrtinirdeśa-sūtra.* Thus, among these two kinds of Lands of Worldly Purity,
the heavens are a lower form than the lands of those who desire to transcend the world.

Hui-yüan stated further that in terms of the Four Noble Truths these
lands do not escape from the Truth of Suffering. While this is clearly the

case for the lower form, there is some ambiguity about the higher kind. Beings in these lands may seem to transcend the defiled cycle of birth and death either by good karma or by invoking the Buddha's Name, but in fact they do not. This is because in their rebirth they still carry with them their defiled consciousness.

Another reason that Hui-yüan placed the Western Pure Land among the Lands of Worldly Purity is found in his *Wu-liang-shou-ching i-shu.* There Hui-yüan refers to the account in the *Kuan-shih-ying-p'u-sa shou-chi-ching* in which it is stated that Amitābha will be replaced by Kuan-yin and then by Ta-shih.[32] Thus, one day his life will end. How then can Amitābha be called the Buddha of Limitless Life, *Wu-liang-shou-fo?* According to Hui-yüan, this may be understood on two levels. From the point of view of true reality, the life of Amitābha is eternal, *chen-chi-ch'ang-chu.* From the point of view of his life as a manifestation, it is long, *yü-ying-shou-chung tz'u-fo-shou-ch'ang,* but it is limited and has a beginning and an end. Only because common people and members of the Two Vehicles have inadequate understanding do they say his life is unlimited, *wu-liang.*[33] The implication of these remarks by Hui-yüan is that those with true understanding realize that the view of Amitābha and his land as being specific realities to be singled out and sought after is only a limited understanding, one that is helpful at a beginning stage only.

The Lands Pure in Appearance are the places where śrāvakas, pratyekabuddhas, and various bodhisattvas live. Quoting the *Ta-chih-tu-lun,* Hui-yüan described these lands as being marvelous pure lands "beyond the Three Realms." Because these lands are realized through meditation on causality and the suppression of passions, they are free of defilement. Nevertheless, these lands are also shaped by the thoughts of those who have been reborn in them. "Although this type of land is pure, it is generated by erroneous thoughts and, hence, is as empty and unreal as what is seen in a dream." Therefore, they are only "pure in appearance." Basically, the Lands Pure in Appearance are also of two kinds: (a) the lower form of these lands is attained by śrāvakas and pratyekabuddhas through their good capacities dedicated to rejecting evil, but for their own benefit; these lands are serene and without form, like a peaceful resting place, but are devoid of the compassionate resolve to help others; and (b) the higher form of these lands is attained by various bodhisattvas owing to their improved capacities developed through saving others. Rather than being resting places, these are areas which evolve and change in terms of the needs of sentient beings which are to be met.

The Land of True Purity is a place in which live bodhisattvas from the first *bhūmi* on up to Buddhahood. Unlike the previous Lands Pure in Appearance, this land lacks deluded thoughts and the obstructions associated with the rise of illusions. This "land" is truly pure, for its beings are unattached to conditioned phenomena. Therefore, it is without any particular form, color, or shape. Because it lacks any specific attachments in regard to its causation, it has no definite location. Moreover, because it does not depend on any particular cause or condition, it does not discriminate between this and that, between self and others. But even though it has no distinct form, it is not a "no-land," *wu-t'u*.[34] Although marvelous and serene, it also manifests all things. In spite of its utter purity, it is not separate from defilement. Rather, like a pure pearl, it is not restricted to any particular color for there is nothing which is not shown in it. As the *Shih-ti-ching-lun* states: "Although we know that the various Buddha Lands are nonsubstantial, *k'ung,* yet we cultivate the practices [that will enable us to realize] the lands of unlimited adornments."[35]

Hui-yüan then showed how true reality can be considered as twofold. Echoing the familiar Chinese paradigm of essence and function, *t'i-yung,* he treated reality in its nature as the True Land, *chen-t'u,* and in its function as the Response Land, *ying-t'u.* He then explained how true reality can also be seen from a threefold perspective as the Three Lands of the Three Bodies of the Buddha *(trikāya).*

The first Land of the Three Bodies of the Buddha is the Land of Dharma-nature, synonymous with ultimate reality. It is "perfectly homogenous with respect to its characteristics," *chu-i t'ung-t'i,* so that none of its attributes obstruct other dimensions. All things interpenetrate the Ultimate like Indra's net. This land is like space, unmoving, without limits, and without specific location.

The second land is the Land of True Reward, the name of which refers to the unlimited variety of adornments that results when the bodhisattva cultivates the inexhaustible practices of the *dharmadhātu.* When these two lands shine like a pure jewel reflecting the capacities and needs of sentient beings in every different kind of way without defect, they then are called the Lands of Perfect Response. This represents the third kind of land, and is occupied by the Third Body of the Buddha, the *nirmāṇakāya.* Hui-yüan followed the discussion in the *Shih-ti-ching-lun* by describing seven aspects in which the purity of perfect response may be manifested. For example, he cited the Purity of a Common Essense, wherein each Buddha Land contains every other Buddha Land within it. He also cited the Purity of Function, the Purity of Adornments, the Purity of Causes, and others.[36]

According to Hui-yüan's classification of the Pure Lands, anything less than the True Land, the *dharmadhātu,* is to be considered as worldly or artificial. However, after one adopts the perspective of the True Land, then all else can be seen as manifestations, *ying,* of it. All forms and events become functions, *yung,* of true reality in the all-inclusive interpenetration of nonsubstantiality. Ultimately, this position is not derived from the *trikāya* doctrine, for underlying the *trikāya* doctrine are two basic Buddha forms: the True Body, *chen-shen,* and the Response Body, *ying-shen.*

This is a very important position which Hui-yüan stated at some length in many passages. Following his section on "the meaning of entering the gate of nonduality" in his *Ta-ch'eng i-chang,* he composed a section on "the Two Truths" which is particularly interesting.[37] In order to illustrate the alternatives in interpreting the polarity of the Two Truths, he set forth a fourfold classification of doctrine, *p'an-chiao.* First is the Abhidharma teaching which, although it mistakenly affirms a real existence to dharmas, is not heterodox since dharmas are said to be causally produced. Second is the *Ch'eng-shih-lun* teaching in which dharmas are false and without self-nature but still have form, *hsiang.* Third is the teaching of the Wisdom and Lotus traditions, which deny a self-nature or form to dharmas but which do not go beyond the position that form is emptiness and emptiness is form. Fourth is the *Tathāgata-garbha* tradition which teaches that although dharmas are illusory and without essence, the *ālayavijñāna* itself is not empty, *pu-k'ung tsang.* This is the teaching in which true reality is manifested, *hsien-shih tsung.*[38] This is the interpretation advocated by Hui-yüan, and is a very positive affirmation of the value of nonsubstantial phenomena and Conventional Truth. In this teaching there is a mutual identity, *hsiang-chi,* between the Two Truths, in which essence, *t'i,* gives rise to function, *yung,* and function is identical with essence.[39] Hui-yüan expressed the idea again in a later section when he wrote that *li* was "the one reality of the Two Truths which gives rise to the *dharmadhātu,*" *erh-ti i-shih yuan-ch'i fa-chieh.*[40] This theme of the harmony of the Conventional and Absolute Truths was crucial for Hui-yüan as the foundation of his interpretation of the Pure Lands, and was echoed by other thinkers of the period.

T'IEN-T'AI CHIH-I (538–597)

The writings of T'ien-t'ai Chih-i on the nature of the Pure Lands carry on the Vimalakīrti tradition and also reflect the influence of Hui-yüan. Chih-i's major discussion of the Pure Lands is to be found in his commentary on the *Vimalakīrtinirdeśa-sūtra,* the *Wei-mo-ching wen-shu* comprising twenty-eight fascicles.[41] The sūtra was a perennial favorite of Chih-i, being among the half-dozen scriptures he quoted most often.[42] The actual reason for his compiling the commentary was a request in 595 from the royal prince Yang Kuang. Accordingly, the *Wei-mo-ching wen-shu* not only represents the mature thought of Chih-i but may even have been his last work, since it was presented to Yang Kuang after Chih-i's death.[43] The book was highly valued by later disciples who circulated it in an abridged form of ten fascicles that had been compiled by Chan-jan in 764.[44] Although certain commentaries on several Pure Land sūtras have been attributed to Chih-i, their authenticity is in doubt;[45] hence, the present discussion will be limited to the ideas found in the *Wei-mo-ching wen-shu.*

Chih-i began his discussion of the Buddha Lands with a general explanation that emphasized particularly the distinction between the two lands that are associated with the two bodies of the Buddha—the Response Land, *ying-t'u,* connected with the Apparitional Body, *nirmāṇakāya,* and the True Land, *chen-t'u,* associated with the Dharma-body, *dharmakāya.* He explained the relationship between these two lands as being a manifestation of the relationship between phenomena, *shih,* and inherent reality, *li,* or between the traces [left by the source], *chi,* and the source itself, *pen.*[46] Not only are these idioms very Chinese in spirit but they also recall the manner in which Seng-chao classified the Reward Land on one side and the True Land of the Dharma-body on the other. Of course, the two lands associated with the two bodies of the Buddha are a more exact reflection of the scheme of Hui-yüan in which the two main lands were the True Land and the Response Land.

In the next section of the *Wei-mo-ching wen-shu,* Chih-i presented his detailed explanation of the Pure Lands. There are four kinds: (1) the Land Where the Common and Saintly Live Together, *fan-sheng t'ung-chu-t'u;* (2) the Land of Expediency with a Remnant [of fundamental ignorance], *fang-pien yu-yu-t'u;* (3) the Land of True Reward without Obstruction, *shih-pao wu-chang-ai-t'u;* and (4) the Land of Eternal Serenity and Illumination, *ch'ang-chi kuang-t'u.* Following is a summary of these four lands as described in the *Wei-mo-ching wen-shu.*[47]

Of the common and saintly beings who live in the first land, the common beings include all those of the four evil rebirths, plus men and gods. The saintly beings include śrāvakas and pratyekabuddhas, plus bodhisattvas up to the first *bhūmi.* These are called real saints, *shih-sheng.* In contrast are bodhisattvas of the first *bhūmi* on up to the Buddha, who reenter the lower level of sainthood for the sake of saving others. These are called provisional saints, *ch'üan-sheng,* and are also included in this first land. In addition, the Land Where the Common and Saintly Live Together can be divided into a defiled land, *hui-t'u,* and a pure land, *ching-t'u.* The defiled land is filled with impurities like those in our pres-

ent *sahā*-world. The pure land lacks the four evil rebirths, and includes
men and gods with pure embellishments, much like the Western Pure
Land of Amitābha.

The second land is the Land of Expediency. Here one can still be
reborn because the remainder of fundamental ignorance has not yet been
cut off; but, at the same time, one is beyond the Three Realms to the degree that the mortal body is discarded and all other false ideas and wrong
attitudes have been cut off. Such a stage is called the stage of nonretro-
gression since it is beyond the seventh *bhūmi*. There is no dichotomy between self and others, between cause and effect, or between inherent reality, *li,* and phenomena, events, *shih.* Hence, one does not cling to merits,
but is able to save others and practice the *dharma* completely. This is the
dwelling place of all those in the Three Vehicles who have realized the expedient path, which means that things can be used as if they were substantial even though they are nonsubstantial. This is called the two views
of nonsubstantiality and temporary substantiality, *k'ung chia erh-kuan.*

In the third land, the Land of True Reward without Obstruction, the
one real truth, *i-shih-ti,* is viewed, fundamental ignorance is refuted, and
the Dharma-nature, *fa-hsing,* is manifest; thus, true reward without
defilement is obtained. In spite of the fact that in this land fundamental
ignorance is not completely eliminated, all other realms are included here
and this realm is included in all others. Thus, like Indra's net, there is
mutual interpenetration and total freedom without obstruction. This is
the dwelling place of the Reward Body *(pao-shen,* Skt. *saṃbhogakāya).*
Chih-i included here the seven purities from the *Shih-ti-ching-lun,* which
Hui-yüan had listed under the Lands of Perfect Response.

The name of the fourth land, the Land of Eternal Serenity and Illumination, is drawn from the *Kuan-p'u-hsien-ching* where it is the name
for the dwelling place of Śākyamuni in the form of Vairocana.[48] Chih-i
quoted the *Jen-wang po-jo-ching* to the effect that sages and saints abide
in their states of attainment and reward, but "the Buddha alone dwells in
the Pure Land."[49] This refers to the Land of Eternal Serenity and Illumination, which is the dwelling place of the Dharma-body. It is also
called the Land of Dharma-nature, *fa-hsing-t'u.* This is said figuratively,
however, because, strictly speaking, the Buddha-nature of Suchness has
no body and no land, *chen-ju fo-hsing fei-shen fei-t'u.*

Implied in the foregoing statements of Chih-i is the idea that the Land
of Eternal Serenity and Illumination refers simply to the world just as it
is when seen without illusion. At the end of this section, Chih-i makes the
interesting comment that he chose to explain the Pure Lands according
to the fourfold scheme in order to parallel the Four Doctrines, *ssu-
chiao,*[50] while at the same time he recognized that there are other classifi-

cations that he could have used. Based upon the Four Doctrines, the high claims of the Pure Land tradition for Amitābha and His land can be acknowledged as being valid at their level. However, as viewed from the Complete Teaching of T'ien-t'ai these claims represent only a preliminary stage of understanding belonging to the Tripiṭaka Teaching, and the Buddha is but an Inferior Apparitional Body, *lieh-ying-shen*.[51] This attitude undermines the enduring significance of all the Pure Lands short of the Land of Eternal Serenity and Illumination. Thus, it dissolves the fourfold scheme of classification back into the duality of *li* and *shih, pen* and *chi,* True Land and Response Lands, which Chih-i invoked at the beginning of his discussion.

It has become clear that Seng-chao, Hui-yüan, and Chih-i (in spite of the differences among their Pure Land classifications) are united in considering these classifications as being secondary elaborations of the more fundamental motif of true reality, *chen,* and its manifestations, *ying.* For Chih-i and his Hua-yen contemporary Tu-shun (557–640) this motif was expressed by juxtaposing *li* and *shih* and at the same time asserting their ultimate nonduality. Seng-chao summarized the idea in many striking phrases, such as "establishing finite positions is identical to true reality," *li-ch'u chi-chen,* and "in the realm of conditioned phenomena which is no different from true reality," *ch'u-shih erh chen.*[52] This theme of the "one reality of the Two Truths" and the immanence of the Buddha-nature was seen by Kamata Shigeo as pervading Buddhism during the Northern and Southern Dynasties (420–589) and culminating in the Sui-T'ang schools.[53] He traced the concept of Buddha-nature from Bodhiruci's translation of the *Nirvāṇa-sūtra* up to the time of Hui-yüan and Seng-ts'an (529–613), who had a chapter on mutual identity, *hsiang-chi,* in his *Shih-chung Ta-ch'eng-lun.*[54] Although this theme continues into the development of Hua-yen schemes of mutual interpenetration and identity, it is beyond the concern of this essay. Suffice it to say that Chih-i also identified the Two Truths by means of his scheme of Three Truths.[55] Seng-chao, Hui-yüan, and Chih-i believed that underlying the polarity of *chen* and *ying,* or *li* and *shih,* is a postitive sense of their ultimate nonduality through the presence of the absolute in the finite.[56]

In this context, there is no room for a strong concept of the Pure Lands or Reward Buddhas at an intermediate stage between ordinary life and true reality, since they are but two aspects of the same thing. Accordingly, it is not surprising to see these thinkers ignore the highly developed Indian visions of elaborate Pure Lands and heroic Buddhas. The duality of existence can be unified here and now, and need not be projected beyond the Three Realms onto a celestial Buddha or postponed until one is reborn in a Pure Land. This seems to be in marked contrast

to the stand taken by those steeped in the tradition of Pure Land devotionalism as exemplified by Tao-ch'o. But before one can draw concrete
conclusions, one must examine Tao-ch'o's position in some detail.

Tao-ch'o (562–645)

The spiritual predecessor of Tao-ch'o in the Pure Land lineage was T'an-
luan (ca. 488–554). An examination of his writings shows that he did not
live when the classification of the Pure Lands was an important issue. He
offered no scheme and really did not discuss in detail the Western Pure
Land of Amitābha in relationship to other lands. While advocating
reliance on Amitābha and rebirth in the Pure Land, T'an-luan only in-
directly referred to the place of the Pure Land within Buddhist
cosmology. Briefly, he stated that the Western Pure Land is beyond the
Three Realms; that is, it transcends the cycle of birth and death.[57] His
authority for this statement is the *Ching-t'u-lun*[58] attributed to Vasubandhu, and the *Ta-chih-tu-lun*.[59] It is interesting that Hui-yüan later referred to the same passage in the *Ta-chih-tu-lun*, but there he argued that
the Western Pure Land does not qualify.[60] Thus, Hui-yüan placed it
firmly within the Three Realms, and added that it is the dwelling place of
the *defiled* form of the Reward Body, a status not significantly higher
than an Apparitional Body. This also contradicts T'an-luan who argued
that the Pure Land is beyond the Three Realms because of the special
merit built up by Amitābha when he was Bodhisattva Dharmākara.[61]

If this land of Amitābha is a reward for good merit, then Amitābha is
a bona fide Reward Body, *saṃbhogakāya,* and his Buddha Land quali-
fies as a Reward Land. However, T'an-luan did not explicitly say this.
Chi-tsang wrote about a "northern master" who held that (1) Amitābha's Pure Land was not in the Three Realms, and (2) that when Bodhisattva Dharmākara attained the eighth *bhūmi* he created a purified land
based on his vows, which Chi-tsang called a "Reward Land."[62] Mochizuki Shinkō identified this "northern master" as T'an-luan to support
his contention that in the eyes of T'an-luan, Amitābha was indeed a
saṃbhogakāya, and his Pure Land was a Reward Land.[63] Whether true
or not (and I tend to believe that it is), the fact that Mochizuki had to
resort to such an oblique reference shows the paucity of our sources.
This, in turn, points up the total lack of development of Pure Land
cosmology at the time of T'an-luan among the devotees of Amitābha and
his Western Pure Land.

This situation had changed drastically by the time of Tao-ch'o. The
nature of the Pure Land of Amitābha is of primary importance to the
structure of his thoughts, and more than half of the twelve chapters of
his *An-lo-chi* have sections dealing with its nature and its relationship

with other lands. In comparison to T'an-luan, he paid much more attention to the place of the Pure Land within Buddhist cosmology. This attention seems to reflect the strong influence of Hui-yüan and the challenge of his interpretations of the Pure Lands.

Chapter 1 of the *An-lo-chi* begins with prefatory remarks affirming that Buddhist teachings must be appropriate to the times and to the capacities of the persons being taught, and acknowledging the scope of Buddhist teaching in terms of its methods, sources, contents, audiences, and aims. The stage having been set, the last three sections of the chapter are then devoted to explaining the Pure Land of Amitābha.[64] Because the basic framework of Tao-ch'o's understanding of the Pure Land is set forth in these sections, I will first summarize these passages and then attempt to refine the ideas through references to later sections.

As if in rebuttal to Hui-yüan and Chih-i, Tao-ch'o stated at the outset that Amitābha is a Reward Body and his land is a Reward Land.[65] All those in the past who identified Amitābha as an Apparitional Body were in error. To support his claim, he argued rather weakly that if his opponents were correct, then the Apparitional Body would dwell in both the Defiled Land and the Pure Land, which he felt to be doubtful. However, Chih-i did divide the Apparitional Body into two kinds, an inferior and a superior *nirmāṇakāya*.[66] Moreover, the *Vimalakīrtinirdeśasūtra* advocates the ultimate nonduality of these two lands, which also weakens the strength of this distinction between the Defiled and the Pure Land.

More forcefully, Tao-ch'o quoted from the *Ta-ch'eng t'ung-hsing-ching* where Amitābha clearly is located in the Pure Land and is identified with the Reward Body rather than with the Apparitional Body, *hua-shen,* or the True Body, *chen-shen.*[67] But rather than lock himself into a substantialist system of classification implying separate and enduring Buddha-bodies, Tao-ch'o went on to admit that Amitābha manifests an Apparitional Body when born into the Defiled Land to save sentient beings. Similarly, Śākyamuni manifests a Reward Body when in the Pure Land. Amitābha, in fact, involves all three bodies.[68] As proof, Tao-ch'o quoted the *O-mi-t'o ku-yin-sheng-wang t'o-lo-ni-ching,* which shows Amitābha dwelling in a country called Ching-t'ai, having a father and mother, and living with śrāvakas. In this context, Amitābha was in his Apparitional Body.[69]

Not only does Amitābha have all three Buddha-bodies, but Tao-ch'o believed that his Reward Body is eternal, *ch'ang-chu,* and, because of the illusions of sentient beings, only appears to have disappeared into nirvāṇa. Similarly, the essense of the Pure Land is neither created nor destroyed, *t'i fei ch'eng huai.*[70] The Pure Land, from the point of view of its essential nature, cannot be considered pure or defiled, *fa-hsing-t'u tse pu-lun ch'ing cho*. But because of the great compassion which led to the creation of the Reward Body and the Apparitional Body, it cannot be said that the Pure Land and the Defiled Land do not exist.[71] Thus, Tao-ch'o also invoked an underlying duality as a basic paradigm to assess the true nature of the Pure Land, as did the thinkers who were not devotees of the Pure Land. Amitābha is eternal and his land is unchanging beyond the distinctions of purity and defilement insofar as Amitābha is an expression of the True Body *(dharmakāya)* and his land is a part of the True Land *(dharmadhātu)*.[72] However, in response to the needs of sentient beings caught in illusion, Amitābha and his land apparently change and can be distinguished from the realm of impurity. These manifestations of the body and land of Amitābha are the Response Body and Response Land of the *dharmakāya*.

Tao-ch'o established that Amitābha in the present is a Reward Buddha.[73] However, the *Kuan-shih-yin-p'u-sa shou-chi-ching* says that in the future after the disappearance of the true teachings of Amitābha, Kuan-yin will become a Buddha and replace Amitābha.[74] This implies that the Reward Land and the Reward Body endure as permanent categories or manifestations of the *dharmakāya*. Thus, true reality, *chen,* perpetually radiates a response, *ying,* which takes the form either of reward, *pao,* or apparition, *hua*. The Pure Land of Amitābha is not the true reality, *chen,* in its essense or in its fluctuating transformations, *hua,* for the sake of sentient beings, but is its ever-shining reward, *pao*.

Thus, the Pure Land can be seen in three different ways according to the capacities of sentient beings. Tao-ch'o outlined these ways as follows: as reward, which is the reward granted from the *dharmakāya, chen-ch'ui-pao,* as the rays of light come from the sun; as transformation, which is the sudden transformation of apparently permanent things into ashes, or the sudden transformation of barrenness into richness, so that sentient beings will give up attachment to transient things and seek enlightenment; and as pure, which is the purity [inherent in all things due to the nonduality of existence] as revealed in the *Vimalakīrtinirdeśa-sūtra* when the Buddha touched his toes to the ground to display that there was nothing that was not pure.[75]

Having listed these three possibilities, Tao-ch'o then affirmed the reality and importance of the first interpretation as being especially pertinent to the Pure Land of Amitābha: that is, as the Reward Land emanating from the *dharmakāya, ts'ung-chen ch'ui-pao-kuo*. If Amitābha's Pure Land were only the second, it would be transient and ultimately unreal. If it were the third, it would imply merely the diffuse purity of all things.

Having established the elevated and permanent position of the Western Pure Land, Tao-ch'o then proposed that common as well as saintly beings could be reborn there, *fan-sheng t'ung-wang.* This idea was rejected by Hui-yüan and Chih-i. However, Tao-ch'o reasoned that owing to the power of Amitābha the merits of both the common and saintly are supplemented and they are able to attain such a high rebirth.[77] The implication is that when they are dwelling in the Pure Land they are no longer "common and saintly"[78] but are transformed through the power of Amitābha. Tao-ch'o added the qualifying remark that if common beings seek rebirth through dependency on form, *i-hsiang,* such as Mañjuśrī did after looking only once at the form of the Buddha,[79] then they see merely an apparitional form of the Buddha of the Reward Land. This rebirth is of a lower rank than is the rebirth of "those who know that the essense is nonform and no-thought and yet in the midst of causal relations seeks rebirth [in the Pure Land]."[80]

The significant distinction, therefore, is not between monks and laymen, *tzu-su,* but between those who are dependent on form and those who are not—those who know that birth is identical to birthlessness, *sheng wu-sheng,* form is equal to nonform, *hsiang wu-hsiang,* and who do not ignore the Two Truths, *erh-ti.* Although the latter attain a superior rebirth, *shang pei sheng,* the Pure Land of Amitābha includes both of these categories of persons. "Common people in the burning house [of illusion] who depend exclusively on form, *i-hsiang ch'eng hsiang,* also are reborn [in the Pure Land]."[81]

It appears, therefore, that Tao-ch'o believed that two Buddha-bodies exist in the Reward Land: the limited apparitional form of the Reward Body for those still dependent on form, and the eternal Reward Body for those who go beyond form. "Because the wisdom of common people is shallow, many seek [rebirth in the Pure Land] by relying on form. Although they definitely attain rebirth [in the Pure Land], the power of goodness with form is minute, and they merely are reborn in a land of form, *hsiang-t'u,* and see only the apparitional form of the Reward Buddha, *pao-hua-fo.*[82]

In explaining further, Tao-ch'o quoted the *Ching-t'u-lun* to the effect that if one meditates on the twenty-nine kinds of pure adornments of the Buddha Land, of the Buddha, and of the bodhisattvas, "they condense into, *lüeh-ju,* the one true reality, *i-fa-chü.*[83] The one true reality is to be understood as utter purity, *ch'ing-ching.* Utter purity means the unconditioned *dharmakāya* of true wisdom, *chen-shih chih-hui wu-wei fa-shen.*"[84] Tao-ch'o then appended the following unacknowledged commentary by T'an-luan as part of the quotation:

Why are the expanded, *kuang* [twenty-nine kinds of purity], and the condensed, *lüeh* [one true reality], mutually inclusive? The various Buddhas and bodhisattvas have two kinds of *dharmakāya:* (1) the *dharmakāya* in its inherent nature, *fa-hsing fa-shen,* and (2) the *dharmakāya* of expedient means, *fang-pien fa-shen.* The *dharmakāya* of expedient means arises from and is based on the *dharmakāya* in its inherent nature. The *dharmakāya* in its inherent nature becomes manifest because of the *dharmakāya* of expedient means. These two kinds of *dharmakāya* are one but are not identical. Therefore, the expanded, *kuang,* and the condensed, *lüeh,* are mutually inclusive.

If bodhisattvas do not know the expanded and the condensed are mutually inclusive, then they cannot benefit themselves or others. . . . However, [bodhisattvas] know that in viewing the two dimensions of broad and specific, *tsung-pieh,* in terms of their causal connections, there is nothing which has not the character of reality, *shih-hsiang.* Based on the knowledge of the character of reality, they know that all beings in the Three Realms are in delusion. Knowing about the delusion of sentient beings gives birth to the compassion based on true reality, *chen-shih-tz'u-pei.* Knowing the *dharmakāya* or true reality gives rise to taking refuge in true reality.[85]

This quotation reinforces the paradigm used by the other thinkers examined previously which proposed an underlying duality that ultimately is a nonduality. Instead of the two dimensions of *li* and *shih,* or *chen* and *ying,* T'an-luan used the categories or images of (1) the condensed, *lüeh,* the one true reality, *i-fa-chü,* or the *dharmakāya* in its inherent nature, and (2) the expanded, *kuang,* adornments, or the *dharmakāya* of expedient means. Insofar as Tao-ch'o quoted this passage in the context of a discussion of the nature of the Pure Land, we may conclude that he wished to emphasize the interrelationship and ultimate nonduality of the two kinds of Pure Land: the one of form, *hsiang,* and the one of nonform, *wu-hsiang.*

In the final part of chapter 1, Tao-ch'o briefly asserted that the Pure Land of Amitābha is supreme, *sheng-miao,* and beyond the Three Realms and the cycle of birth and death.[86] Again Tao-ch'o showed the influence of T'an-luan, for as proof texts he used passages from the *Ta-chih-tu-lun*[87] and the *Ching-t'u-lun*[88] both of which are found in T'an-luan's writings.[89] Moreover, he ended the chapter with a verse composed by T'an-luan and based on the *Wu-liang-shou-ching.*[90]

The foregoing survey of Tao-ch'o discussion of the Pure Land drawn from chapter 1 of the *An-lo-chi* is detailed enough to suggest a few preliminary conclusions. (1) Although Tao-ch'o did discuss the Pure Land in terms of the *trikāya* doctrine, he also used the paradigm of two principal lands, the True Land and the Response Land, *chen-ying erh-t'u,* paralleling the True Body, *chen-shen,* and the Response Body, *ying-shen,* of the Buddha. In fact, in the table of contents to chapter 1, this is the title he gave to section 7.[91] (2) The Pure Land of Amitābha is one expression of the Response Land, *ying-t'u.* (3) Because there is no reality separate from that of the True Land, *chen-t'u,* of the *dharmakāya,* ultimately the Pure Land is eternal and beyond the distinctions of purity and defilement. (4) In the Response Land, there are distinctions between the Reward Land, *pao-t'u,* and the Apparitional Land, *hua-t'u.* The Reward Land may appear in different ways to ignorant sentient beings, but is ultimately an enduring manifestation of the *dharmakāya.* On the other hand, the Apparitional Land consists of temporary expediencies and transformations. (5) The Pure Land of Amitābha is a Reward Land. It is beyond the Three Realms and the cycle of birth and death. (6) Nevertheless, in the Reward Land of Amitābha there are two levels of rebirth: one for those dependent on form and the other for those aware of the Two Truths and the identity of form with nonform, birth with birthlessness.

Accordingly, if an adequate perspective is to be given to the Reward Land of Amitābha, the scheme of Three Bodies and Three Lands, *san-shen san-t'u,*[92] should be reworked as follows:

I. True Land *(chen-t'u)* of the *dharmakāya*
II. Response Land *(ying-t'u)*
    A. Reward Land *(pao-t'u)*
       1. Land of Nonform *(wu-hsiang-t'u),* that is the true expression of the *saṃbhogakāya.*
       2. Land of Form *(hsiang-t'u),* that is a temporary manifestation for those still dependent on form; and that has an apparitional form of the Reward Buddha *(pao-hua-shen).*
    B. Apparitional Land *(hua-t'u)* of the *nirmāṇakāya*

The popular Pure Land devotionalism with which Tao-ch'o is identified and which he defended focused on the details of practice and rebirth in a Pure Land of form. The Pure Land of Amitābha, according to Tao-ch'o, includes both form and nonform, and it was the land of form that needed defending to his contemporaries. This he attempted to do in a number of ways in the *An-lo-chi.* For example, Tao-ch'o found it hard to believe that devotion to the Buddha could involve harmful attachment to form. To support his feeling he quoted passages from the *Nirvāṇa-sūtra* and the *Ching-t'u-lun* that advocate worship and love of the true dharma. Tao-ch'o concluded: "Therefore, although this is grasping onto form, *ch'ü-hsiang,* such grasping does not correspond to binding attachment, *chih-feng.* In addition, the form of the Pure Land which we are discussing is identical to form without defilements, form which is true form, *wu-lou hsiang shih-hsiang hsiang.*"[93]

Nevertheless, these arguments from the devotional tradition of Buddhism still did not seem to satisfy the Mahāyāna commitment to nonform. As Tao-ch'o posed the question: "Those of the lower grade who attain rebirth [in the Pure Land] through invoking [the name of Amitābha] ten times, how can they possibly not grasp it as real birth?''[94] The answer that he gave was that just as a luminous pearl clears muddy waters, the purifying power of Amitābha removes illusions, so that those who are attached to rebirth will be transformed into a state of birthlessness:

> It is like lighting a fire on top of ice. As the fire intensifies, the ice will melt. When the ice melts, then the fire will go out. Those people of a lower grade of rebirth who rely on the power of reciting the Buddha's name with the purpose of attaining rebirth and with the resolve of being reborn in his land, even though they do not understand the birthlessness of the dharma-nature, will attain the realm of birthlessness and will see the flame of rebirth spontaneously disappear at that time.[95]

Thus, Tao-ch'o's position regarding those of a lower rebirth is somewhat paradoxical. First, because such persons rely on form, they are reborn in a Pure Land of form and see an apparitional form of the Reward Body of Amitābha. However, because they have invoked the name of Amitābha, they are ultimately destined for a rebirth into birthlessness and a Pure Land of nonform.

This did not conclude Tao-ch'o's struggle with this issue, however, for he also wished to argue for the validity of a Pure Land with form in terms of those who do have a higher understanding. Earlier in chapter 2, he stated the problem this way:

> Question: Some people say that the Mahāyāna doctrine of nonform, wu-hsiang, does not discriminate between this and that. If one aspires to be reborn in the Pure Land, then such aspiration is attachment to form and increasingly adds to the fetters of illusion. What use is there in seeking [rebirth in the Pure Land]?
>
> Answer: Those who think like this are wrong. Why? The various teachings of the Buddha must all possess two conditions: they [must] rely on dharma-nature, the true reality, fa-hsing shih-li, and they [must] comply with the Two Truths. Those who understand the Mahāyāna doctrine of no-thought, wu-nien, only in terms of dharma-nature, while at the same time slandering the quest [for rebirth in the Pure Land] without [relying on the principle of] causality, do not comply with the Two Truths. Those who have views like this lapse into holding a nihilistic idea of śūnyatā.[96]

Tao-ch'o then quoted from the chapter on enlightenment in the Wu-shang-i-ching,[97] a text that represents the tathāgata-garbha theory ''in its full and pure aspect.''[98] He extracted from this text the crucial importance of manifesting the principle of causality so that rewards are not lost. Accordingly, he urged practitioners that ''although reality is birthless, li sui wu-sheng, in terms of the way of the Two Truths reality is not without causality and the quest [for rebirth in the Pure Land], *jan erh-ti tao li fei wu yuan ch'iu.* [As a consequence] all can attain rebirth in the Pure Land."[99]

Similarly, Tao-ch'o gleaned support from the *Vimalakīrtinirdeśa-sūtra* by finding passages that reflected this double aspect of the Ultimate Truth of nonform, birthlessness, and nonsubstantiality, and of the Conventional Truth that takes seriously the world of form and causal relationships. "Although the bodhisattva sees that all Buddha Lands and sentient beings are empty, yet in order to save sentient beings he constantly cultivated a land of purity."[100] "The life of a bodhisattva is to realize the state of non-purposive activity, *wu-tso,* and yet to take on bodily existence."[101]

We can gather from the above references some idea of the position of Tao-ch'o regarding those of a higher rebirth. As in the case of those of a lower rebirth, his theory is somewhat paradoxical. Those of a higher rebirth who understand the Ultimate Truth of *śūnyatā* and the identity of form and nonform are reborn in a birthless Pure Land beyond form and see the true Reward Body of Amitābha. However, because they understand the Two Truths and have compassion for other beings, they seek a middle path between form and nonform and reenter the conditioned world to purify that world for the sake of others.[102]

DOCTRINE OF THE TWO TRUTHS

The preceding discussion makes it clear that the key philosophical principle used by Tao-ch'o to legitimize the idea of rebirth in the Pure Land of form was the doctrine of Two Truths. In his frequent reference to the concept—it appears at least a dozen times in his *An-lo-chi*—Tao-ch'o assumed that his readers shared with him a common understanding of the doctrine and had adopted it as a fundamental of Buddhism. Thus, he did not feel the need either to define or to defend the Two Truths. In general his use of the term implies the legitimacy of Conventional Truth as an expression of Ultimate Truth and as a vehicle to reach Ultimate Truth. Even though all form is nonform, it is acceptable and necessary to use form within the limits of causality, because its use is an expedient means of saving others out of one's compassion for them and because even for the unenlightened the use of form can lead to the revelation of form as nonform.

An appeal to the Two Truths as a justification for the use of form as an expedient device was then well established. Chih-i was critical of those who reject Conventional Truth in favor of Ultimate Truth but who are not able to move back into the sphere of Conventional Truth. They are limited in their understanding and cannot, in the words of the *Lotus-*

sūtra, "purify a Buddha Land through the free enjoyment of supernatural powers, *yu-hsi shen-t'ung.*"[103] These are members of the Two
Vehicles, wrote Chih-i, who have not reached the fuller understanding of
the Two Truths achieved by members of the bodhisattva vehicle.

> [The members of] the Two Vehicles are not able to perfect sentient beings
> nor to purify a Buddha Land. Therefore, they do not receive the name of
> "free enjoyment [of supernatural powers]" . . . . Although [the members
> of] the Two Vehicles view the Two Truths, they understand only how to
> move from temporary existence into *śūnyatā, chia-ju-k'ung* . . . .
> Bodhisattvas also view the Two Truths, and, starting from the [first]
> stage of dry wisdom and ending with the [fourth] stage of beholding [the
> truth], they operate mostly from temporary existence into *śūnyatā.* . . .
> [However], from the [fifth] stage of thinner [defilements, and on to seventh
> stage], they learn the free enjoyment of supernatural powers, mostly
> cultivating the view which involves moving from *śūnyatā* to enter tem-
> porary existence, *ts'ung-k'ung ju-chia kuan.* They obtain the dharma-eye
> of various knowledges about the path mostly by using Conventional Truth,
> *su.*[104]

It seems clear from this passage that Chih-i is in full agreement with
Tao-ch'o. If an individual only knows how he or she can move from temporary existence into *śūnyatā* then that person has a partial view of the
Two Truths and only a one-sided understanding of nonform.[105] Such a
view affirms that "all Buddha Lands are empty," but does not assert, as
does the *Vimalakīrtinirdeśa-sūtra,* that bodhisattvas should purify a
Buddha Land nonetheless.[106] Only when one is able to move from *śūnyatā* back into this temporary world, and to use this world expediently
from the point of view of *śūnyatā,* has one learned the "free enjoyment
of supernatural powers" and developed the ability to perfect sentient beings and purify a Buddha Land. This is the doctrinal basis on which Tao-
ch'o also justified the creation of a Buddha Land as a place of salvation.

Tao-ch'o recognized like Chih-i that neither the creation of Pure
Lands nor their appropriation by believers was the final goal. The purpose of all sentient beings is the attainment of enlightenment. In fact, no
one can be reborn in the Pure Land until he or she awakens the resolve to
attain enlightenment, *bodhicitta.* To support this assertion, Tao-ch'o
quoted from the *Wu-liang-shou-ching.* However, this sūtra refers only to
awakening the *bodhicitta* for those who wish to see the Buddha of
Limitless Life in this world.[107] Tao-ch'o altered this in an important way,
for he said that all those who wish to be reborn in the Pure Land must
first awaken the *bodhicitta.*[108] The emphasis that Tao-ch'o placed on the
bodhicitta can be seen by the fact that his chapter on the *bodhicitta* is the
longest one in the *An-lo-chi,* occupying more than a quarter of the text.

But in spite of these high goals, Tao-ch'o felt that man's capacities in this age are so low and conditions so bad that his only hope is to seek rebirth in the Pure Land as an intermediate stage on the way to enlightenment.[109] Of course, Chih-i did advocate calling on the compassionate power of Amitābha in certain meditations.[110] Shortly before he died he allegedly said that he felt that he himself had not gone beyond the five preliminary grades which are preparatory to beginning the fifty-two stages of a bodhisattva.[111] Thus, in actual practice Chih-i may not have felt it possible to go much beyond the level of the Pure Land devotion advocated by Tao-ch'o. However, he did not want to rule out the possibility of enlightenment here and now. Rather, he suggested that it was possible at a relatively early stage to take responsibility for purifying a Buddha Land for *others,* not just to seek to be reborn in a Buddha Land *oneself.* In contrast, Tao-ch'o actively warned against this premature compassionate activity as being certain to bring disaster because it would be misguided and unenlightened.[112]

Far from advocating such elevated activity to his readers, Tao-ch'o directed his efforts toward recommending and justifying the elementary devotional practices of invoking the Buddha's name and seeking rebirth in the Pure Land. He seems to argue that if we accept the *Vimalakīrtinirdeśa-sūtra* when it says that bodhisattvas are supposed to purify a land for the sake of others, then we must also acknowledge that those for whom the lands are purified are justified in using these lands to progress along the path toward enlightenment.

> If a person is able exclusively and continously without interruption only [to invoke the Buddha's name], then he definitely will be reborn before the Buddha. Now I urge future students that if they wish to understand the Two Truths, they need merely to know that continuous thought beyond reason is identical to the "gate of wisdom," and that being able to think actively without ceasing is identical to the "gate of virtue." Therefore, the *[Vimalakīrtinirdeśa-] sūtra* says that "bodhisattvas-mahāsattvas constantly cultivate their minds by means of virtue and wisdom." If anyone who is just beginning cannot transcend form, then merely by depending on form and exclusively going to [Amitābha] that person will be reborn [in the Pure Land]. There is no doubt.[113]

This passage draws upon the two dimensions of wisdom and compassion that underlie the paradoxical life of a bodhisattva. However, Tao-ch'o inverted the argument of the *Vimalakīrtinirdeśa-sūtra* in an interesting way. In the sūtra, a bodhisattva first understands that all form is empty, and then uses form constructively without attachment or illusion in order to save others. But Tao-ch'o seems to be suggesting that those who do not yet fully understand the emptiness of form can legitimately indulge in discrimination and utilize phenomenal forms for their own benefit because their activity is consistent with and in response to the virtuous activity of bodhisattvas.

How he connected this to his doctrine of the Two Truths Tao-ch'o never discussed in detail. Apparently he saw Conventional Truth both as an expression of Ultimate Truth and as a vehicle to reach Ultimate Truth. This is in radical disagreement with the Mādhyamika tradition as represented by Candrakīrti who only understood Conventional Truth *(saṃvṛti)* as a negative term. Nagao Gadjin found that Candrakīrti interpreted *saṃvṛti* as ''(1) falsehood through ignorance, (2) contingent existence without substance, and (3) conventional terminology, manner of speaking, and name.''[114]

On the other hand, the *Vijñāna-vāda* tradition interpreted Conventional Truth very positively. Nagao Gadjin concluded that the *Madhyānta-vibhāga* and the *Commentary* on it by Sthiramati agreed with Candrakīrti only insofar as believing that *saṃvṛti* refers to events that have dependent origination and to temporary verbal designations or conventional terminology. However, Sthiramati radically differed with the interpretation of *saṃvṛti* as falsehood through ignorance or a covering of truth. Rather, he used the term *udbhāvanā-saṃvṛtti,* meaning ''manifestation'': ''*Saṃvṛtti* is thus an utterance, attempting to express the inexpressible Absolute. In this respect, *saṃvṛtti* is . . . . placed closer to *paramārtha* . . . . Such a state of being may be appropriately compared with the notion of *marga* the way which leads to the Absolute on the one hand, and which emerges from the Absolute on the other.''[115]

This sense of *saṃvṛti* as manifestation is in substantial agreement with the very positive interpretation of Conventional Truth advocated by Hui-yüan. As we have seen, he favored the teaching which understood *saṃvṛti* as manifesting true reality, *hsien-shih tsung,* and which was based on the *tathāgatha-garbha* tradition. Similarly, Tao-ch'o invoked the *Wu-shang-i-ching* from the same tradition in order to explain the validity of Conventional Truth.[116] In addition, Seng-chao, Hui-yüan, and Chih-i all shared a commitment to a position of nonduality between the phenomenal and the absolute. It seems clear from the arguments of Tao-ch'o that he also advocated this idea, and, in fact, used it as the very foundation for his Pure Land ideas and practices.

CONCLUSIONS

The doctrine of Tao-ch'o concerning Amitābha and his land fits into the pattern which developed within Mahāyāna Buddhism from the fourth century on. This pattern involved an increased preoccupation with the second body of the Buddha, the reward body, *sambhogakāya,* because it bridged the gap between ordinary illusory existence and the Ultimate Truth. The *saṃbhogakāya* embodied the upward aspirations and achievements of merit as exemplified by the resplendent bodhisattvas and celestial Buddhas. On the other hand, as the dharma developed transcendent dimensions which were immovable, impenetrable, and absolute, the *saṃbhogakāya* became the visible manifestation of its self-expression and its compassionate activity for others.

> Thus, we know that the *sāṃbhogika-kāya* is composed of a twofold character. While, on the one hand, there is the aspect of transcending the human Buddha, the *nairmāṇika-kāya,* there is, on the other hand, the concretization of the absolute, the *svābhāvika-kāya.* Therefore, the *sāṃbhogika-kāya* has the two aspects of being at once transcendental and phenomenal, and at once historic and super-historic.[117]

This dual character of the *saṃbhogakāya* became clearly etched as the *svasaṃbhogakāya, tzu-shou-yung,* and as the *parasaṃbhogakāya, t'a-shou-yung,* in the translations of Hsüan-tsang (ca. 596–664).[118] However, already in the writings of Ching-ying Hui-yüan this tension was expressed by a fourfold scheme attributed to the *Laṅkāvatāra-sūtra.*[119] Besides the Transformation Buddha, *ying-hua-fo,* and Suchness Buddha, *ju-ju-fo,* there are the two bodies of the Merit Buddha, *kung-te-fo,* and Wisdom Buddha, *chih-hui-fo.* Hui-yüan then equated these latter two with the Reward Buddha, *fo-pao-shen,* [120] which anticipated the distinctions made by Hsüan-tsang.

Amitābha and his land, as an expression of the *saṃbhogakāya,* obviously occupied the central role in the thoughts of Tao-ch'o. The twofold paradigm of *chen* and *ying, li* and *shih,* root and branches, or essence and function, so dominated the thinking of the other scholars we have considered that the middle dropped out of the *trikāya* doctrine and Amitābha became identified with the derivative and inferior position of "response," *ying.* Moreover, because these extremes implied each other, there was no need for a third element to unite them. However, Tao-ch'o so despaired of contemporary conditions that he had to place their union beyond history in the figure of Amitābha. In this regard he was true to the mainstream of Indian Mahāyāna Buddhism where the *saṃbhogakāya* "occupies the central position in the triple-body doctrine; especially, the soteriology in Buddhism is developed revolving around the axis of this double-character of the *sāṃbhogika-kāya.*"[121]

Seen in retrospect, the efforts of Tao-ch'o were all bent toward legitimizing Pure Land devotional practices and images that were accessible to the masses and had caught the popular imagination. Common people who understand only at the level of Conventional Truth are redeemed if they rely on the forms of Amitābha because of his saving power and because of the doctrine of the Two Truths. Even though Hui-yüan wrote approving commentaries on various Pure Land sūtras, and Chih-i recommended invoking the help of Amitābha, this was not their primary message. In contrast, because of the times and the low capacities of men, Tao-ch'o advocated rebirth in the Pure Land above all else. Even wise persons who understand the Two Truths also need to be reinforced in their understanding through rebirth in the Pure Land. Thus, Tao-ch'o transferred the principle of the Two Truths and the identity of form and nonform, birth and birthlessness, to his discussion of the Pure Land. On the other hand, Seng-chao, Hui-yüan, and Chih-i expressed confidence that these principles are also applicable here and now in the midst of this conditional world. For them the intermediate level of the Pure Land is incomplete and even expendable.

In conclusion, a common stock of underlying principles was utilized in fifth- and sixth-century China when the Pure Buddha Lands were discussed. The *trikāya* doctrine was widely acknowledged as an organizing principle for the Pure Lands, but the paradigm of *chen* and *ying* manifested itself as more basic for all thinkers. The Two Truths were generally appealed to as a vehicle for authenticating expedient practices, but eventually they coalesced into an ultimate affirmation of the nonduality of True Reality, of which the Two Truths are but a function.

The differences between Pure Land devotees and nondevotees seem to have been based less on *doctrine* or philosophy than on the degree of *confidence* that they had as individuals as to their ability to actualize the Buddhist experience effectively in their own lifetimes. The Pure Land devotees felt compelled to look to another place, the Pure Land, and to another time when they would be reborn there, as the best occasion for the realization of these principles. On the other hand, the nondevotees gave limited value to the Pure Lands because they could see these same principles illuminating the landscape of their present existence. In both cases, however, we see that similar underlying structures of thought were used by Chinese thinkers to assimilate the complex variations of Indian Buddhism.

NOTES

1.   This is a slightly revised version of a part of my Ph.D. dissertation, "Tao-ch'o (562–645), A Pioneer of Chinese Pure Land Buddhism" (Yale University, 1976).
2.   See Stanley Weinstein, "Imperial Patronage in the Formation of T'ang Buddhism," in *Perspectives on the T'ang,* ed. Arthur Wright and Denis Twitchett (New Haven: Yale University Press, 1973), pp. 265–274.

3.   Tsukamoto Zenryū, *Shina Bukkyōshi Kenkyū, Hokugi-hen* (Tokyo: Kōbundō Shoten, 1942), p. 380.

4.   The first mention that we have of a "Pure Land School," *ching-t'u-tsung*, was by Wŏnhyo in the seventh century. See *Taishō Shinshū Daizōkyō*, "Taishō Tripiṭaka," 100 vols. (Tokyo: Daizō Publishing Co., 1924–1932) (hereafter cited as T), 47.119b.20. Cf. T 47.110a.22-23 where the *Hsi-fang yao-chüeh* also speaks about "a school," *i-tsung*.

5.   Fujita Kotatsu, *Genshi Jōdoshisō no Kenkyū* (Tokyo: Iwanami Shoten, 1970), pp. 141–161 and 431–438.

6.   See the *Wu-liang-shou-ching* (T 12.267b.12) where the land of Amitābha is described as "like nirvāṇa."

7.   Fujita Kotatsu, *Genshi Jōdoshisō no Kenkyū*, pp. 486–505.

8.   Ibid.

9.   Teresina Rowell, "The Background and Early Use of the Buddha-kṣetra Concept," *Eastern Buddhist* VI.3 (July 1934), 199 ff.

10.   Lewis R. Lancaster, "Discussion of time in Mahāyāna texts," *Philosophy East and West* XXIV.2 (April 1974), 209–214.

11.   Fujita found references to Buddha Lands in almost three hundred Mahāyāna texts, including the earliest sūtras such as the *Aṣṭasāhasrikā-prajñāpāramitā-sūtra, Lotus-sūtra, Gaṇḍavyūha-sūtra,* etc. (Fujita Kotatsu, *Genshi Jōdoshisō no Kenkyū*, pp. 474–486.)

12.   Hīnayāna Buddhism also had a *dharmakāya* doctrine, but this referred to the "body of truth" which the historical Buddha Śākyamuni discovered and with which he identified himself. There are a number of famous passages in which the Buddha identified his teaching or *dharma* as the essence of his being: e.g., "those who see the *dharma* will see me; those who see me will see the *dharma*." (See *Saṃyutta-Nikāya* III.120, and cf. *Dīgha-Nikāya* II.100 and 154.) In addition, Abhidharmists considered the elements (also called *dharmas*) of the Buddha's body to have been cleansed of illusions and defilements. Hence, they called the Buddha's body of purified elements a *dharmakāya*. See the *Abhidharmakośa* VI.50 ff; VII.34; and VIII.34 ff.

13.   Fujita Kotatsu, *Genshi Jōdoshisō no Kenkyū*, pp. 506–512.

14.   D. T. Suzuki, *Studies in the Laṅkāvatāra Sūtra* (London: Routledge & Kegan Paul, 1930), pp. 308–338.

15.   The most popular Chinese translations of these three sūtras are T 12.346-348; T 12.340-346; and T 12.265-279 respectively.

16.   This date is based on Tsukamoto Zenryū, *Jōron Kenkyū* (Kyoto: Hōzōkan, 1955), pp. 120–121.

17.   There are three major Chinese translations extant: T 14.519-536, translated by Chih Ch'ien during 222-229 (T 55.119b); T 14.537-557, translated by Kumārajīva in 406; and T 14.557-588, translated by Hsüan-tsang in 650 (T 55.555c).

18.   Already in Chih Ch'ien's translation there is a passage describing Buddha Lands that contain everything excellent, *i-chieh hao-ta,* and lands that are bad, *pu- hao-t'u,* and admonishing that bodhisattvas should neither favor one nor seek to avoid the other. Rather, Buddha Lands do not differ in respect to their purpose of saving beings. "Ānanda, just as Buddha Lands have a number of paths on earth, but are unified in heaven, so the various *tathāgatas* take a number of forms [to save beings], but are unified in their unobstructed wisdom" (T 14.533b.25-c.1). Nevertheless, a simple statement that the "Pure Lands are manifest because of the desire of the Buddha to save beings" (T 14.532b.16-17)

became lengthened in the Hsüan-tsang version to the effect that "because the various world-honored Buddhas desire to perfect beings, they manifest all kinds of Buddha Lands in accordance with the desires of these beings. Some are defiled, some are pure, and others have indefinite qualities. But in reality the Buddha Lands are all pure without any distinctions" (T 14.579b.26–28).

19. For the Pure Land section of chapter 1, see T 14.520b.24–c.22; 538c.6–539a.6, and 559c.26–560b.4. For the Pure Land section of chapter 11, see T 14.533b.14–29, 553c.17–554a.9, and 582a.7–b.11. Cf. Étienne Lamotte, *L'Enseignement de Vimalakīrti* (Louvain: Institut Orientaliste, 1962), pp. 120–125, 342–344, and appendix 1, note 1, pp. 395–404.

20. T 38.327–420.

21. See the textual critique by Inaba Enjō in *Bussho kaisetsu Daijiten,* edited by Ono Gemmyō (Tokyo: Daito Shuppansha, 1932), vol. 8, p. 53.

22. T 38.334b.15–28.

23. I am indebted to Stanley Weinstein for pointing out that when Seng-chao writes *pao-ying chih-t'u* he is *not* referring to two lands, a Reward Land, *pao-t'u,* and a Response Land, *ying-t'u.* Rather, he uses *pao-ying* as a compound meaning the Land of Reward and Recompense, which is in contrast to the True Land, *chen-t'u.*

24. T 38.334b.21–27.

25. T 38.405a.2–3.

26. Mochizuki Shinkō, *Chūgoku Jōdokyōrishi* (Kyoto: Hōzōkan, 1964), p. 90.

27. Stanley Weinstein, "On the Authorship of the *Hsi-fang yao-chüeh,*" *Transactions of the International Conference of Orientalists in Japan* 4 (1959): 22–23.

28. T 37.173–186 and T 37.91–116, respectively.

29. Shinkai Jikō, "Jōyōji Eon no Mida Jōdokan," *Bukkyō Daigaku Kenkyū kiyō* 55 (1971): 133–164.

30. T 44.465–872.

31. The account which follows is a summary of T 44.834a.25–836a.21. Portions of this treatment of Hui-yüan have benefited from the helpful criticisms and suggestions of Stanley Weinstein.

32. T 12.357a.12–18.

33. T 37.92a.1–7. "Two Vehicles" is a term devised by Mahāyāna Buddhists to categorize the established forms of Buddhist practice as preliminary stages in preparation for their own form of practice which they considered more advanced and which they called the Third Vehicle or Bodhisattva Vehicle. See the *Lotus-sūtra,* chapter 2.

34. T 44.835b.10–13.

35. T 26.174a.5–6, quoted by Hui-yüan in T 44.835a.24–25.

36. T 26.139c.26–140a.6, discussed by Hui-yüan in T 44.835c.1–836a.19.

37. T 44.482c.2–485b.8.

38. T 44.483a.11–b.28.

39. T 44.485b.7–8.

40. T 44.649a.27–28.

41. *Dai-Nihon Zoku-zōkyō,* 150 boxes (Kyoto: Zōkyō Shoin, 1905–1912) (hereafter cited as *ZZK*), 1.27.5–28.2. Reprint ed. (Hong Kong: Fo-ching liu-t'ung-chu, 1967), vol. 27, p. 429–vol. 28, p. 193.

42. Satō Tetsuei, *Tendai Daishi no Kenkyū* (Kyoto: Hyakka-en, 1961), pp. 418–419.

43. Ibid., p. 439.

44. *Wei-mo-ching lüeh-shu,* T 38.562–710.

45.   Satō Tetsuei, *Tendai Daishi no Kenkyū,* pp. 555–658.

46.   *ZZK,* Hong Kong edition, 27:432, recto a.

47.   Ibid., p. 432, recto b–433, verso b.

48.   T 9.392c.15–20.

49.   T 8.828a.1.

50.   For an outline of the Four Doctrines of Tripiṭaka, Shared, Special, and Complete, see Leon Hurvitz, *Chih-i (538–597), Mélanges chinois et bouddhiques* 12 (1960–62): 248–271.

51.   Mochizuki Shinkō, ed., *Bukkyō Daijiten* (Tokyo: Sekai Seiten Kanko Gakkai, 1968), vol. 1, p. 334c.

52.   T 45.153a.4–5.

53.   Kamata Shigeo, *Chūgoku Bukkyō Shisōshi Kenkyū* (Tokyo: Shunjū-sha, 1968), pp. 312–327.

54.   This work is no longer extant, but its table of contents is listed in the *Li-tai San-pao-chi,* T 49.106a.

55.   The Three Views, *san-kuan,* were explained by Chih-i in his *San-kuan-i* (*ZZK* 2.4.1; Hong Kong edition, 99:37–52), which originally was part of Chih-i's commentary on the *Vimalakīrtinirdeśa-sūtra.* Although Chih-i claims an Indian source, the *Ying-lo-ching,* for the idea (T 24.1019b.22–23), the concept did not have importance until it became a solution to a problem created by the negative interpretation of *śūnyatā* by the Chinese.

56.   For a recent discussion of this as reflected in the thought of Tu-shun (557–640), see Robert Gimello, "Apophatic and kataphatic discourse in Mahāyāna: A Chinese view," *Philosophy East and West* XXVI.2 (April 1976): 117–136.

57.   T 47.1a.

58.   T 26.230c.21.

59.   T 25.340a.10–21, and compare T 25.714a.10–13. For another elaboration of this issue by T'an-luan, see his *Wang-sheng-lun-chu,* T 40.828a.16–b.1. For a discussion in English, see Roger Corless, "T'an-luan's Commentary on the Pure Land Discourse: An Annotated Translation and Soteriological Analysis of the *Wang-sheng-lun Chu* (t.1819)" (Ph.D. dissertation, University of Wisconsin, 1973), pp. 108–112.

60.   T 44.834b.23–28.

61.   T 47.1a.

62.   T 37.235a.18 ff.

63.   Mochizuki Shinkō, *Chūgoku Jōdokyōrishi,* pp. 86–87.

64.   *An-lo-chi,* chapter 1, section 7–9, T 47.5c.11–7b.10.

65.   T 47.5c.11–16.

66.   Mochizuki, *Bukkyō Daijiten* I.334c.

67.   T 16.651b.4–6, c.6–18, summarized by Tao-ch'o in T47.5c.17–29.

68.   T 47.6a.15–19.

69.   T 12.352b.21–26, quoted by Tao-ch'o in T 47.6a.19–24. See also T 47.153a.20–24.

70.   T 47.6b.1–3. This disagrees with the interpretation of Hui-yüan, outlined earlier, who claimed that Amitābha did disappear into Nirvāṇa and his life ended.

71.   T 47.6b.7–8.

72.   Mochizuki Shinkō argues that because the *dharmakāya* is colorless, formless, invisible, and without a dwelling place, according to the *Ta-ch'eng t'ung-hsing-ching* quotation to which I referred previously, then it does not have a Pure Land. However, I here follow the scheme of "Three Bodies and Three Lands,"

san-shen san-t'u, used by Tao-ch'o (T 47.5c.11); in this scheme the True Land is merely symbolic of all reality when reality is truly seen. See Mochizuki Shinkō, *Chūgoku Jōdokyōrishi,* pp. 141–142.

73.   T 47.5c.12–13.

74.   T 12.357a.12–18, summarized by Tao-ch'o in T 47.6b.20–21.

75.   T 14.538c.20–21.

76.   T 47.6b.8–20.

77.   .T 47.6b.23–6c.1.

78.   T 47.17b.24–c.6.

79.   T 47.6c.5–7a.4, which slightly abridges T 15.687c.28–688b.11.

80.   T 47.7a.5–6.

81.   T 47.7a.23–24 and 18b.18–20.

82.   T 47.6c.3–5.

83.   Rather than translating *i-fa-chü* as "one essential part" (Corless, "T'an-luan's Commentary," p. 296) or "one law" (Yamamoto Kosho, trans., *Shinshu Seiten* [Honolulu: Honpa Hongwanji Mission, 1955], p. 119), I have translated it as "one true reality" (Oda Tokunō, *Bukkyō Daijiten,* 2nd ed. [Tokyo: Okura Shoten, 1954], p. 84, who defined *i-fa-chü* as *shinnyo ichiri* and quoted the *O-mi-t'o-ching-shu* as his authority).

84.   T 26.232b.22–25. Cf. Yamamoto, *Shinshu Seiten,* p. 118.

85.   T 40.841b.12–17, 842a.5–9; quoted in the *An-lo-chi,* T 47.7a.9–15, 19–22.

86.   T 47.7a.25–b.10.

87.   T 25.340a.10–21.

88.   T 26.230c.21–22.

89.   T 47.1a; T 40828a.16–b.1.

90.   T 47.423a.3–4, 7–8.

91.   T 47.4a.22–23.

92.   T 47.5c.11.

93.   T 47.18c.15–17.

94.   T 47.11c.16–17.

95.   T 47.11c.27–12a.2.

96.   T 47.8b.10–15.

97.   T 16.471b.8–9.

98.   Takasaki Jikido, "Structure of the *Anuttarāsraya-sūtra* (Wu-shang-i-ching)," *Indogaku Bukkyōgaku Kenkyū* 8 (2): 744.

99.   T 47.8b.15–22.

100.   T 14.530a.1–2, quoted in T 47.8b.22–23.

101.   T 14.545c.9–10, quoted in T 47.8b.24–25.

102.   T 47.18b, 8c.10–19. This describes the mission of a bodhisattva, which is illustrated by a quotation from the *Vimalakīrtinirdeśa-sūtra* (T 14.538a.26–29).

103.   T 9.16b.16–17.

104.   T 33.730b.16–26. For an extended discussion of *chia-ju-k'ung* by Chih-i, see T 46.71b.29 ff, particularly 75b.27–78b.9. For *ju-chia-kuan* specifically, see T 46.76a.19 ff.

105.   T 47.8b.9–c.7.

106.   T 14.545c.26–27, 550a.1–2.

107.   T 12.272b.21–23.

108.   T 47.7b.15–23.

109.   T 47.4a.26–4c.2.

110.   T 46.12b.19 ff.

111. Leon Hurvitz, *Chih-i (538–597)*, p. 270, n. 2.

112. T 47.9a.8–25.

113. T 47.11b.9–14.

114. Nagao Gadjin, "An Interpretation of the Term 'Saṁvṛti' (Convention) in Buddhism," in *Silver Jubilee Volume of the Zinbun-Kagaku-Kenkyu-syo* (Kyoto: Zinbun-Kagaku-syo, 1954), p. 553.

115. Ibid., p. 555.

116. T 47.8b.15 ff.

117. Nagao Gadjin, "On the Theory of Buddha-Body *(Buddha-kāya)*," *Eastern Buddhist* n.s. 4, no. 1 (May 1973): 36.

118. *Ch'eng-wei-shih-lun*, T 31.57c.24–58a.2; *Fo-ti-ching lun*, T 26.326a.22–24.

119. Nagao Gadjin considers this distinction to be based on a mistranslation from the Sanskrit. See "On the Theory of Buddha-body," p. 42, n. 24.

120. T 44.841b.22–27.

121. Nagao, "On the Theory of Buddha-body," p. 37.

3   Taoist Alchemy: A Sympathetic Approach through Symbols

THOMAS BOEHMER

Immortality is a matter that has concerned the Taoist for more than two thousand years. It is the central concern of meditative, ritual, gymnastic, dietary, pharmacological, and alchemical practices, the ultimate aim of which is to be "wafted up into heaven in broad daylight." The Taoist believes that the centrifugal forces of the microcosm that lead to dissolution, darkness, and death can be reversed, thus effecting a centripetal cohesive tendency whereby the usual movements of the cosmos and nature can be reverted. The sequence of progression from life to death, light to darkness, yang to yin, spring and summer to fall and winter, will move in a new progression from death to life, yin to yang, to the eternal state of the newborn child, *ch'ih-tzu,* also known as *ch'ang-sheng,* eternally born anew. The Taoist conceives of immortality in the Inner Elixir, or *nei-tan,* tradition as a goal which can be met in the present life. This is not to be thought of as a physical immortality, though there are stories of Taoists living extraordinarily long lives, but rather as a state which the adept attains during life which exempts him from the descent into the fiery underworld.[1]

Taoist alchemy does not present a doctrine of universal salvation; rather, each person must obtain salvation through his own efforts toward realizing immortality.[2] It is the individual's responsibility to seek out a master from whom he may receive explanations of and initiation into the obscure doctrines of the ancient canons.

The individual has available two basic approaches to immortality: thus, there are two types of *hsien-shu.* One, which is external, involves the preparation and use of various elixirs and pharmaceuticals, *wai-tan.*

The other, which is internal, involves the calling forth and ordering of the attendants of the interior of the body, *nei-tan.* This chapter will be concerned primarily with the internal aspect of Taoist alchemy. However, before I engage in a discussion of Taoist internal alchemy, I would first like to attempt to place it in historical and symbolic perpectives.

Although still a matter of considerable controversy, available evidence suggests that alchemy as an art, *wai-tan,* originated in China. Tsou Yen (circa 350–270 B.C.), from the state of Ch'i (presently known as Shantung), is credited by some texts with the discovery of alchemy.[3] He is also traditionally regarded as the founder of the yin-yang five element school of philosophy which became popular during the Han dynasty.[4] I shall discuss the importance of the yin-yang five element theory later, but for now I would like merely to note that this theory is the foundation of Taoist alchemy, including both the *nei-tan* and *wai-tan* traditions. In the *Shih-chi,* a work of Ssu-ma Ch'ien, also of the Han period, we learn that people from the state of Yen practiced methods for obtaining immortality and that the kings from this part of China sent people to the present Gulf of Penchili to seek magical islands or mountains where immortals were said to live.[5]

The *Huai-nan-tzu,* also of the former Han dynasty, contains what appears to be the earliest mention of the alchemical metal mercury. This work also mentions the natural metamorphoses of the five metals (gold, lead, copper, silver, and iron) in a period of 500 to 1000 years from a mineral, to mercury, to metal, to subterranean springs, to clouds, and finally to the sea.[6] Ko Hung in his *Pao-p'u-tzu* referred to various accounts of gold in treatises dealing with gods and immortals. Ko stated that Liu An (died 122 B.C.), prince of Huai-nan and reputed author of the *Huai-nan-tzu,* used these accounts to compose his books, the *Huang-pao* and *Cheng-chung.*[7]

The origins of books dealing with internal alchemy are veiled in legends. Traditionally, the earliest work of internal medicine that may be considered the precursor to internal alchemy is the *Huang-ti Nei Ching Su Wen, The Yellow Emperor's Classic of Internal Medicine,* attributed to the legendary Yellow Emperor. Although it is not possible to state precisely when this work first appeared in written form, it probably was not earlier than the Tang dynasty.[8] We find in this classic the following dialogue:

> [The Yellow Emperor said] "I urge you to bring into harmony for me nature, Heaven, and Tao . . . . There must be an end and a beginning. Heaven must be in accord with the lights of the sky, and the celestial bodies, and their courses and periods. The earth below must reflect the four seasons, the five elements, that which is precious and that which is lowly and

without value—one as well as the other. Is it not that in Winter man responds to Yin . . . ? And is it not that in Summer he responds to Yang . . . ? Let me be informed about their workings."

Ch'i Po replied: "Truly a subtle question! It demands that one decypher Nature to the utmost degree."

The Emperor exclaimed: "I should like to be informed about Nature to the utmost degree and to include [information] about man, his physical form, his blood, his breath of life, his flowing and his dissolution; and I should like to know what causes his death and his life and what we can do about all this."[9]

Other much earlier references to internal alchemy can be found. In the early poem by Ch'ü Yüan (died ca. 288 B.C.) entitled "Wandering in the Distance," we find reference to breathing techniques in the attainment of Tao. Freely translated the poem reads:

Eat six kinds of air and drink pure dew in order to preserve the purity of your soul. Breathe the essence of air in and the foul air out. The *Tao* is minute and without content, and yet it is large and without limit. Do not confuse your soul—the *Tao* is spontaneous. Concentrate on the breath and the *Tao* will remain with you in the middle of the night.[10]

The fundamental and earliest existent Taoist text on meditative breathing is found in the *Ts'an-t'ung-ch'i,* or *Meditation on Identity and Unity* (ca. A.D. 142). This work, which was famous in the twelfth and thirteenth centuries, has been attributed to Wei Po-yang.[11]

It is interesting to note that the earliest Chinese alchemical texts extant precede those of the West by several centuries. Evidence presently available indicates that alchemical practices were not to be found in the West before the Christian era. The most important evidence to support this comes from Pliny the Elder (A.D. 23–79), who wrote extensively of metallurgy but did not speak of alchemy per se. The various observations and beliefs concerning the nature and process of metals mentioned in Pliny's writings, however, indicate a climate of thought favorable to the emergence of alchemy as an art.[12]

THE SYMBOLIC PERSPECTIVE

The alchemical perspective proceeds from the view that the cosmos, or macrocosm, and man, or microcosm, correspond to one another as reflections; whatever is present in one is also present in the other. This metaphoric symbolism is to be understood, however, not in the physical sense in which the reflected image is reversed, but rather in the sense that each presents a true image of the other. This correspondence may be understood in terms of the subject and object, knower and known. The cosmos as object appears in the mirror of the human subject. While these poles may be distinguished intellectually, however, they are, in and of themselves, inseparable. Each one is to be conceived of only in relation to the other.[13] Thus, if man is a reflection of the cosmos, the principles of yin and yang must be at work within man just as they are in the cosmos.[14]

This system of correspondences between the macrocosm and microcosm exists in the *Weltanschauung* of both the Chinese and Western alchemical traditions. However, the symbol system present in the Taoist tradition is far more complex. The round head of man corresponds to the arch or Heaven, the mountain K'un-lun which supports the sky corresponds to the cranium, the sun and moon which are attached and revolve about each other represent respectively the left and right eyes, the veins correspond to the rivers, the blood is their flow, the hairs of the body represent the stars and the planets, grinding the teeth imitates the rolling thunder. All of the gods of the sun and moon, rivers and seas—all of the cosmic processes have their parallels and loci in the microcosm of the human body.[15]

However, it is essential that we realize that for the Taoist there is no separation between the symbol and what it signifies, between the macrocosm and microcosm. Each, being a true reflection of the other, may stand in the other's stead.[16] The functions of the cosmos, of the earth, of the state, of man, and of man's internal organs all may be understood as the hierarchical correspondent of the other. Further, it should be understood that this system of correspondences exists both within and between the material and physical realms. Here too, although we may make this intellectual distinction for the purpose of discussion, it must be understood that no such distinction exists for the Taoist. In light of this, our previous distinction between external alchemy, *wai-tan,* and internal alchemy, *nei-tan,* is seen to be merely a theoretical distinction made for the purpose of discussion.

The symbol system of universal identification between the microcosm and macrocosm appears in a well-ordered fashion. In the *Huai-nan-tzu* we find the following symbolic correlations:

> Heaven has four seasons, five elements, nine divisions, and three hundred and sixty days. Similarly man has four limbs, five internal organs, nine orifices, and three hundred and sixty joints. Heaven has wind, rain, cold and heat; man similarly has joy, anger, taking and giving.[17]

The movement of the five elements in the yin-yang five-element theory presents the movements of the cosmos, a movement which is, of course, reflected in the body of man. In the writings of Tung Chung-shu of the early second century A.D. we find the following correlations:

Heaven comprises five elements: the first is wood, the second fire, the third earth, the fourth metal, and the fifth water. Wood is the beginning of the cycle, water the last, and earth is in the center of the circle. Such is the order given by nature. Wood produces fire, fire produces earth, earth metal, metal water, water wood. This is the father-son relationship.

The five elements move in a circle in proper order, each of them performing its specific functions. Therefore, wood is located in the East and characterizes the *ch'i* or ether of Spring. Fire is located in the South and characterizes the *ch'i* of Summer. Metal is located in the West and characterizes the *ch'i* of Autumn. Water is located in the North and characterizes the *ch'i* of Winter . . . . Earth dwells in the center and is called Heavenly Nourisher . . . .[18]

Earth, the center, through the movements of yin and yang, radiates and receives powers from the peripheries. According to the *Ts'an-t'ung-ch'i,* not only the seasons, directions, and metals, but also the five internal organs of man are related to one another.[19] Other correspondences exist, according to the *Huai-nan-tzu,* between the five sacred mountains, the five emperors, the five imperial assistants, the five planets, and the five colors (Table 3.1).[20] Further, there is a numerical correspondence in this symbol system in which the numeral 1 corresponds to water, 2 to fire, 3 to wood, 4 to metal, and 5 to earth. The even numbers correspond to yin and the odd numbers correspond to yang. This symbol system will be better understood perhaps by referring to Figure 3.1, in which the possible relationships among the symbols may be seen.

Table 3.1

ELEMENT	DIRECTION	EMPEROR	ASSISTANT	SEASON	PLANET	
Wood	East	Fu Hsi	Chü Mang	Spring	Jupiter	3
Fire	South	Shen Nung	Chu Jung	Summer	Mars	2
Earth	Center	Huang-ti	Hou-t'u	*Fang* months*	Saturn	5
Metal	West	Shao-hao	Ju-shou	Autumn	Venus	4
Water	North	Chüan-hsu	Hsüan-ming	Winter	Mercury	1

ORGAN	MOUNTAIN	COLOR	ANIMAL	ORIFICE	ATTRIBUTE	
Liver	T'ai Shan	Blue	Dragon	Eyes	Benevolence	3
Heart	Heng Shan	Red	Bird	Ears	Propriety	2
Spleen	Sung Shan	Yellow	(Crucible)	Mouth	Faith	5
Lungs	Hua Shan	White	Tiger	Nose	Righteousness	4
Kidneys	Heng Shan	Black	Tortoise	Urethra and rectum	Wisdom	1

NOTE: This table, in different form, appears in Michael Saso's *Taoism and the Rite of Cosmic Renewal,* p.54.

* third, sixth, ninth and twelfth months.

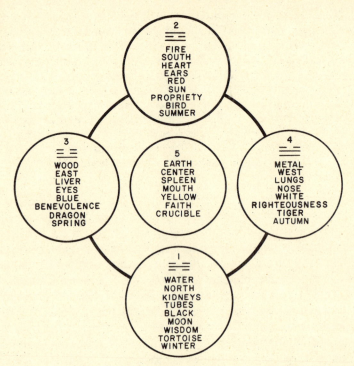

Figure 3.1   The five elements arranged in a mandala of the five directions.

It is important, however, to understand that these relationships are not merely symbolic play; as is the case with all symbols, they have a transcendent function. The union of 2 and 3, the yin and yang, fire and wood, produce the center, 5, which is earth. The union of 4 and 1, metal and water, also produce the center, 5. Thus, through meditation, alchemy, ritual, or circulation of breath, the union of yin and yang elements can be seen as leading to the center, the void or origin, the preontological and preontogenetic ground. It is through the union of opposites that the return to the undifferentiated source is effected. The five elements are not to be thought of as material elements, but rather as spatiotemporal qualities involved in the successive stages of the eternal cyclical process.[21]

It is interesting to note that many of the alchemical formulas of the *wai-tan* tradition are reducible in the symbol system of the ying-yang, five-element theory to various planetary essences, *ching,* and to the five central organs of the body. In an explanatory note, attributed to Liu An, regarding an alchemical formula for compounding the five-mineral elixir, we find the following correlations:

The five minerals are the vital essences of the five celestial bodies. Cinnabar is the vital essence of great yang, Mars. Magnetite is the vital essence of great yin, Mercury. Malachite is the vital essence of lesser yang, Jupiter. Realgar is the vital essence of Divine Earth, Saturn. Arsenolite is the vital essence of lesser yin, Venus. An elixir compounded from the vital essences of the five celestial bodies can impart immortality to a man.[22]

The five substances cited in this formula are those which are commonly employed in the compounding of the alchemical elixir. These minerals can be identified with the five elements through their associated colors, planetary essences, and associated hexagrams. That these compounds are extremely poisonous is obvious as they contain such chemicals as arsenic sulphide (realgar), mercuric sulphide (cinnabar), and carbonate of copper (malachite). Indeed, there is reason to believe that the Taoist alchemist understood that his mineral elixirs were toxic. It was an accepted fact among pre-T'ang and T'ang Taoists that the consumption of alchemical concoctions led to a quick death. To "attain longevity" or to "ascend to heaven in broad daylight" meant mercury or gold poisoning, in many cases. Poisoning by slower stages—by consuming the elixir a little at a time—was also possible.[23]

Indeed, the reading and translation of the alchemical texts, whether they be overtly of the *wai-tan* tradition or of the *nei-tan* tradition, involves the careful correlation of an immense body of obscure matter. We find in the *Keng Tao Chi:*

The mastery of the major elixirs does not surpass lead and mercury. Compounds made from lead and mercury are the basis of the great potions. The common reverberation and mutual tempering of lead and mercury does not lie beyond the principles of heaven and earth, of male and female. Lead is of the nature of yin. . . . Mercury is of the nature of yang. . . . Therefore the trigram *k'an* is lead, water, and moon; the trigram *li* is mercury, fire, and the sun. Compounding *k'an* and *li,* lead and mercury, together is the union of the sun and moon. The mutual conflict of lead and mercury is the sexual union of the dragon and the tiger. If they are not of unequal valence, then they will mutually temper each other.[24]

It is interesting to note here that the conjunction of the *k'an* and *li* also provides the basic current of the Taoist breathing practices in the *nei-tan* tradition.[25]

The *Ts'an-t'ung-ch'i* devotes a great deal of attention to the problems of the obscure symbolism of the alchemical texts along with warnings about the interpretation of these treatises. For example, we find in the sixty-second chapter:

> The immortals of old . . . their sympathy for those of posterity who might have a liking for the attainment of the Tao led them to explain their writings of old with words and illustrations. They couched their ideas in the names of stones and in vague language so that only some branches, as it were, were in view and the roots securely hidden. Those that had access to them wasted their lives over them.[26]

. Again, in the fifty-second chapter of the *Ts'an-t'ung-ch'i* we find advice concerning the interpretation of the alchemical treatises:

> By searching far and wide for reputed medicines, they fell into bypaths that were incompatible with the Tao. One should make inferences from clues and signs just as one would from the appearances of a stranger he meets. The thing to do is to compare things by classes and to trace their beginnings and ends.[27]

And once again in the twenty-eighth verse:

> The way to make oneself a *fu-shih hsien* [drug-using supernatural being] lies in the use of drugs similar to oneself.[28]

It is apparent then that whatever form the Taoist practice may take in this system of universal correspondences, meditation, breath regulation, alchemy, or liturgy, the function, process, and effect are the same: a reenaction of the cosmic processes and a return to the undifferentiated ground. The Taoist does not see his actions as being merely an imitation of the celestial process; but, rather, he actually is participating in the cosmic process. Because of the total pervasiveness of this symbol system, it is extremely difficult for an individual to read, translate, and comprehend the Taoist texts. In many cases the Taoist texts may be interpreted variously according to the application intended. The following verse from Ko Hung's *P'ao-p'u-tzu Nei-p'ien*, 3.1b, may demonstrate this point.

> He who consumes cinnabar
> and preserves the One
> Does not end until the heavens do.
> He who returns the essence
> and practices fetal breath
> Will have longevity without limit.

The first line "consumes cinnabar" makes obvious reference to the ingestion of the alchemical elixir. The second line "preserves the One" may be understood as suggesting the Taoist meditative practice known as "preserving the One." The fourth line makes apparent reference to the sexoyogic practice of reverting the semen in intercourse immediately prior to ejaculation. "Fetal breath" refers to the circulation of breath in the

Taoist practice of rhythmic breathing. However, this poem may be interpreted in terms of any or all of these practices.

We may regard Taoist alchemy as a process aimed at rebirth, in which the outward transmutation of base metals into noble ones, the production of reverted cinnabar or gold, serves as a highly evocative symbol for an inner process.[29] From this perspective, whether we regard alchemical directions as outward in nature, *wai-tan,* such as we find in Ko Hung's *P'ao-p'u-tzu,* or primarily inward in nature, *nei-tan,* such as we find in the *Chou-i Ts'an-t'ung-ch'i,* the goal is the same, that of returning the soul to the original, preontogenetic state of union. The symbolic transformation occurs against the resistance of the dark, chaotic forces of the cosmos which tend toward dissolution and death, yin; the attainment of an "inward gold" demands the conquest of these centrifugal forces so that the soul may return to its original state of luminosity and purity, yang.[30] The alchemical work, insofar as it was conceived of and executed as an external process, serves then as a "mesocosm" or median ground through which the forces of the macrocosm and microcosm may be understood and manipulated. "Inward gold," or, rather, the fact that gold has a microcosmic as well as macrocosmic reality, is the natural outcome of the contemplative way of thought; the essence of gold is recognized spontaneously in both man and the cosmos.[31] Gold, then, can be understood as a symbol for the original, pure, luminous, unified essence of the cosmos. It is not a substance which is newly produced, but rather is a cosmic principle, or essence, that is uncovered and revealed.

Alchemy, in Chinese thought, is neither theological nor metaphysical in nature; it regards the play of the powers of the soul from a purely cosmological perspective and treats them as a "substance" which is to be purified and crystallized anew. In this regard, though alchemy appears in the garb of a physical science, or art of nature, in reality it is not. Nor is it "protoscientific" or "pseudoscientific" as many would have us believe; rather, it is a soteriological doctrine of being which regards the processes of man and the cosmos as being inseparable. Thus, aside from its symbolic, ritual nature, alchemy either as a pure art or science probably never existed in China.[32]

The Pursuit Of Immortality

Dietary Concerns

We shall consider the Taoist practices in pursuit of immortality in the order of their relative complexity and importance. According to Ko Hung, the most basic practice in pursuit of immortality consists of a severe restriction of the diet. The alchemist's diet demands abstinence from grains, starches, meat or other animal flesh, wine, and the five flavors (onion, garlic, leek, absinthe, and mustard).[33] Indeed, in the *T'ai-p'ing Ching, The Book of Great Peace* (a work attributed to Yü Chi of the second century, the present text of which is of the sixth century), it is stated that the best diets are those that exclude the consumption of solid food altogether. The regular diet is to be replaced by "fetal nourishment," *t'ai-shih,* and "nourishing the breath," *t'ai-hsi,* which will be discussed later.[34]

Starches are to be avoided because their essence is the same as that of earth, yin, and also because they nourish the "three worms." They are said to enter the interior of man and to destroy him at his three roots. The upper worm, known as the "clean old woman," consumes the brain, causing man's internal and external vision to fail. The second worm, known as the "white old crone," devours the central part of man, the five internal organs. The third worm consumes the belly, causing the gate of life, the right kidney, to weaken so that seminal essence is dispersed.[35] We may note here the following correspondence with the *Tao-te-ching,* verse 12:1-3:

> The five colors cause one's eyes to be blind.
> The five tones cause one's ears to be deaf.
> The five flavors cause one's palate to be spoiled.[36]

The flavors of blood, onion, garlic, leek, absinthe, and mustard are said to be offensive to the spirits of the body; they will not perform their proper functions if they are disturbed. Tao Yen is said to have abstained from the consumption of cereals for fifteen years while surviving on berries and finally gave up food altogether in favor of nourishing his blood, *t'ai-chih.* However, the abstention from starches, strong flavors, wine, and animal flesh is not sufficient for the attainment of immortality. Ko Hung wrote in the *P'ao-p'u-tzu:*

> By dispensing with starches a man can only stop spending money on grains, but that alone cannot bring fullness of life. When I inquired of people who had been doing without starches for a long time they said that they were in better health than when they had been eating starches . . . but when they swallowed their breaths, ate paper amulets, or drank brine, only decreased appetite resulted and they did not have the strength to do hard work.[37]
>
> The genii classics say that although several centuries of life may be acquired by eating the leaves of certain plants and trees, it is quite impossible to attain immortality without knowledge of divine cinnabar. On the basis of this we can realize that plants and trees can only protract life, but they are not medicines for bringing fullness of life. They may be taken only to keep oneself whole until the elixir has been successfully prepared.[38]

Nevertheless, Ko believed that a strict diet is essential to the practice of breath circulation:

> For the circulation of breaths, it is essential that the practitioner refrain from overeating. When fresh vegetables and fatty meats are concerned, the breaths, becoming strengthened, are hard to preserve.[39]

However, before we embark on a discussion of the practice of breath circulation it may be helpful to consider the Taoist schematization of the body.

The Schematic Basis

In Chinese thought the body is divided into three major regions. These are known as the higher, lower, and middle cinnabar fields. (Cinnabar is the major constituent parts of the Taoist alchemical elixir.) The higher cinnabar field encompasses the head, the arms, and the palace of *ni-wan*.[40] It contains the five primary organs of sense: ears, eyes, nose, tongue, and fingers (which are the primary organs for the sense of touch). The middle cinnabar field is the chest and is the realm of the Red Palace. It contains the five central organs: the heart, lungs, kidneys, liver, and spleen. The lower cinnabar field encompasses the area below the navel, the sides, and the legs, and is known as the Palace (or Field) of Cinnabar. These sections of the body contain the spirits and divinities of the macrocosm.

The higher section corresponds to Green Heaven and contains the spirits of the hair, brain, eyes, nose, ears, teeth, mouth, and tongue.[41] In addition, it is the center of the nine realized men. They are known as the *Ming-t'ang* Palace Realized Man, the Cinnabar-Field Palace Realized Man, the *Tung Fang* Palace Realized Man, the *Ni-wan* Palace Realized Man, the Ultimate Truth Palace Realized Man, the Flowing Pearl Palace Realized Man, the Heavenly Court Palace Realized Man, the Great *Ti* Palace Realized Man, and the Great *Huang* Palace Realized Man. These men are arranged in two parallel lines running horizontally from the front to the back of the head. The upper line of four contains the Heavenly Court Palace Realized Man, the Ultimate Truth Palace Realized Man, the *Ni-wan* Palace Realized Man, and the Great *Huang* Palace Realized Man. The lower line of five contains the *Ming-t'ang* Palace Realized Man, the *Tung Fang* Palace Realized Man, the Flowing Pearl Palace Realized Man, and the Cinnabar Field Palace Realized Man.[42] Two spirits guard the nine palaces of the head in an area called the Yellow Porch, over the right eye, *huang-ch'üeh,* and the Red Terrace, over the left eye, *chiang-t'ai.*[43]

The lower and middle cinnabar fields also have their respective divinities and spirits. The middle cinnabar field corresponds to the color yellow and to the element earth and contains the throat spirit, the heart spirit, the liver spirit, the spleen spirit, the stomach spirit, the gall bladder spirit, the lung spirit, and the three-tracts spirit, *san chiao*.[44] The *san chiao* are the esophagus, urethra, and the large intestine.[45] In addition, there are also nine realized men residing in the middle cinnabar field who have their residences in the organs. They are the Cinnabar Origin Palace Realized Man, located in the kidneys; the Vermilion Palace Realized Man, residing in the heart; the Orchard Pavilion Palace Realized Man, residing in the liver; the Shang Book Court Palace Realized Man, the lungs; the Yellow Court Palace Realized Man, the spleen; the Heaven Soul Palace Realized Man, the gall bladder (a sixth organ posited by the Taoists and said to govern the six organs of the abdominal region); the Eternal Spirit Palace Realized Man, the large intestine; the Body *Aula* Palace Realized Man, the bladder; and the Primordial Spirit Palace Realized Man, small intestine. The five central organs correspond to the five central peaks, the five directions, and the five elements.[46]

There are also eight spirits located in the lower cinnabar field, corresponding to the element water and the color white. They are known as the lower abdomen spirit, the large intestine spirit, the bladder spirit, the left *yang* spirit, the right yang spirit, the right kidney spirit and the left kidney spirit.[47]

The twenty-four spirits (eight in each of the three cinnabar fields) correspond to the twenty-four divisions of the cosmos, the twelve double solar months (i.e. two for each lunar month), and the twenty-four hours of the day. The nine realized men correspond to the nine heavens.[48] The three cinnabar fields correspond to heaven, earth, and man.

THE INNER ELIXIR THEORY

The Inner Elixir theory involves the compounding of *ching,* seminal essence; *ch'i,* breath; and *shen,* spirit. Each of these three principles has a dual aspect, one which is visibly manifested in material form and another which is an invisible, primordial aspect of the cosmos. The visible aspect is manifested in the microcosm of man. The latter has as its realm the macrocosm, heaven and earth. Thus, within this dual perspective, *ching* has a visible manifestation in the cosmos as semen; while at the same time, it has an undifferentiated, unmanifested aspect as essence.[49] The macrocosmic primordial aspect of *ching* is known as *Tao-te* Heavenly Worthy, *Tao-te T'ien-tsun,* lord of man.[50] Similiarly, *ch'i* has its manifestation in the microcosm as the material breath of respiration, but it is also the primordial breath of the macrocosm known as Primordial Heavenly Worthy, *Yüan-shih T'ien-tsun,* lord of heaven. In the same manner, *shen* is known in the microcosm as spirit or consciousness as obtained through the various spatiotemporal patterns of sensa; it may also be spirit or consciousness of the macrocosm known as *Ling-pao* Heavenly Worthy, *Ling-Pao T'ien-tsun,* lord of earth.[51]

Each of these three principles has its corresponding realm in the body. *Ching* has as its realm the lower cinnabar field; *ch'i* has as its realm the superior cinnabar field; *shen* has as its realm the central cinnabar field. These three fields correspond to man, heaven, and earth, or *Tao-te* Heavenly Worthy, Primordial Heavenly Worthy, and *Ling-pao* Heavenly Worthy.[52] The essence of these three heavenly worthies is *yang,* and their presence in the body is directly contrary to that of the "three worms" whose essence is *yin.*[53]

There are three interrelated practices for the attainment of immortality. These are meditation, sexoyogic procedures, and the circulation of breath. As we shall see, the inner alchemical elixir is composed of the three life principles. The compounding of the inner elixir is described in the Taoist yogin motto: *Lien ching hua ch'i, lien ch'i hua shen,* "Through the compounding of seminal essence, the breath is transformed; through the compounding of breath, the spirit is transformed."[54]

Circulation of Breath

Circulation of breath was a popular technique employed in the pursuit of immortality during the early T'ang dynasty and other periods of Chinese history. The circulation of breath consists, basically, of a special manner of rhythmic breathing that was regarded as being vital to man. The breathing process consists of two series of respirations which correspond to the two breaths of the cosmos. They are inhalation, known as the living breath, *chen ch'i,* containing the essence of yang and corresponding to the period from midnight to noon; the other is exhalation, known as the dead breath, *szu-ch'i,* which contains the essence of yin and corresponds to the period from noon to midnight.[55] As we mentioned previously, the breath, *ch'i,* has a dual significance. It may be thought of as physical inhalation and exhalation; but in the esoteric tradition, as the circulation of psychic energy throughout the body. This is known as "embryonic breathing," "fetal breathing," or "primordial breathing."[56] In the following passage from the *Pao-p'u-tzu,* Ko Hung wrote:

> Through circulation of the breaths illnesses can be cured, plague need not be fled, snakes and tigers can be charmed, bleeding from wounds can be halted, one may stay under water or walk on it, be free from hunger and thirst, and protract one's years. The most important part of it is simply to

breathe like a fetus. He who succeeds in doing this will do his breathing as though in the womb, without using nose or mouth, and for him the divine process has been achieved.

When first learning to circulate the breaths, one inhales through the nose and closes up that breath. After holding it quietly for 120 heartbeats [approximately two minutes] it is expelled in tiny quantities through the mouth. During the exhalations and inhalations one should not hear the sound of one's own breathing, and one should always exhale less than one inhales. A goose feather held before the nose and mouth during the exhalations should not move. After some practice the number of heartbeats may be increased very gradually to one thousand before the breath is released [at the usual pulse rate this is well over fourteen minutes]. Once this is achieved, the aged will become one day younger each day.[57]

There are two basic currents in the circulation of breath. One is known as the lesser heavenly circulation, and the other is known as the great heavenly circulation. The lesser heavenly circulation begins with the living breath, *chen-ch'i,* descending by the force of yin to the heart (corresponding to Mars, fire, south, the sun, and the central cinnabar field) and then to the kidneys (corresponding to lead, water, north, the moon, and the central cinnabar field). We then have the union of the two primordial movers, the sun and the moon, the heart and the kidney, great yin and great yang, *k'an* and *li,* lead and mercury (see Figure 3.1). This basic current, as we have previously mentioned, parallels the basic twofold process of the cosmos: expansion and contraction, waxing and waning.[58] In the union of the heart and kidney, the mutual tempering of yin and yang leads to unity.

The lesser current serves as the foundation for the great heavenly circulation which begins at the tip of the spine, the lower cinnabar field, moves upward along the spine to the head, the higher cinnabar field, forward, down through the face and over the sides, and descends again to the tip of the spine. The breath is conducted by interior vision, *nei-kuan,* throughout the various centers of the body, uniting the fivefold elements (the five internal organs), and rising and falling with the lesser current. The pulse and breath stop. The current then ascends spontaneously to the higher field of cinnabar, the head, where it is conducted once again by the force of interior vision to its origin in the central cinnabar field.[59]

The union of metal and water, the lungs and kidneys, yields seminal essence, *ching (Tao-te* Heavenly Worthy), and the number 5 (4—metal, lungs + 1—water, kidneys). The union of wood and fire, heart and liver, yields spirit, *shen (Ling-pao* Heavenly Worthy), and the number 5 (2—heart, fire + 3—liver, wood). The breath (Primordial Heavenly Worthy), in moving through the three centers of the body, effects the union of the three principles, *shen, ch'i,* and *ching,* the Three Pure Ones, *Ling-*

pao Heavenly Worthy, Primordial Heavenly Worthy, and *Tao-te* Heavenly Worthy, compounding them in the mysterious, void center known as the Yellow Court.[60] Primordial *ch'i* has thus been produced and compounded with primordial *ching,* and primordial *shen;* the inner elixir has been compounded and immortality has been realized (see Figures 3.2 and 3.3).

Sexoyogic Procedure

The circulation of breath and the compounding of the inner elixir were considered by some Taoists, particularly those of the later Mao Shan and Wu-tang Shan traditions, to be incomplete without development of the seminal essence, *ching,* through sexoyogic procedures.[61]

Briefly, this procedure consists of engaging in sexual intercourse and reverting the semen flow immediately before ejaculating by pressing it into the urethra. In this manner, the yang aspect of *ching* is increased and the yin aspect is gathered from the woman (if the Taoist is a woman the reverse is the case, i.e., orgasm is suppressed), thus preventing vital essences from flowing outward, and thereby protracting longevity.[62] In

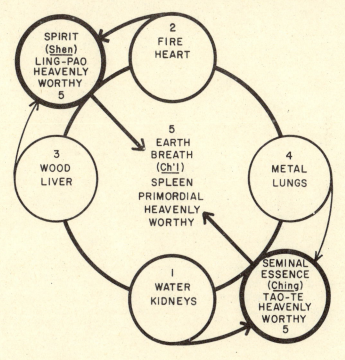

Figure 3.2   The refining of the inner elixir.

三家相見圖

大道立微見此圖分明有象不模糊
先將一二爲之用三四中當共一都

身心意是誰分作三家

肝青爲父
肺白爲母
心赤爲女
脾黃爲祖
腎黑爲子
于五行始
三物一家
都歸戊已

不用五金併八
石只求三品共一室
煉成一顆如意珠軟似塊羅紅似日

精氣神由我合成一箇

精　神　氣

Figure 3.3　The three principles, *ching, shen,* and *ch'i,* are brought together in the center of the microcosm to form "One." Ch'ing dynasty woodblock print, from the *Hsing-ming Kuei-chih,* unpublished manuscript, editor's collection.

the *Pao-p'u-tzu* Ko Hung wrote on the necessity of following correct sexual procedures:

> Though one were to take all the famous medicines, without the knowledge of this essential one would find it impossible to attain Fullness of Life. Man may not, however, give up sexual intercourse entirely, for otherwise he would fall into melancholia through inactivity, and die prematurely from inactivity through the many illnesses resulting from depression and celibacy. On the other hand, overindulgence diminishes one's life, and it is only by harmonizing the two extremes that damage will be avoided.[63]

In conjunction with the circulation of breath the seminal essence is compounded in the lower field of elixir (corresponding to water and *Tao-te* Heavenly Worthy) with primordial breath from the higher field of elixir (corresponding to heaven and Primordial Heavenly Worthy). As we have seen in our discussion of breath circulation, this compounding of primordial *ch'i, ching,* and *shen* effects the union of the three principles or the Three Pure Ones in the Yellow Court, thus producing the internal elixir, or the newborn ruddy child, *ch'ih-tzu,* and eternal life, *ch'ang-sheng*.

The Meditation of Orthodox Shang-ch'ing Taoism

Concomitant with the development of primordial *ch'i* and primordial essence *(ching)* is the development of primordial spirit *(shen)*. Such development is known variously as "preserving the One" or "obtaining the One," *te-i;* it may also be spoken of as uniting the three principles or the Three Pure Ones into One. The One of the microcosm is but a phenomenal manifestation of the primordial One of the macrocosm.[64] The development of the primordial spirit is also referred to as concentrating the One, *shou-i.*[65]

The method of preserving the One, *te-i,* is called by the Shang-ch'ing Taoists *tso-wang,* sitting and forgetting, or *ts'un-szu,* maintaining the thought.[66] It is explained by referring to the *Tao-te Ching,* verse 48:

> The pursuit of learning is to increase day by day,
> The pursuit of *Tao* is to decrease day by day.

> It is to decrease and further decrease until one reaches the point of taking no action.

> No action is taken, and yet nothing is left undone.[67]

Externally, the method is similar to yogic or Zen meditation; the goal of union is essentially the same. Sitting and forgetting, the Taoist dissolves the outward-flowing, dissipating perspective of representative thought,

thought which is limited and distorted by consciousness tempered by the various spatiotemporal patterns of sense. Through the dissolution of the dichotomous mode of thought, distinctions between subject and object, knower and known—the whole of representational thought—are dissolved. The method of sitting and forgetting has been well described in *Chuang-tzu,* chapter 6:

> Once Yen Huei, a student of Confucius, reported to the Master that he was making progress. He said, "I forget the moral distinction of benevolence and righteousness." The Master said: "Good, but not perfect." Another day Yen Huei said: "I forget rituals and music." The Master said: "Very well, but still not perfect." The third time this earnest student came to the Master saying: "I forget myself while sitting." The Master was surprised and asked: "What do you mean, that you forget yourself while sitting?" The student answered: "It is to free oneself from bodily form and to disregard hearing and seeing. Through the transcendence of bodily form and the elimination of sensations one identifies oneself with the Infinite. This is what I meant by forgetting myself while sitting."[68]

Maintaining the thought means returning to and preserving the primordial thought once it has been attained. It means preserving the mind of no mind, the transcendent mind, *wu hsin,* or preserving the thought of no thought, *wu nien.* Having attained this, the Taoist has emptied his mind of the immanent, dissipating, outflowing, changing things and has united himself with the act that moves without losing its state of original, undifferentiated, primordial purity. The Taoist encounters the transcendent unity of the Tao. Thus we find in the *Chuang-tzu,* chapter 8: "Heaven, earth, and I live together and all things and I are One."

The Threefold Approach

The pursuit of immortality through the compounding of the inner elixir is, as we have briefly demonstrated, threefold. This threefold approach derives from and relates to the three primordial principles of the cosmos: *ching, ch'i,* and *shen.* These three approaches are complementary in compounding the inner elixir. However, it is important that we understand that while these approaches are complementary, they are not necessarily interdependent. Frequently, the practices of breath circulation, meditation, and sexoyoga are employed together; at other times they are employed separately. As we have seen, members of the higher grades of the orthodox *Cheng-i* tradition do not practice the sexual procedures. [69] Circulating one's breath through the three cinnabar fields while swallowing saliva is considered to be sufficient for the compounding of the inner elixir. Meditation may also appear as a distinct practice without the circulation of breath. In this case, the concentration of thought in meditation effects the compounding of the three life-principles into the elixir. Indeed, Chuang-tzu suggested that meditation is the only necessary practice; we find in chapter 15:

> When man breathes in and out, or inhales in order to release the old air and take in the new, man hibernates like a bear and stretches his neck like a bird; he is merely striving for longevity. Such a man, wishing to live as long as Peng-tzu, indulges in breathing in order to develop his physique. . . . If one achieves longevity, not through breathing but through emptiness of mind, forgetting everything and possessing nothing, he has reached purity and infinity. All good qualities come with it. This is the Tao of heaven and earth.[70]

However, the three practices have the same essential goal, that of dissolving, purifying, and crystallizing the three principles (whether they be conceived of as purely material, material and spiritual, or purely spiritual) into their original unified state. Regardless of the method employed, each of these three practices effects the same transformation; that is, the return to the transcendent void, the cosmic center which is known as the original source of all things and is called the Yellow Court, the Great One, *T'ai-i,* or the Tao.

The Moral Aspect

Unlike Western alchemy, Taoist alchemy had an ethical aspect. According to the moral doctrine, the alchemical work was not to be pursued until the requisite number of virtuous acts had been performed. The idea behind this doctrine was that misdeeds of any sort develop the yin aspect of the soul. Conversely, meritorious acts develop the yang aspect of the soul.

The yang aspect of the soul is known as *hun* and is characterized by the virtues of benevolence, righteousness, propriety, wisdom, and faith (see Table 3.1). The yin aspect of the soul is known as *p'o* and is characterized by the seven passions of joy, anger, sorrow, fear, love, hate, and lust. Thus, acts associated with yang lead to lightness and purity of the soul and the union of the three life-principles in the center. Those who cultivate the *hun* aspect of the soul attain fullness of life and may be wafted up into the bright heavens. On the other hand, those who cultivate the *p'o* aspect of the soul are subject to suffering, illness, and untimely death due to the dissipation of the three life-principles by the outflowing emotions.[71] Thus, longevity is associated with virtuous acts that are unifying and death is associated with dissipating acts and transgressions.[72] It is in this context that Ko Hung wrote in the *Pao-p'u-tzu:*

> *Yü ch'ien ching* says further, "Those wishing to become earth genii must do three hundred consecutive good deeds; those wishing to be heavenly genii must acquire twelve hundred. If, after acquiring 1199, one commits a single bad deed, all the ones previously acquired are lost, and one must begin anew." Therefore, there is no question of the good merely outweighing the evil. Even though no wrong has been committed, if one merely speaks of one's own deeds and demands a reward for alms, the merit from the one vaunted deed will be lost immediately; but the whole series of merits will not be lost. It further says, "No benefit is to be derived from taking geniehood medicine before the full quota of merits has been acquired." If the medicine is not taken but the good deeds are performed, geniehood may not be acquired, but one can at least avoid the misfortune of sudden death. Personally, I am much inclined to suspect that old P'eng and others like him were prevented from mounting to heaven because their full measure of merits had not yet been accumulated.[73]

The ancient Taoist alchemists thought that a man was born with a predetermined lifespan, which was shortened for each transgression. These deductions, which were decided by the Director of Fates, varied from three to three hundred days, depending on the degree of transgression. Thus, when a man's alloted lifespan was used up, he would fall ill and die.[74]

Though not entirely in an ethical context, other requirements and injunctions were imposed on alchemical work. The processor was enjoined to protect the area in which the work was done from "stupid and profane persons" and from disbelievers, or else the alchemical work would fail. Furthermore, upon completion of the elixir, the alchemist was to make offerings to the gods in a prescribed manner.[75]

Conclusions

It is apparent, then, that in Taoist alchemy we are dealing with a highly complex symbol system in which there are universal correspondences from the infinite magnitude of the macrocosm to the infinitesimal degree of the microcosm. The essential nature of the centeredness of the Tao embraces the ultimate polarities of both the macrocosm and microcosm while itself remaining unpolarized. The Tao is the source of all differentiation, but is, in and of itself, nondifferentiated. Through the threefold approach of internal alchemy, *nei-tan*—meditation, circulation of breath, and sexoyogic procedures—the three nondifferentiated principles *ching, ch'i,* and *shen* are attained and unified in their original, void, nondifferentiated state, the transcendent Tao of the void center. In this manner the mandala of the macrocosm is realized and fixed within the microcosm. The play of powers of the microcosm as they are associated with change, life, and death are replaced by the purified powers of the macrocosm which are eternally situated in the unchanging. The alchemist becomes the perfect mirror of the cosmos. Upon attaining this state, the alchemist effects a return to the original, primordial instant of creation. He thus participates in the source of creation and is thereby renewed or reborn. Because the source and process of creation is eternal, the alchemist, being centered in the source of the eternal, is rendered immortal.

The pursuit of physical immortality, either through internal alchemy, *nei-tan,* or external alchemy, *wai-tan,* occurs because of a misunderstanding of the essential nature of the alchemical symbols. Without an intuitive realization of the transcendent nature of these symbols (and this in no way implies the recognition of symbol as symbol or the intellectual correlation of symbols), one cannot attain immortality; indeed, it does not exist. This is exemplified in fact by the many documentations of poisoning that resulted from the consumption of an alchemical elixir. Insofar as the alchemical elixir was compounded and consumed with the hope of attaining immortality, it was properly done only after the corresponding internal elixir has been compounded. Thus the consumption of the alchemical elixir was frequently regarded as the proper response to a divine summons, indicating that the processor had, in fact, completed the internal alchemical work. [76] The alchemist who died as the result of the consumption of the material elixir was thus referred to as a corpse-freed immortal.[77] Thus, the perfection of the external elixir implied the perfection of the internal elixir. It is in this context that we read in the Yellow Court Canon that "the one spirit divides and becomes many spirits; the many spirits return and become one spirit." The one spirit, *chen,* is real and the many phenomenal spirits, *ching,* are unreal. The Taoist alchemist sought to realize that the myriad creatures and the myriad spirits are unreal insofar as they are subordinate to the process of change and to refine them gradually to a state of permanence or eternal life, *ch'ang-sheng,* by union with the Yellow Court of the Center.[78]

NOTES

1. Of course this is only true of the Inner Elixir, or *nei-tan,* tradition of Taoist alchemy. As Joseph Needham has pointed out, the alchemists of the External Elixir, or *wai-tan,* tradition conceived of a physical immortality and sought to obtain it by compounding and consuming organic and inorganic elixirs. See Joseph Needham, *Science and Civilisation in China,* vol. 5, pp. xxxi, 71, 82, 114–115.

2.   Strictly speaking, this is so; however, we find in such Taoist liturgical practices as the *Cheng-chiao* the doctrine that allows for the transfer of merit. The adept, in this case the Taoist priest, having successfully obtained "immortality" (literally a state of continual rebirth, *ch'ang-sheng*) can use his accumulated stock of merit to help others attain immortality for the entire community. (See Michael Saso, *Taoism and the Rite of Cosmic Renewal* [Pullman: Washington State University Press, 1972], pp. 80–83). Furthermore, we find in the *Pao-p'u-tzu* of Ko Hung that once the divine elixir has been successfully made, longevity is guaranteed and baser metals can be transmuted into gold. The gold, once made, must be used to finance a large-scale religious ceremony with offerings to the various gods on behalf of the ghosts, ancestors, house, and village. (See James R. Ware, trans., *Alchemy, Medicine and Religion in the China of A.D. 320* [Cambridge, Mass.: MIT Press, 1966], p. 80.)

3.   Homer Dubs, "The Origin of Alchemy," *AMBIX*, IX, no. 1 (February 1961): 28.

4.   Schuyler Camman, "The Magic Square of Three in Old Chinese Philosophy of Religion," *History of Religions* I, no. 2 (summer 1961): 41.

5.   Homer Dubs, "The Origin of Alchemy," p. 29.

6.   Ibid., p. 30.

7.   James R. Ware, *Alchemy, Medicine, and Religion in the China of A.D. 320,* p. 51.

8.   Ilza Veith, *Some Philosophical Concepts of Early Chinese Medicine,* transaction no. 4 of the Indian Institute of Cultures (Basavangundi, Bangalore, December, 1950), p. 1.

9.   Ibid., p. 2.

10.   Chang Chung-yuan, *Taoism and Creativity: A Study of Chinese Philosophy, Art, and Poetry* (New York: Harper & Row, 1970), p. 128.

11.   Ibid., p. 134.

12.   Kurt Seligman, *Magic, Supernaturalism, and Religion* (New York: Pantheon, 1948), p. 79.

13.   Titus Burckhardt, *Alchemy: Science of the Cosmos, Science of the Soul* (Baltimore: Penguin, 1971), p. 34.

14.   Michael Saso, *Taoism and the Rite of Cosmic Renewal,* pp. 11–12.

15.   Henri Maspero, *Mélanges Posthumes sur les Religions et l'histoire de la Chine:* Vol. II, *Le Taoisme* (Paris, 1950), pp. 33–34.

16.   Tillich mentioned six characteristics of symbols which may be useful here. The symbols (1) point beyond themselves to something else; (2) they participate in that to which they point; (3) they open up levels of reality otherwise closed to us; (4) they unlock dimensions and elements of reality; (5) they cannot be produced intentionally; and, finally, (6) they may grow old and die. Paul Tillich, *Dynamics of Faith,* pp. 41–43.

17.   Chang Chung-yuan, *Taoism and Creativity,* p. 138.

18.   Chang Chung-yuan, *Taoism and Creativity,* p. 139.

19.   Ibid., p. 141.

20.   Michael Saso, *Taoism and the Rite of Cosmic Renewal,* p. 54.

21.   Laurence G. Thompson, *Chinese Religion: An Introduction* (Belmont, Calif.: Dickenson, 1969), p. 54.

22.   *T'ai ch'ing shih pi chi, Tao-tsang,* 582:A:13a.

23.   The classic example of Chou Tzu-Liang, the 6th Century adept who died from

alchemical poisoning, is found in *Tao-tsang,* Vol. 152, *Chou-shih Ming Tung Chi.*

24. *Tao-tsang,* Vol. 602, chap. 4, pp. 4a–b.
25. Chang Chung-yuan, *Taoism and Creativity,* p. 142.
26. Wu Lu-chiang and Tenney L. Davis, *"Ts'ang T'ung Ch'i,"* *Isis* 18 (1932): 257.
27. Ibid., p. 253.
28. Ibid., p. 241.
29. Titus Burckhardt, *Alchemy,* p. 23.
30. Ibid., p. 13.
31. Ibid., p. 15.
32. Ibid., p. 27.
33. Henri Maspero, *Le Taoisme,* p. 21.
34. Ibid., p. 21.
35. Michael Saso, "On the Ritual Use of the Yellow Court Canon," *Journal of the China Society* IX (Taipei, 1972): 14.
36. Wing-tsit Chan, *The Way of Lao Tsu* (Tao-te Ching) (New York: Bobbs-Merrill, 1963), p. 121.
37. James R. Ware, *Alchemy, Medicine, and Religion,* p. 243.
38. Ibid., p. 196.
39. Ibid., p. 140.
40. There is some dispute regarding the translation of *ni-wan.* Henri Maspero and Chang Chung-yuan regard the word as a transliteration of the Sanskrit word Nirvāṇa. Michael Saso agrees with this point but adds that many of the esoteric texts in the Taoist canon describe the *ni-wan* as being one of the nine palaces of the *ming-t'ang* in the brain. Cf. *Teng-chen Yin-chueh* (TT 193, Ch. *Shang*).
41. Michael Saso, "On the Ritual Use of the Yellow Court Canon," p. 7.
42. Michael Saso, "On the Ritual Use of the Yellow Court Canon," p. 9.
43. Henri Maspero, *Le Taoisme,* p. 94.
44. Michael Saso, "On the Ritual Use of the Yellow Court Canon," p. 7.
45. Henri Maspero, *Le Taoisme,* p. 91.
46. Michael Saso, "On the Ritual Use of the Yellow Court Canon," p. 8.
47. Ibid., pp. 7–8.
48. Ibid., pp. 8.
49. Chang Chung-yuan, *Taoism and Creativity,* pp. 135–136.
50. Michael Saso, "On the Ritual Use of the Yellow Court Canon," p. 15.
51. Ibid., p. 15.
52. This is, of course, an oversimplified schematization since all three principles function in each level of the body, the microcosm, and in the external world of nature, the macrocosm. Their "place of residence" is thus distinguished from their macrocosmic and microcosmic spheres of influence.
53. Henri Maspero, *Le Taoisme,* p. 139.
54. Chang Chung-yuan, *Creativity and Taoism,* p. 136.
55. Henri Maspero, *Le Taoisme,* p. 108.
56. Chang Chung-yuan, *Creativity and Taoism,* p. 135.
57. James R. Ware, *Alchemy, Medicine, and Religion,* pp. 138–139.
58. Chang Chung-yuan, *Creativity and Taoism,* pp. 142–143.
59. Ibid., pp. 144–146, 156, 157.
60. Michael Saso, "On the Ritual Use of the Yellow Court Canon," p. 4. The esoteric Yellow Court is not to be confused with the three centers or the "fields

of cinnabar" that are mentioned in various Taoist texts, that is, the *ni-wan* (brain), the heart, and the *tan-t'ien* (belly), which are sometimes called the Yellow Court, See Michael Saso, "On the Ritual Use of the Yellow Court Canon," p. 10.

61.   Michael Saso, "On the Ritual Use of the Yellow Court Canon," p. 4. It should be noted here that those of the orthodox *Cheng-i* tradition do not practice the sexual procedures; instead, the swallowing of saliva is said to be sufficient for developing the seminal essence. See Michael Saso, "On the Ritual Use of the Yellow Court Canon," p. 4.

62.   Wei Hua-ts'un disapproved of the sexoyogic practices in the fourth and fifth chapters of the *Chen-kao*. The passages in the *Yellow Court Canon* with ambiguous meaning must always be interpreted in the spiritual sense, according to the orthodox *Shang-ch'ing* interpretation.

63.   James R. Ware, *Alchemy, Medicine, and Religion,* p. 140.

64.   Henri Maspero, *Le Taoisme,* p. 37.

65.   Ibid., p. 138.

66.   Ibid., p. 147.

67.   Wing-tsit Chan, *The Way of Lao Tsu (Tao-te Ching),* p. 184.

68.   Chang Chung-yuan, *Creativity and Taoism,* p. 132.

69.   Michael Saso, "On the Ritual Use of the Yellow Court Canon," p. 4.

70.   Chang Chung-yuan, *Creativity and Taoism,* p. 132.

71.   It should be noted that yin has two meanings: one, the visible, which is associated with dissipation; and the other, the invisible, which is the esoteric source from which yang is reborn. The two are not identical and the *p'o* aspect of the soul is associated with the former.

72.   Michael Saso, *Taoism and the Rite of Cosmic Renewal,* pp. 11-12.

73.   James R. Ware, *Alchemy, Medicine, and Religion,* pp. 66-67.

74.   Ibid., p. 115.

75.   Ibid., pp. 92-93.

76.   *Chou-shih Ming T'ung Chi* 3.4a, *Tao-tsang,* vol. 152.

77.   *Chen-kao* 10.5a, 14.16a ff.

78   Michael Saso, "On the Ritual Use of the Yellow Court Canon," pp. 10-11.

4 A Description of the *Fa-ch'ang* Ritual as Practiced by the *Lü Shan* Taoists of Northern Taiwan

JOHN KEUPERS

EDITOR'S INTRODUCTION

The following paper of John Keupers represents the first study in English of the complicated and dramatic ritual of the redhead *Lü Shan* Taoists of northern Taiwan.[1] According to the common usage of the people of Taiwan, there are two kinds of Taoists who minister to the spiritual and temporal needs of the popular religion: the strictly orthodox blackhead Taoists, who descend from the classical orders of antiquity, and the popular local redhead Taoists, who are commonly seen throughout Taiwan, Fukien, and other provinces of southeastern China. The redhead Taoists are known for their highly instructive and colorful rituals, their frenzied exorcisms and cures, and their ubiquitous presence throughout the villages and countryside of Taiwan. Since the redhead Taoists are so readily visible, many fieldworkers from foreign universities as well as Chinese scholars from local universities have judged Taiwanese Taoism to be quite degenerate, a far cry from the classical orders and monasteries of mainland China. Although nothing could be farther from the truth, the fewer numbers of blackhead Taoists and the highly secretive and esoteric nature of classical Taoism have kept the blackhead rituals out of the sight of foreign and Chinese research scholar alike. The only exceptions have been an occasional glimpse of the classical *chiao* rituals of renewal or the acceptance of a few scholars into the inner coterie of an orthodox master.[2]

There are more than eighty recognized orders and sects of Taoists throughout China, of which a small representative group now resides in Taiwan. The majority of the Chinese inhabitants of Taiwan come from the southern part of Fukien province and the borders of neighboring Kwangtung. It is not surprising, therefore, that the greater number of Taoists in Taiwan comes from the same two areas, and represents Taoism much as it has been practiced in southeast China from the late Ming period onward. There are at least four groups or orders of

Taoists which can be recognized among the blackhead Taoists. These are (1) the classical *Shang-ch'ing* order from Mao Shan near Nanking; (2) the military *T'ai-chi* or *Pei-chi* (Polestar) order from Wu-tang Shan in Hupei province; (3) the highly esoteric, prestigious *Ch'ing-wei* or Thunder Magic sect from Hua Shan in Shensi Province; and (4) the Heavenly Master *Cheng-i* (orthodox one) order from Lung-hu Shan in Kiangsi Province. Since the center of Taoism closest to Fukien and Taiwan is the residence of the Heavenly Master of the *Cheng-i* sect in Kiangsi province, the Heavenly Master's sect has had the greatest influence on the Taoists of Taiwan. Thus, all four of the classical orders mentioned above have been assimilated into the orthodox *Cheng-i* order and have received licenses of ordination from the Heavenly Master in Lung-hu Shan.

There are likewise at least four or five sects of Taoists which can be recognized among the redheads of Taiwan. These include the local or heterodox Heavenly Master sect, the *Ling-pao* sect, the *Lau-chün* sect, the *Shen-hsiao* sect, and the above-mentioned redhead *Lü Shan San-nai* order.[3] All of the Taoists of local origin, who perform ritual for the living only and do not bury the dead, are classified by the people of Taiwan as redhead Taoists. Only the *Lü Shan* Taoists treated in this chapter by John Keupers actually wrap red cloths around their heads when performing ritual; but their influence has been so deeply felt in Taiwan that many of the other orders, especially in southern Taiwan, have learned their highly colorful rites and also wrap red cloths around their heads when performing ritual. Thus, in southern Taiwan, many of the blackhead Taoists wrap red cloths around their heads and use *Lü Shan* redhead rituals as a means of enhancing their liturgical services and of competing in the ritual market.

The use of the term redhead does not refer solely to the red cloth wrapped around the head during ritual ceremony. The *Shen-hsiao, Ling-pao,* and *Lao-chün* orders often dress exactly as do the blackhead orders, with the black skull-cap and gold knob headpiece typical of the Heavenly Master sect Taoists. The reason for the similarity in dress between the redhead and blackhead orders ultimately can be ascribed to the same cause, that is, the dominance of the Heavenly Master at Lung-hu Shan over Taoism in southeast China. From the Sung dynasty onward, Taoists were required to obtain a license of ordination from the Heavenly Masters. Whatever the local sect or belief of the many Taoists who came to Lung-hu Shan for a license, the imprint of the Heavenly Master was set both on the ritual and the dress of the Taoists who came away with the blessing and permit to operate granted (for a fee) by the Heavenly Master.

The order or sect of the Taoist who came to the Heavenly Master for a license of ordination was not a problem. No matter what the belief or the persuasion of the Taoist, he had to be legally granted the official sanction to operate. By examining the ordination manual used by the Heavenly Master, we see that Taoists coming to Lung-hu Shan were granted licenses in five different kinds of ritual orders.[4] These were (1) the *Shang-ch'ing* sect; (2) *Ch'ing-wei* sect; (3) the *Pei-chi* sect; (4) the *Cheng-i* sect; and (5) the mid-Sung dynasty order called *Shen-hsiao* sect.[5] Although Taoist supplicants were required to purchase a license from the Heavenly Master, they were ordinarily not allowed to choose which sort of license. Rather the Heavenly Master traditonally granted licenses according to the theoretical and practical knowledge of the ritual possessed by individual Taoists. All of the local, popular, or heterodox orders were given titles and manuals deriving from the *Shen-hsiao* order. The other titles were extremely esoteric and were traditionally passed on by inheritance, from father to son or from master to disciple, only after strict vows of secrecy had been taken to preserve the knowledge within the Taoist's own family. Only the *Shen-hsiao* ritual and rubrics were allowed to be divulged freely, and thus *Shen-hsiao* and redhead Taoists became synonymous. All popular orders were ordained by the Heavenly Master as *Shen-hsiao*.

John Keupers makes the distinction very clearly when he states in the beginning of his chapter that the *chiao* rites, which the *Lü Shan* Taoists received from the Heavenly Master sect, take only three months to learn, while the difficult *fa-ch'ang* ritual of the *Lü Shan* order itself takes a very long time to perfect. When they made the journey to Lung-hu Shan, the local Fukien and Taiwan Taoists rarely spent longer than three months learning the *chiao* rites of renewal at the source of orthodoxy. Indeed, the rites of the *Shen-hsiao* order were a weak and shortened mimicry of the orthodox and stately *chiao* liturgies of renewal performed by the blackhead orthodox orders. It was possible to progress upward within one's own order and learn the *chiao*, the exorcisms of the *T'ai-chi* sect, and the powerful Thunder Magic of the *Ch'ing-wei* sect. It was even possible to learn burial ritual and to wear the dress of the orthodox orders. But such local Taoists as did these things were still classified as *Shen-hsiao*, and they signed their official ritual documents as such. That is, the *Shen-hsiao* Taoists always addressed the spirits of the highest heavens with their official titles, which betrayed their origins and their ritual knowledge to whoever could read the memorials, rescripts, and passports addressed to the heavenly realms. Once a *Shen-hsiao*, always a *Shen-hsiao;* that is to say, the disciple or the son of the Taoist could not surpass his teacher in ritual perfection.

But whatever the weakness and mimicry of the *Shen-hsiao* style of liturgy, the rituals proper to the *Lü Shan* order itself are both powerful and exceedingly entertaining to behold. Since the *Lü Shan* rites are not bound by the taboo of inheritance, one can, for a fee, learn *Lü Shan* rituals from any master willing to part with the information. For this reason, the rites are extremely popular and widespread throughout Taiwan and other parts of southeast China, and John Keupers was able to view the grand rite of curing as practiced by the *Lü Shan* Taoists of southeast China. The rite is found not only in Taiwan but throughout Fukien, Chekiang, Kiangsi, and parts of Kwangtung. Like the highly entertaining and Impressive drama called "climbing the 36-sword ladder," the *fa-ch'ang* described here is typical of *Lü Shan* Taoism. Taoists of the other orders learn certain parts of the ritual and even learn to climb the 36-sword ladder (not described here) in order to embellish and improve their own acceptance by their local clientele. But in fact the magic and ritual of *Lü Shan* is basically opposed to that of the orthodox Taoist orders. Though there is mutual respect and a union of brethren against the outsider, within the ranks of Taoism the vulgar rites of the *Lü Shan* Taoist, as with the *Shen-hsiao* Taoist, bear a stigma which one must be rid of before ascending the heights of Taoist perfection. The difference lies, as

I have indicated elsewhere,[6] in the distinction between ritual as an expression of the meditations of internal alchemy and ritual as a means to exorcise, cure, and make a living in the external forum alone. To the *Lü Shan* and *Shen-hsiao* Taoists, the meditations of the Yellow Court Canon are irrelevant to the practice of external ritual. It is at this point that a parting of the way occurs between the orthodox and the heterodox Taoist.

A DESCRIPTION OF THE FA-CH'ANG RITUAL

Lü Shan San-nai Taoists are commonly classified by the people of northern Taiwan as belonging to one of the redhead orders. Though called upon to perform the classical *chiao* festival in a slightly simplified version, the *Lü Shan* Taoists are especially known in the ritual market for their highly dramatic and popular rites of healing and exorcism. The orthodox *chiao* rites of renewal are called *tao-ch'ang* by the *Lü Shan* Taoists, while the heterodox rites of exorcistic cures are called *fa-ch'ang*. The latter term is not to be confused with *fa-hui*, which is a general term in northern Taiwan for all sorts of lengthy rites performed by the popular redhead Taoists. As the *Lü Shan* Taoists themselves tell it, the orthodox *tao-ch'ang* rites of renewal require only three to six months to master, according to the redhead traditions, while the highly entertaining *Lü Shan* rituals require a much longer time to perfect. The reverse is true for the blackhead Taoists, who require years to perfect the difficult rubrics of the orthodox *chiao* rites of renewal, but use a simplified form of redhead rites to bolster their image in the public forum. One of the most noticeable differences between the classical rites of renewal and the popular rites of exorcism is the use or nonuse of literary materials. In the case of the *tao-ch'ang,* both redhead and blackhead use written texts. For the *fa-ch'ang,* however, no texts are used. The words of the exorcism are memorized and passed down from master to disciple with various difficult details recorded only in a notebook. The words are committed to memory. Gestures with dramatic dance and acting play a much more important role in the rituals of the redhead Taoists.

The *fa-ch'ang* described below was an extremely elaborate ritual, which lasted an entire day. In modern Taiwan it is quite exceptional to perform such a lengthy rite because of the costs involved. The man who called in the Taoists was a well-to-do Chinese herb doctor, who lived in a two-block, three-story modern apartment building. He had been ill for some time, and neither Western nor Chinese medicine seemed to help. The *fa-ch'ang* ritual was performed to catch the evil spirits who were preventing the normal medicine from being effective.

There were seven Taoists involved in the rite of curing. All related, they usually worked together as a group except for smaller, everyday rites requiring only one Taoist to perform. For major performances like the one described here, they were forced to cooperate: none of them had a full set of ritual texts in his own possession, for each specialized in a certain part of the overall ritual. During the day each took turns performing one of the rituals or playing musical instruments such as the drums, cymbals, trumpets and the *sona,* the double reed flute. The *Lü Shan* style rites were always performed throughout the day by a single Taoist who wrapped a red cloth around his head; while he worked, the others assisted. Except for the red cloth, no special vestments or clothes were used during the dramatic *Lü Shan* style rituals.

The family shrine was located in a small room on the roof of the apartment building. Behind the altar the Taoists had set up the three scrolls of the *Lü Shan* sect. These depicted the *San-nai* Three Lady spirits, Ch'en, Lin, and Li, who are tutelary spirits of the *Lü Shan* sect. They are known in popular terms as the three matrons, and they correspond to the Three Pure Ones of the orthodox Taoist sects. On each of the three scrolls were pictured the various helpers of the three sisters in their fight against evil spirits, as well as the Three Pure Ones themselves who appeared above and behind the three women as the highest deities in the Taoist heavens. The three women were thus given the most honorific position in the hierarchical realm of the redhead Taoists.

The Taoist altar, whether set up by blackhead or redhead Taoists, is always arranged after the manner of classical Chinese ritual. The place of honor, that is the back wall toward which the priest faces when peforming ritual, is located at what is considered to be the north side, that is, the ritual north. The deities of the highest order are depicted in scrolls hung along the ritual north side of the altar, the same ritual area where the emperor sat during imperial audiences. On the ritual east and west sides of the altar were hung scrolls depicting the eastern and western heavens, respectively. In this case, the deities of the redhead Taoists were represented by scrolls hung on either side of the altar. On the ritual east wall two scrolls were hung. The first represented Tung-wang Kung, who is identified by the redhead orders with Hsü Chen-jen[7] and two judges of the infernal regions. Next to Hsü Chen-jen was Chang-sha, the powerful pupil of Lady Ch'en, holding the left-headed peach in his hand. His body was covered with eyes and he rode on a fire wheel.

Against the west wall was hung first the scroll of Hsi-wang Mu with the two lady judges who assist her in the fight against evil spirits. The second scroll hung on the west wall depicted Yü-yüan, the other disciple of Lady Ch'en. In his hand was held the right-headed peach and his body was also covered with eyes. With his left foot he tread on the infamous spirit of Chang K'eng-kuei. On the family altar itself, beneath the scrolls of the three ladies, were various statues of popular local deities, the temple god of the area (Ching Shen), and the patron of powerful magicians (Pei-ti).[8] On the northwestern corner of the altar was placed the bushel of white rice, in which the Taoist priest set his ritual paraphernalia—the five army flags of the generals of the five directions, the seal for stamping official heavenly documents, the thunder block carved of date wood into a rectangular shape with a pyramid on top and on which was inscribed the letters "five thunder magic,"[9] and the great Taoist sword.

In front of the main family altar was placed a lower altar on which the Taoists had arranged three tablets dedicated to the Three Pure Ones, as is done in the orthodox *chiao* ritual. On the table was an incense burner, cups with wine, plates with cakes, fruit, and cookies, and, finally, a special bowl in which were placed five duck eggs, arranged on top of white uncooked rice. The five duck eggs symbolized the power to suppress, the term for duck, *ya,* being homonymous with the sound for suppress. On each of the five eggs was drawn the esoteric Taoist characters for one of the five planets. The eggs thus represented the evil-suppressing armies of the five directions.

The ritual began with the usual preparatory rites common to temple services throughout northern Taiwan. Incense was lit and put in the incense burners, and the five-to-ten-minute percussion piece called *nao-t'ien* (also *nao-t'an*), a thundering salute with drums and cymbals, announced the beginning of the *fa-ch'ang*. Following the *nao-t'ien* piece, the Taoists donned the robes of the orthodox blackhead orders and performed the rite called *ch'i-sheng,* appeal to the saints, or, sometimes, invitation to the spirits.[10] The rite has been borrowed from the orthodox *tao-ch'ang* and requires three Taoists in ceremonial robes but not wearing the red cloths around their heads, speaking the classical texts of the Taoist Canon. During the rite the main spirits of the Taoist pantheon, such as the Three Pure Ones and the spirits peculiar to the *Lü Shan* sect (the register, *lu,* of the *Lü Shan* order), are called upon to be present. The spirits depicted on the scrolls, namely the three ladies, Tung-wang Kung, Hsi-wang Mu, the many-eyed marshalls, and others, were invited to be present.

The third ceremony, called *an-tsao an-ching,* in which the spirits of the hearth and the kitchen were appeased, and the fourth ceremony, in which the memorial, *shen-tsou wen-chuang,* was presented to the Great South Pole Emperor of Long Life, *Nan-chi Ch'ang-sheng Ta-ti,* followed in quick succession. The memorial contained the eight life characters of the sick man (year, month, day, and hour of birth) and a petition for peace and life. Before the presentation of the memorial to the Great

South Pole Emperor, a dramatic dance was performed by one of the Taoists after the pattern of the *lo-shu,* that is, the arrangement of the five elements in the order in which they destroy each other, from metal (west) to wood (east), water (north) to fire (south), and finally to earth (center). While dragging his left foot after his right, the Taoist paced off the five directions of the cosmos in the ancient dance steps called the pace of Yü, thereby suppressing all of the evil earth spirits in the five directions, by the use of mudras and mantras. The Taoist himself performed the role of the mediator, or principal messenger, to convey the prayers of the sick man to the heavenly emperors. The Taoist became the immortal on the white crane, *Pai-ho Hsien-jen.* After the dance, he mounted a small stool, which symbolized the carapace of a golden turtle engraved with the eight trigrams. In his hand he held a white feather fan, symbolizing the white crane. He held the memorial, together with three sticks of incense atop his head, and mounted to the celestial South Pole star to present the memorial.

As soon as the memorial had been read, a typically *Lü Shan* ritual called *P'ao-fa,* magic for making evil specters flee, was performed. Three strips of white cloth, each a yard or so in length, were rolled up like a scroll and used for the event. In crude red painting were depicted (1) the five fierce generals, *wu-ch'ang meng-chiang,* riding on tigers with demon-destroying weapons in their hands; (2) the three Mao Shan brothers, *Mao-shan shih-yeh,* with sharp swords, accompanied by a huge serpent; and, finally (3) the Five Thunder marshalls, *wu-lei yüan-shuai,* birdlike warriors with knives and axes walking on clouds. An incantation was chanted over each of the three pieces of cloth, which were then dropped to the ground, thus making present what was depicted on them. Through the incantations and the dropping of the scrolls, the spiritual power of the immortals pictured on the scrolls was summoned to be actively present. The three pieces of white cloth were immediately picked up by one of the members of the sick man's family and hung over his bed.

The next ritual, called *ch'ih-fu,* giving imperial power to the talismans, was performed in order to give supernatural power to the weapons and instruments used in the fight against the evil spirits. The talismanic charms and the Taoist's sword were given spiritual power to vanquish the evil demons who were causing the illness. First the sword was brandished in the air as the Taoist, now wearing a red cloth around his head, spoke magic formulas that activated the power of the weapon. Next, the sword was used to bless a small metal bowl of holy water, the water being used to purify the area. Next the thunder block was used to draw magical seal characters in the air, making the documents and the prayers of the Taoist valid in the fight against evil. Finally a wild dance was performed in which blood was drawn from the comb of a cock and the tongue of a duck.[11] The blood was used to actify and validate five yellow and five red talismanic charms. The five yellow charms were taken to the room of the sick man and hung in the four directions and the center of the room. The five red talismans were worn by the other members of the family to protect them from attack by the exorcised evil spirits.

With the rites of preparation completed, the central part of the exorcistic cure now began. In the first of the rites of exorcism, the redhead Taoist must determine the origin and the consequence of the sickness. He must learn which of the five elements and, therefore, which of the five directions was responsible for the illness. The rite is called "the five bowls that contain the trigrams of King Wen," *Chou Wen-wang wu wan kua*.[12] The bowls, which were made of wood or plastic, were thrown at random over the shoulder of the Taoist, and the direction in which they landed was used to determine the source of the illness. The ritual was done in the following manner. The head Taoist of the group wrapped the red cloth around his head, and sat on the floor of the room, facing the south, with his back to the main altar in the north. Before him were placed the five dishes with the duck eggs, five glasses filled with sacrificial tea, and the five small wooden bowls. Fat meat was put in each of the bowls as an offering to the five fierce generals. The meat was then removed from the bowls, and the Taoist collected all five of them into his hands, stacked up one on another. He thereupon sang a lengthy song, while beating the bowls rhythmically on the ground. Then he threw the bowls one by one over his head, while a member of the family ran forward to place a number in each bowl, one through five, as they landed on the floor. The five bowls stood for (1) the living place of the sick man; (2) his life; (3) the location of the tomb of his ancestors; (4) the spirit of yin, that is, the lone soul from outside who came into collision with the sick man and caused his illness; and (5) the tutelary spirit, *kuei-jen,* of the sick man.

Once all five bowls had landed and their identity had been established, the Taoist then calculated in which direction they lay—north, south, east, west, or center—by noting the ritual area in which they had fallen. The most important of the bowls, the fourth container, betrayed the direction, the element, and the organ in the sick man's body where the evil spirit was hidden.[13] When the location of the evil spirit had been determined, the head Taoist then asked the consent of the spirits effectively to carry out the exorcism. Consent was asked and obtained by a throw of the fortune blocks, the moon-shaped bamboo crescents commonly used in Taiwan for asking favors of the gods. The exorcising rites then began in earnest.

The first rite used by the Taoists on this occasion was the famous "rolled fire mat," which consisted of a rattan mat that had been rolled up with two kerosene torches enclosed at either end. The torches were lit, and the rolled mat was twirled around the head of the Taoist like a baton. With the terrifying instrument of exorcism prepared, the Taoist then went to the room of the sick man and performed the rite called "turning over the earth." The rolled mat was carried to the four corners and the center of the room, where the Taoist beat the earth, thus scaring out all evil spirits hidden there. The *chia-i*, evil wood influences of the east,[14] the *ping-ting*, evil fire influences of the south, the *wu-chi*, evil earth spirits of the center, the *keng-hsin*, evil metal influences of the west, and, finally, the *jen-kuei*, baleful water influences of the north, were all scared out from their hiding places and assembled in the center of the room. Next, while twirling the fire baton in his hands again, the Taoist sent the baleful heavenly spirits back to heaven, buried the evil earthly humors, returned the yearly demons to their year and the monthly evils to the moon, scattered the evils of the day to the sun, and buried the hourly demons in the earth.

The next rite was also performed in the sick man's room. There the Taoist faced outside of the room, through the open door. The ritual, called "carrying off the evil spirits," was begun with the Taoist squatting on the ground, with a bowl of rice by his feet. In the bowl of rice were placed three paper figures. The first represented the evil heavenly dog; the second, the white tiger; and the third, the five ghosts that represent all evil spirits. There was also a paper figure of a man, *t'i-shen*, which substituted for the sick person. Accompanying himself to the melodic tinkling of a small handbell with a *vajra* handle, the Taoist summoned the spirit armies of the five directions and burnt offerings of paper money to them. Next, he went to the sick man's bed and scattered rice mixed with salt around the room to purify the area. The paper figures were all tied to the sick man's body with a thin thread, and the evil spirits were summoned forth and entered the paper effigies. Finally, the thread was cut from the man's body with the great exorcising sword. The evil spirits, now imprisoned in the substitute paper effigies, were placed in a sack and kept until the proper hour arrived to carry them away and bury them in a far-off place, from whence they could never return.

Meanwhile, the heavenly army of the five directions, which had been waging the war against the evil spirits, was fed and paid in a special ceremony that occurred on the altar atop the roof of the sick man's residence. The rite for feeding the five armies took place with the Taoist facing the south, that is the door of the family shrine, with his back to the ritual north. The five armies were again represented by the five duck eggs,

laid on an altar now facing the outside or the south of the area. Great
quantities of food, paper money, and incense were offered as payment
for their services. Later in the afternoon, the offended lonely yin soul
outside was also given a banquet, and paper money offered on a table
placed outside by the front door of the residence. The rite is called "wor-
shipping the exterior yin," *pai wai-yin*.

As an added blessing, the Taoists performed at this point a ritual seen
commonly throughout Taiwan and Chinese communities of Southeast
Asia. The rite, called "honoring the dipper and praying for old age," is
ordinarily performed for a man or woman over 60 years of age; while for
a younger man or woman, "offering to the birth star" is commonly performed.[15] In this case, because of the sick man's age, the offering to the
dipper was made. The Taoist again performed the rite toward the outside, that is, facing the ritual south with his back to the Taoist altar. Two
tables were set up by the door of the family shrine, one higher than the
other. Meanwhile over the window, a large piece of cloth was hung, and
a charm which read "true charm to prolong life" was drawn on the cloth
in white chalk. Then on top of the higher table were laid sacrificial offerings to the mother of the polestar, *Tou-mu hsing-chun*. The sacrificial
offerings were only of the purest substances—wine, sweets, and incense.
On the lower table, meat and other offerings were laid out for all the
other heavenly spirits.

Next, a seven-branched candelabra, representing the seven stars of the
Big Dipper, was carried to the sick man's room, and the seven small oil
lamps were lit. Incense was lit and quantities of paper money were
burned, after which the Taoist recited the scripture of the Big Dipper.[16]
During the recitation of the scripture, the Taoist again dressed in the
black skull cap and the gold crown, after the manner of the orthodox
blackhead Taoists. The clothes with the talismanic charm were left in the
upstairs altar room, for later use. At the end of the reading, the Taoist
then began to perform the last of the exorcising rites, known as "carrying off of the yin fire."

The fever of the sick man was considered to be caused by a special fire
spirit, which was extinguished and carried off after a reading of the
Canon of the Big Dipper. The "carrying off of the yin fire" was begun by
the Taoist, now dressed again as a redhead, drawing two talismans on
white paper, burning them, and putting the ashes in a glass of water for
the sick man to drink. The first charm was meant to purify the body of
the sick man and the second, the "snow mountain charm," to extinguish
the fires of fever. Next the Taoist took a bundle of symbolic spirit money
(ming-chih), and rolling up individual bills into a cone-shaped torch, lit
them and drew magic talismanic charms in the air with the flaming mon-

Figure 4.1 The Taoist, wearing a red cloth around his head, offers *Lü Shan* ritual during the performance of a *Chiao* near Tainan in south Taiwan.

ey (see Figure 4.1). After drawing a charm, he then placed the flaming paper in his mouth and devoured the flame to overcome the evil fire spirit. Shortly after, the evil fire spirit and the other demons that caused the disease were all taken in the Taoist's bag to a distant place and buried.

It was a very dangerous period of time when the fire spirit and those imprisoned earlier were carried out of the house. Before the Taoist left with his well-tied sack of evil spirits, he hid the magic seal used to stamp the talismanic charms by tying it inside of a bundle of paper money, thus protecting it from the rage of the departing spirits. A small rite called "gathering into the incense burner" was performed to protect the family members from the wrath of the demons. The bedroom of the sick man was locked, and one of the family remained inside to ring the Taoist's handbell, while the spirits were being finally exorcised. The sick man remained in bed during the entire time required to remove the exorcising bag from the house.

The Taoist then took the bag, now filled with malevolent spirits, and began to blow on the special horn of exorcism, a cow horn, the inside of which had been painted red (see Figure 4.2). As he stepped out of the door, he blew repeated notes on the trumpet, summoning the helpful spirits under his command and frightening all others away. Jumping on his motorbike, he whisked the spirits away to an unknown place and dis-

Figure 4.2   Redhead *Lü Shan* ritual. While blowing a trumpet, the Taoist mas-. ter, wearing a red cloth wrapped around his head, throws a duck under the temple altar.

posed of them. After fifteen minutes or so he returned and was welcomed by the burning of charms by the door, the freeing of the seal enclosed in the paper money, and the opening of doors by the people of the household who were hiding from the baleful influences of the sickness-causing spirits.

With the return of the Taoist, the rite of exorcism was technically ended, but the catechetical aspects of the ritual were now repeated again for the benefit of neighbors and friends, in sort of dramatic interlude which symbolically represented the power of the Taoist over the forces of evil. As the neighbors gathered to watch, the room which served as the family altar atop the roof was readied for the redhead Taoists' performance. On top of a table in the center of the room was placed a cardboard box, with some of the clothes of the sick man inside. The clothes were all of a white color. A blue cloth was then affixed around the sides and legs of the table, and over all was spread a net. The net was then fastened around the four legs of the table by means of four locks, hooked through the mesh of the net. Under the table was placed an incense pot with two handles, offerings of tea in cups, and an earthenware pot with two spouts. The earthenware pot represented the instruments used to prepare medicine to cure the illness of the sick man. Two Taoists then began to perform the ritual, called "breaking open the net of heaven and earth," a dramatic presentation of the liberation of the sick man from the bonds of the king of demons *(Muo-wang).*[17] (See Figure 4.3.)

The first Taoist dressed like a tiger-like creature with a mask on which was written "demon king" *(Muo-wang),* the custodian of the net of heaven and earth. The second Taoist dressed as a *Lü Shan* Taoist with the red cloth around his head, under the title of General of *Lü Shan, T'ai-pao,* with the yellow army flag of the Heavenly Master in his right hand. A free dialogue ensued between the redhead Taoist and the demon concerning the fate of the sick man. During the debate, the Taoist tried

Figure 4.3   The Taoist high priest spears the demon king, *Muo-wang.* A *Shen-hsiao* Taoist uses *Lü Shan* ritual, Tainan city, south Taiwan.

to win the freedom of the sick man by bribing the demon king with paper money. The demon king laughed at this idea, and they began to fight (Figure 4.3).[18] The Taoist used the sword, and the demon king, a heavy wooden stick. The latter was forced to give in and removed one lock from the net. The game was repeated until all of the locks and the net had been removed. The demon then snatched the clothes (the soul of the sick man) out of the box and tried to hold onto them, but in the last fight he was conquered and had to flee in the evening darkness outside. The soul of the sick man was freed at last from the attacks of the demon and thus he was cured. The Taoist then took the earthenware pot from beneath the table and smashed it, this being a definite sign that the power of the demon had been broken and that the medicine would not be needed anymore. The Taoist then mounted onto a chair and, with the yellow flag and the *vajra* bell in his hands, chanted over the sick man's clothes. When the song had ended, the clothes were taken back for the sick man to wear.

At the end of a long day indeed, by then late in the evening, a table of offerings was set out for the Jade Emperor, *T'ien-kung,* who rules over the spirits of heaven and earth. The last offering was made toward the outside, that is, with the Taoist facing the south and looking out the door of the family altar room. The final ceremony was called "seeing off the spirits" and is common to all Taoist ritual ceremony.

In conclusion, it must be noted that the lengthy ritual was clearly divided into the preparation for the exorcism, the exorcism itself, and the final dramatic presentation in which the whole rite was summarized in the form of a play for the benefit of the neighborhood onlookers. Such rites are typical of the *Lü Shan* redhead Taoists of northern Taiwan, and demonstrate the vast difference between the popular, theatrical ritual of the redhead Taoists and the stately, classical, and literary rites of the orthodox blackhead orders. The explanations offered here are those of the Taoist master who officiated at the rite.

EDITOR'S CONCLUSION

The foregoing description of the *Lü Shan* Taoist's rite of exorcistic curing provides a rare insight into the popular local ritual of southeast China commonly associated with heterodox Taoism. Northern and southern Taiwan are separated by only a few hundred miles, nevertheless, each section is very different in the purity or lack of it found in the Taoist master's use or nonuse of *Lü Shan* ritual. In northern Taiwan *Lü Shan* style redhead ritual may not be mixed with the orthodox literary rituals of the blackhead Taoists. The *Cheng-i* Taoists of the Heavenly Master sect actually take a vow against the evil spirits of the *Lü Shan* order and promise not to use *Lü Shan* style rituals during the *chiao* festivals of renewal, in order that they might be ordained into the secrets of the higher eso-teric forms of interior meditation. In southern Taiwan, however, the Taoists commonly mix *Lü Shan* ritual with the orthodox *chiao* rites of renewal and do not maintain a pure form of classical Taoist meditation in their liturgical per-formances. Thus, the *Lü Shan* rites described here can be seen during the classi-cal *chiao* festival of renewal in cities such as Tainan and Kaohsiung in southern Taiwan (see Figures 4.1, 4.2, and 4.3).

The reason for such an anomaly is to be found in the documents which the Taoist masters compose, which are read during ritual and sent off to the heavens by being burned. In these documents, one of which is reserved for the Taoist's own archives, are listed the true title and the register, *lu,* of the Taoist's liturgical powers. The Taoists of southern Taiwan are members of the *Shen-hsiao* sect and so list themselves when signing their heavenly memorials.[19] Thus, the mixture of *Lü Shan* ritual with classical orthodox style is permitted in southern Taiwan, where *Shen-hsiao* Taoists are referred to as "red-black two-tiered masters" when they perform both heterodox and orthodox styles of ritual. The *Lü Shan* ritual has been described in such a manner that the field researcher will easily be able to identify the style and thus the order of the performing Taoist. The order or sect of the Taoist can also be known from the register of spirits, *lu,* whom the Taoist can summon under his power and command. Taoists who use the spirits described here belong to the pure *Lü Shan* order or to the Sung dynasty *Shen-hsiao* sect, which mixes orthodox with popular styles of Taoism.

NOTES

1. For a recent work in Chinese which deals with some of the redhead rituals, see Liu Chih-wan, *Chung-kuo Min-chien Hsin-yang Lun Chi,* Academia Sinica Special Monograph no. 22 (Taipei, Taiwan, 1974).

2. For a description of the orthodox blackhead rituals, see Michael Saso, *Taoism and the Rite of Cosmic Renewal* (Pullman: Washington State University Press, 1972), pp. 65–83.

3. Saso, *Taoism and the Rite of Csmic Renewal,* pp. 84–87.

4. *Chi-lu T'an-ch'ing Yüan-k'o.* Library of the 61st Heavenly Master, Lung-hu Shan, 1886.

5. The *Shen-hsiao* sect, founded by Lin Ling-su; cf. *Tao-tsang* [Taoist Canon] 148, chap. 53 (hereafer cited as *TT*).

6. Michael Saso, "Orthodoxy and Heterodoxy in Taoist Ritual," in *Religion and Ritual in Chinese Society,* ed. Arthur P. Wolf (Stanford: Stanford University Press, 1974).

7. The identification of Hsü Hsun (Hsü Chen-jen), the Legendary Founder of Thunder Magic, with Tung-wang Kung is peculiar to the myth of *Lü Shan* style Taoism.

8. *Ching-shen,* identified with Ch'eng-huang, god of the city, and *Pei-ti,* powerful god of the north.

9. The thunder block is the insignia of the Tantric Taoist *Ch'ing-wei* sect. The

mid-Sung Dynasty *Shen-hsiao* sect borrowed the rituals from the orthodox orders and incorporated them into the rites of popular Taoism. The earliest notice of the block is to be found in *TT* 324, the work entitled *T'ai-shang Ch'ih-wen Tung-shen San Lu,* ca. A.D. 623.

10. See Michael Saso, ed., *Chuang-lin Hsü Tao-tsang,* 25 vols. (Taipei: Ch'eng-wen Press, 1975), pt. 4, *Chüan* 19, p. 7099 for the text of the *Ch'i-sheng* ritual.

11. This ritual is used by the *Shen-hsiao* Taoists of Tainan and southern Taiwan as a part of the orthodox *chiao* ritual of renewal. However, the Taoist wraps a red cloth around his head and faces the south when performing the rite.

12. That is, the five bowls represent the five directions and the corresponding trigrams of change, arranged after the manner of King Wen into a *Lo-shu* or magic square.

13. Each of the organs in the body corresponds to a direction. Thus liver = east, lungs = west, heart = south, kidneys = north, and spleen = center.

14. Each of the elements has a baleful aspect. Thus, for each of the following directions, the harmful elements are east's harmful wood, south's harmful fire, center's harmful earth, west's harmful metal, and north's harmful water.

15. The offering to the birth star *yüan-ch'en,* or the *Pen-ming* spirit.

16. See Saso, *Chuang-lin Hsü Tao-tsang,* pt. 1, *Chüan* 35, p. 2417.

17. It must be pointed out here that *Muo-wang* means demon king, not "ghost," i.e., the soul of an ancestor. Many fieldworkers in the social sciences have made the mistake of dividing Chinese spirits into three categories, gods, ghosts, and ancestors, thereby giving an anthropomorphic aspect to the entire panoply of Chinese spirits. Such a division was justified perhaps by the Confucian interpretation of the term *kuei* in the sole sense of a departed soul or ghost. The *Muo-wang* depicted by the Taoist, however, is a truly demonic spirit, and must not be translated as "ghost." To limit the notion of evil spirits to "ghost" is to neglect the entire Buddhist and Taoist traditions in Chinese religion.

18. A version of this ritual is used by the *Shen-hsiao* Taoists of Tainan city during the *chiao* ritual of renewal. The demon king attempts to steal the handheld incense burner from the community leader but is repelled by the power of the sword-wielding chief Taoist.

19. The biography of Lin Ling-su, the founder of the heterodox *Shen-hsiao* order, is to be found in *TT* 148, *Chüan* 53. It is also found in the *Lieh-chuan* (biographical) section of the Sung Dynasty history, *Chüan* 221, pp. 12b–14, where the Hui-tsung emperor is seen to approve of Lin's new order. The *Pen-chi* section of the Sung history, chap. 21, p. 7b, contains notice of Hui-tsung's decree in the biography of the Hui-tsung emperor himself. Rather like an ancient Roman emperor, Hui-tsung is seen to be meddling with heterodox Taoism while northern China burns. Lin Ling-su was a Taoist from southern Chekiang. The influence of the new *Shen-hsiao* order seems to have been very strong in Chang- chou prefecture in southern Fukien; thus in the area of Tainan and southern Taiwan the immigrants from Chang-chou still preserve the rites of Lin Ling-su to the present day. The *Shen-hsiao* rituals are to be found in *TT* 881–883.

5 The *P'u-tu* Ritual: A Celebration of the Chinese Community of Honolulu

DUANE PANG

EDITOR'S INTRODUCTION

One of the most widely celebrated and popular festivals in the Chinese lunar calendar is the *Chung-yüan Chieh,* the day commemorating the central principle of earth.[1] On the occasion of the festival, which occurs on the fifteenth day of the seventh lunar month, the Chinese community traditionally sponsors a banquet and a lengthy ritual called *P'u-tu,* the merits of which are thought to release all of the suffering souls from a Buddhist-inspired hell, and to integrate all alienated members back into the community. The keynote of the festival is communality; that is, the entire populace is expected to participate. Not only family and friends, but even strangers, tourists, and enemies are invited to be present. In the spiritual order, the merits of the *P'u-tu* ritual and the banquet first free and then feed all of the "hungry and suffering souls" in torment, allowing them to be released from underworld punishment and wafted upward to the heavens.

The concept of a "hungry soul" (Sanskrit *preta*) came from India to China with Mahāyāna Buddhism. It was quickly adapted into the faith of the Chinese people, and became the spiritual symbol for the social outcast, the object of the worship of gambler, prostitute, and beggar. Like social outcasts, "orphan souls" were left in hell with no offspring to pray for them. In the spirit of ecumenical syncretism, Taoist as well as Buddhist priests were called upon by the people to perform the rite for freeing the orphan souls. The Buddhist version of the rite, the earlier of the two, was called *Yü-lan P'en-hui,* from the Sanskrit word *avalambana,* signifying the emptying out of hell, as one empties a bowl by turning it upside down.[2] The Taoist version, devised at a later time, favored the term *P'u-tu,* signifying a general crossing over, or a general amnesty for the souls of the dead in hell.[3] Taoist ritual came to distinguish *Chao-tu,* burial ritual for freeing the soul of an individual from hell, from *P'u-tu,* festival ritual for freeing all of the souls from hell. It was therefore very important, in the context of the Chinese common man's faith, that all the souls in hell be freed at the time of a public festival, rather like a general amnesty declared at some great national event.

The *Chung-yüan Chieh* or festival of earth, celebrated on the fifteenth day of the seventh lunar month, precedes the bringing in of the autumn harvest. The symbolic meaning of the *P'u-tu* ritual celebrated on that day, therefore, is filled with social implications. The feeding of the *preta,* unknown souls who are untended, hungry, and outcast, is directly related to integrating the social outcast, the stranger, and the personal enemies of the community members celebrating the festival. Thus the *P'u-tu* banquet is made especially bounteous in order to feed all of the tourists and strangers who pass by the temple doors during the celebration of the festival. Each member of the community must forgive his or her enemies, or the rite will be inefficacious. Communal unity, a sort of *agapé* in which social solidarity is expressed, is the visible effect of the ritual. In an even deeper sense, the community of man must be seen as imitating heaven in giving, before reaping the bounteous harvest provided by the life-giving warmth of heaven and the fertile depths of the earth. Before receiving the material harvest, the souls of the underworld receive their share of heaven's blessing. The womb of the female principle earth *(yin)* opens to release the souls imprisoned in darkness, before bearing the life-giving crops that sustain the visible community.

The Chinese calendar of festivals is unevenly divided into three cosmic periods, celebrating the origins of heaven, earth, and the watery underworld. The festival of the heavenly principle of light *(Shang-yüan Chieh)* is celebrated on the fifteenth day of the first lunar month, with a dragon dance and a lantern procession.[4] The festival of the earthly principle *(Chung-yüan chieh)* is celebrated on the fifteenth day of the seventh lunar month, usually with the *P'u-tu* ritual if celebrated by a Taoist or the *Yü-lan P'en Hui* if celebrated by a Buddhist.[5] Finally, the fifteenth day of the tenth lunar month *(Hsia-yüan chieh)* is celebrated with the *Chiao* or rite of cosmic renewal, symbolizing the rebirth of the cosmos which takes place each year around the time of the winter solstice *(yin* giving birth to *yang).*[6] Thus the 7/15 *Chung-yüan Chieh* is seen as the central festival in the calendar of liturgical events in the lunar year. It is second to the New Year in importance, and is celebrated both in China and Japan as a time for commemorating the souls of the departed.[7]

The rituals of the fifteenth day seventh month are not limited to the celebration of the *P'u-tu.* In traditional times the *P'u-tu* was preceded by three days of fasting and abstinence, during which period the Buddhist or Taoist priests were called upon to read lengthy canons of merit and litanies of repentance.[8] On the evening before the *P'u-tu* banquet, each family prepared a lantern and carried it in a beautiful procession to be floated out to sea from the nearest river or shoreline.[9] The ritual of floating lantern and the preceding chanting of canons and litanies are not described by Mr. Pang, but are still to be seen in Honolulu on certain occasions.[10] The *P'u-tu* as described below is celebrated each year at the Kuan-yin temple adjacent to the Foster Botanic Gardens in Honolulu, in a three-day festival filled with the chanting of Taoist texts in the traditional manner. It is also celebrated once every third year at the Lum-sai Ho-tang, a temple located at nearby River Street. This temple is dedicated to the popular young lady Ma-tsu, who was worshipped after her death as an imperial concubine of the heavenly Jade Emperor.[11] On this latter occasion, the celebration of the *P'u-tu* is done as a part of the *Chiao* festival of cosmic renewal, performed on the fifteenth day of the tenth lunar month by the Taoists of Honolulu.

The *P'u-tu* therefore is used on more than one occasion during the lunar calendar. First, it is used regularly as a part of the festival of earth celebrated on the fifteenth day of the seventh lunar month. When enacted as a part of the festival of earth, it occurs with the canons of merit and the litanies of repentance only. Second, it is used as a part of the *Chiao* festival of renewal, with a series of rituals which are exceedingly complicated. A list of the basic rituals used in the *Chiao* and the 7/15 festival of earth is given immediately below. Those rituals used only in the *Chiao* are marked with an asterisk (*),[12] while those used on both occasions are left unmarked:

1. *Fa Piao,* a ritual announcing to the spirits and to the community that the festival is to begin.
2. *Ch'ing-shen,* a ritual inviting the spirits to attend.
3. *Chin-t'an,* a ritual for purifying the temple before offering a sacrifice or performing meditation.
4. Canons of merit.
5. Litanies of repentance.
*6. *Su-ch'i,* a ritual for renewing the five elements in the cosmos.
*7. Meditations for union with the eternal Tao.[13]
8. (Floating the lanterns.)
9. *P'u-tu,* for releasing the souls from hell.
10. Thanking and seeing off the spirits.

The festival of earth therefore centers upon the *P'u-tu* and the communal banquet as the single climax of the festival, whereas the lengthier and more esoteric *Chiao* festival of renewal focuses upon the meditation of union with the transcendent Tao. In the latter case, the *P'u-tu* banquet is seen as a concluding act, where union with the community and cosmic renewal follow upon the meditations of union with the Tao. Thus in both cases a *P'u-tu* ritual is an essential part of the festival. It must further be noted that the sacrificial objects used in the various rituals tell something crucial of the spirits to whom the rite is offered. The sacrifices used in the meditative rites of union use only "pure" foods, such as wine, incense, fire, and fruit. The sacrifices offered to the souls in hell include raw meat, while the offerings to the freed souls and to the human participants provide cooked meats in a grand banquet. The dress of the Taoist also reflects the purpose to which the various rites are directed. While performing the meditative rites of union the Taoist wears a flame pin in his cap, symbolizing that his interior is on fire during the rite of union. While freeing the souls in hell, the Taoist

Figure 5.1   The Taoist high priest, wearing the *Wu-lao* hat redolent of Buddhist ritual, offers the *P'u-tu* sacrifice during a *Chiao* festival, Tainan county, south Taiwan.

wears the five-pointed hat described by Mr. Pang. The hat is almost identical with that worn by Buddhists and resembles the crown of *Ti-tsang Wang* (Kṣiti-garbha), the bodhisattva who rescues souls from hell (see Figure 5.1).

The text used by Mr. Pang and the Taoists of Honolulu is found in the Ming dynasty Taoist Canon in volume 217, chapter 60.[14] It is a part of a 320-volume collection called *Ling-pao Ling-chiao Chi-tu Chin-shu,* a work compiled in the thirteenth century containing various kinds of Taoist ritual, both *Chiao* rites of renewal and *Chai* burials. The manual used by the Taoists of Honolulu is length-ier than that found in the canon and the title suggests that it has been influenced by the *Yü-chia Yen-k'ou,* a tantric Buddhist text also used to free the hungry souls from hell.[15] The *Yü-chia Yen-k'ou* is a later Buddhist work which most probably was first used in China during the eighth century A.D. and became very popular during the Mongol period (the thirteenth and first part of the fourteenth centuries A.D.) The text used by the Honolulu Taoists came originally from Chung-shan district in Kwangtung provice, southeast China, the area from which most of the Honolulu Chinese emigrated before coming to Honolulu. Since the text makes use of many mudras (hand symbols) and mantras (conjurations) deriving from esoteric or tantric Buddhism, it shows the influence both of the earlier *Yü-lan P'en Hui* and of the later *Yü-chia Yen-k'ou*. But even though the title and many of the external symbols are obviously derived from Buddhism, the text is in essence Taoist; that is, the nine stages of hell are conceived of after the *Lo-shu* or magic square of Taoism and the spirits invoked are Taoist.

The Taoists of Honolulu belong to the popular Heavenly Master sect with strong influences from the military Pole Star sect, both traditionally orthodox orders.[16] The *Kao-kung Fa-shih* or high priest for the occasion was Li Han, an elderly Taoist who came directly from Kwangtung provice to act as a Taoist for the Chinese community of Honolulu. The chief cantor or *Tu-chiang* was Albert Ch'en, who was trained in Kwangtung as a cantor before coming to Honolulu. The assistant cantor or *Fu-chiang* was Duane Pang himself, who is presently training to become a Taoist and a ritual expert for the Chinese community in Hawaii. His essay represents the first attempt of a practicing Taoist priest to describe the *P'u-tu* in English.

THE P'U-TU RITUAL CELEBRATED IN HONOLULU

The performance of the *P'u-tu* ritual each year on the fifteenth day of the seventh lunar month is considered to be the climax of three days of festive celebration by the Chinese community of Honolulu. At the conclusion of the rite the invisible souls in the underworld and the visible members of the Honolulu community are fed with a great banquet, the merits of which serve to help the living as well as the dead. The entire ritual is performed in such a manner as to represent the symbolic feeding of the "hungry ghosts" in hell, those who have no descendants or loved ones to care for them. The alleviation of the abandoned souls' hunger and suffering is thought to have two objectives: (1) it provides relief from suffering by the general amnesty or freeing from hell; and (2) it brings blessing to the visible community of men and women by appeasing the anger and resentment of spirits harmful to the community's well being. One of the high points of the *P'u-tu* ritual is the reading by the Taoist priests of a document modeled after the memorial sent to the emperor in imperial China. The hungry souls are told to be thankful for the festival banquet, and to bring blessing to the living society which offered the sacrifice for their freedom.[17] The *P'u-tu* thus symbolizes social unity through the giving of a sacrificial banquet, the purpose of which is to right past wrongs and bring accord to the visible world.

Though the Taoist notion of hell was deeply influenced by Buddhist notions of the afterlife, the structure of the underworld described in the *P'u-tu* ritual itself is more Taoist than Buddhist. Modeled after the concept of the magic square or the *Lo-shu*,[18] Taoist hell comprises nine main courts with 145 branch prisons, for meting out punishment due to crimes or sins committed against society during one's visible existence.[19] Hell itself is considered by the Taoist tradition taught in Honolulu to be located under Mt. Feng-tu in Szechuan province, west China.[20] A king rules each of the nine courts of hell, which are numbered after the pattern of the *Lo-shu,* that is, a circle or square of eight courts surrounding a ninth or central court in the middle.[21] In the *P'u-tu* ritual celebrated by the Chinese community of Honolulu, the Nine Stages of Hell and their rulers are as follows:[22]

1. King Ch'in Kuang   Northern Hell of Darkness and Cold
2. King Ch'u Chiang   Southwestern Hell of Butchering and Slicing
3. King Sung Ti   Eastern Hell of Wind and Thunder
4. King Wu Kuan   Southeastern Hell of Iron Posts
5. King Yen Lo (Hindu   Central Hell of Universal Plundering
   God of Death)
6. King Pien Ch'eng   Northwestern Hell of Fire Carts
7. King T'ai Shan   Western Hell of the Indestructible
8. King Tu Ti   Northeastern Hell of Boiling Water
9. King P'ing Teng   Southern Hell of Somber Fire

Above the nine courts is a tenth hall, which is the escape route or the completion of the magic square. Through this tenth court the souls are released, and it is where Buddhist notions of transmigration are syncretistically accounted for in the Taoist cosmos. The lady Meng-p'o gives each soul a potion of forgetfulness so that all past lives are forgotten before recycling into the cosmos.[23]

Upon death the souls of the deceased go initially to the first court of King Ch'in Kuang, who keeps the registers of the living and the dead. King Ch'in Kuang uses a magic mirror which illumines the interior, showing the balance between good and bad deeds performed during the life of the deceased. If good deeds outweigh bad deeds, the soul is taken immediately to the tenth court for release. If bad deeds, that is, offenses committed against the fellow members of the community, are predominant, the soul is sent through various courts of hell where punishments are meted out for specific misdemeanors. During Taoist funeral ritual large scrolls depicting the punishments in the nine hells are hung in the ritual area. Popular manuals and temple murals also give lurid details of the tortures of the damned.[24] It is interesting to note that the demons meting out the torments are the equivalent of politicians in the visible world. Taoist funeral ritual bribes or "buys off" the corrupt officials of hell, much as public officials are dealt with in the real world. It is also worth noting that only the politicians stay permanently in hell, the ordinary folk being allowed release through the meritorious offerings of the living and especially through the ritual of the Buddhist or Taoist priest. The *P'u-tu* ritual therefore can be seen as a grand community celebration of prayer and sacrificial offering, the merit of which wins a general amnesty, or as near to a general amnesty as possible, for the neglected and outcast souls in the underworld. It also stands as a symbol for uniting the divided members of the community in a ritual banquet.

The *P'u-tu* ritual described here follows the customs of Chung-shan district in the province of Kwangtung, whence most of the Chinese of Honolulu, or their ancestors, have come. The ritual itself, however, is classical, and follows the traditions of orthodox Taoism.[25] A strong tradition of martial arts or *Kung-fu* exercise is also found in Honolulu, suggesting similar sources for military Taoists and the military exercises, though this point has not yet been adequately studied. Throughout both Taiwan and the Chinese communities of Southeast Asia similar relationships between military exercises and Taoist ritual have been observed. The use of the sword with the emblem of a turtle and snake derives from Wu-tang Shan in Hupei province, the legendary home of the Pole Star Taoists.

The robes worn by the Taoist priests during the *P'u-tu* are usually red. They are called *Ho-ch'ang*[26] or longevity robes, or more commonly *Hung-p'ao,* red "good luck" robes. On the robes of the high priest, the "Master of Exalted Merit," are embroidered the *pa-kua* or eight trigrams, or eight golden cranes. The embroidered art motifs on the high priest's robes symbolize that he is a heavenly mandarin mediating between the invisible world of the spirits and the visible world of man. On the sleeves, collar, and lower borders of the robe are embroidered the eight treasures, which are symbols of the eight immortals—a fan, lotus, sword, flower basket, flute, gourd, wooden clappers, and a bamboo container. The high priest wears a specially designed hat called the *Chin-k'uan.*[27] It is slightly different from the hat of the orthodox *Cheng-i* Taoist in that the gold crown of the Cheng-i Taoist is, in the case of the Honolulu Chung-shan master, enclosed in an embroidered adaptation of the Buddhist *P'i-lu Mao* of Vairocana[28] or the *Ti-tsang Mao* of Kṣitigarbha.[29] The small golden crown, common to the *Cheng-i* order and to most other Taoists of southeastern China, symbolizes the heavens and the stars. While wearing it the Taoist master stands in the highest heavens, before the thrones of the highest heavenly worthies.[30]

From the top of the Chung-shan Taoist's crown emanates a *Ju-i,* a small mushroom-like emblem which symbolizes the flame of the eternal Tao. The master only wears this flame-pin when performing orthodox Taoist ritual. It is similar to the small gold flame-pin of the *Cheng-i* Taoist which is inserted in the gold crown when performing the meditations of union with the Tao. The *Cheng-i* flame-pin is called *hua* diadem, or *yang,* an emblem of respect in the presence of the eternal Tao.[31] The other Taoist priests, that is, the chief and the assistant cantor, wear simple red robes with green trimming on the sleeves, collar, and lower hem. Usually there is a single golden crane embroidered on the back of the robe. On their heads they wear the *Hua-yang* crown, which the people of Chung-shan also call "fish-tail hat" because of its shape.[32]

PREPARATION OF THE P'U-TU ALTAR

The performance of Taoist ritual in a local temple requires the construction of a special Taoist altar modeled after the mandala of the highest heavens. No matter which direction the altar actually faces, the position of the highest Taoist spirits, the "Three Pure Ones," is conceived of as being in the ritual north.[33] The north is the place where the emperor sits in imperial audience, or the direction toward which the heavens are worshipped. For Taoist ritual, the spirits of the popular folk religion are all moved to the south of the temple, the direction from which the people usually worship. Thus during Taoist ritual the people and spirits of the popular religion all stand in the south, facing the highest Taoist divinities who are situated in the north. The special altar set up in the south area of the temple, the altar on which the statues or scrolls of the popular folk religion spirits are placed, is called the *Yü-huang Tien,* the palace of the Jade Emperor. The Jade Emperor is the highest spirit in the popular folk religion, the deity who fulfills the role of emperor in the heavens. The ritual area thus becomes a sacred mandala in which the highest pure spirits of esoteric Taoism are in the north and the popular divinities of the folk religion are in the south of the temple.

Since the hungry souls or the *preta* represent the alienated and the outcast, their altar cannot be included as a part of the pure area, that is, the temple purified by Taoist ritual. But since they are to be reintegrated into the community, or sent off to the heavens, or at least fed in the communal banquet, a special altar must be set up which connects the ritually outcast souls with the spiritually pure ritual area. This altar is usually set up directly in front of the temple in the plaza, under the open skies. It is ritually connected with the Jade Emperor's altar by a long table on which the sacrificial offerings are laid out. The long table serves to bring the orphan souls into the world of the saved spirits, by leading them up to the temple's incense pot, which always serves as the link between the visible and the invisible. The offerings to the orphan souls are thus set up on a table which links the temple incense pot to the external world.[34] Offerings of tea, wine, vegetarian dishes, buns, fruits, and flowers, always in threes, are laid out on the *P'u-tu* altar.[35]

In most parts of China both the popular Chinese religion and Taoist custom forbid the slaying of any animal during the period of three days which precedes the *P'u-tu* sacrifice.[36] On the third day, the day of the *P'u-tu* sacrifice, a pig is slain, and the raw meat, along with the meat of a goat and other food offerings, is laid out as a sacrifice for the orphan souls. Raw meat thus symbolizes an offering to the alienated dead. The raw meat is then cooked, and a cooked banquet is offered to the orphan souls after the ceremony has finished, showing the transition from the state of alienation to the general amnesty. When the *P'u-tu* altar has been set up, a sacrificial roasted duck is the first cooked food to be offered on the altar. The duck is substituted for the usual sacrificial chicken used for spirits of the popular religion, for the Cantonese believe that on the way to the underworld the chicken's spirit may set to work its beak or sharp claws, which will tear the clothes and other belongings of the dead. Thus the ghosts of the dead may be forced to dress in tattered rags. The duck's flat bill and webbed feet are innocuous, so it is admirably fitted to accompany the material offerings to the underworld.

When the ritual offerings have been laid out on the *P'u-tu* altar, the equipment of the Taoist priest is next brought to the table and arranged in a special order determined by Chung-shan tradition. Five dishes laden with fruit are first put on the table, between a pair of red longevity candles. The candles must be kept burning throughout the ceremony, an assistant being appointed to replace them as they burn low. Next a special bridge-shaped box is put on the table, flanked by another pair of red candles. The box contains the five-pointed hat of Ti-tsang Wang or Kṣiti-garbha, which the Taoist wears when he descends into hell to free the hungry ghosts. The two candles placed by the side of the box are not lit until the very end of the ceremony, after the ghosts have been fed and asked to go home. Lastly an octagonal box is laid on the altar, on top of which are two *Ju-i* or longevity scepters. These scepters are quite artistic, each being shaped like a mushroom with a long curved stem. They are frequently seen in collections of Chinese art, carved from exquisite jade.[37] The eight-sided box thus represents a mandala of the Chinese hells, and the *Ju-i* are the precious symbol of Ling-pao T'ien-tsun, the mediator of the Taoist Trinity, who saves the souls from hell.[38] Finally, on the Taoist's table or altar is placed a dish covered with pure white rice, in the center of which is placed a small slim vase containing fresh water. The vase is symbolic of the *kan-lu,* the viand of sweet dew carried by Kuan-yin, the Buddhist goddess of mercy.[39] A second plate filled with tea leaves is placed next to the dish holding the *kan-lu* vase. In the center of the tea-leaf dish is placed an empty bowl. During the ceremony the water from the *kan-lu* vase will be poured into the empty bowl as a part of the ritual purification.

The table is now ready to be used as the altar for the *P'u-tu* sacrifice. The Taoists sit at the head of the table, the ritual north, acting as the mediators for the highest Heavenly Worthies. The hungry ghosts are conceived of as standing at the south side of the altar, much as do the men and women of the community, guests and strangers, who come to witness the ceremony. The Taoists hang a silk curtain over the north side of the altar, thus protecting themselves from the impure world of the hungry spirits which have just come forth from hell to attend the banquet.[40] The ritual text of the *P'u-tu* is now laid on the altar, in between the *Mu-yü* or "wood fish" and the brass bell on the left and right respectively. These musical instruments are used to accompany the chanting of the Taoists, the wood fish being the instrument of yin and the brass bell or gong the symbol of yang. Thus the playing of the ritual music symbolizes the play of yin and yang in the cosmos.

Since the crowd of hungry ghosts which have been freed from the underworld is thought to be a rowdy group, difficult to control or handle, a huge papier maché figure is made of Ta-shih Yeh or Ta-chung Yeh, the general who controls demonic forces.[41] Colored in lively sequins and bright armor, two great horns extend from the forehead of the blue-faced king of the demons. The statue is thus renamed Kuei Wang (King of demons) or P'u-tu Kung, Lord of the *P'u-tu* amnesty, by the common folk.[42] The true identity of the demon king is however known to the Taoists and to the people. In the very center of the demon king's head is seen to protrude a small likeness of Kuan-yin Buddha, the goddess of mercy. The spirit of Ta-chung Yeh is in fact an avatar or transformation of Kuan-yin Buddha. Previously when Kuan-yin appeared in the underworld as the goddess of mercy, she was taken advantage of by the demonic politicians of hell. Thus she is now transformed into a ferocious general in order to control and frighten the unruly hungry ghosts.[43]

The area in which the orphan souls are thought to stand and wait for the banquet, or assemble for the ritual, is thought to be highly impure and contaminating. All of those people who are ritually impure, that is, who are weak from ritual impurity so as to be unable to counteract the forces of yin from the underworld, are asked to avoid the ritual area. Women who are menstruating, families in mourning for a recent death, and people whose birth date puts them in an unfortunate or inauspicious zodiac sign are asked to keep away from the *P'u-tu* altar.[44] Three bamboo poles are erected to delineate the area, known as *ku-ch'ang,* the field for the orphan souls. A paper lantern is strung from each of the poles to guide the hungry souls to the field. On the face of the lantern is depicted a ferocious lion, a symbol for Chiu-k'u T'ien-tsun, the sovereign spirit who saves all souls from hell.[45] The lanterns and poles thus serve as an invitation to attend the ritual banquet. Food offerings are laid out on a small table by the foot of the bamboo poles, next to a paper house over which is written *Pao-fan Chieh-yin T'ien-tsun,* "A precious banner welcoming Heavenly Worthies." The orphan souls or hungry ghosts (the two terms being practically synonymous) are asked to remain outside in the ritually designated area until summoned inside to attend the *P'u-tu* rite. The Heavenly Worthies and the other Taoist spirits, on the other hand, may go beyond the check point to the designated ritual area north of the Taoist altar.[46] Finally, Hawaiian foods, such as Primo beer and *poi* (taro staple), are laid out as offerings for Polynesian ghosts which might attend.

The P'u-tu Ritual

The *P'u-tu* ritual is most complex and takes a total of three or more hours to perform. The various stages are described in the following paragraphs, numbered according to the *P'u-tu* manual used by the Chung-shan Taoists. The ritual described here is used in common for the Chinese community in Hawaii, whether of Chung-shan, Lung-tu, or Hakka ethnic origins.[47] The manner of performance does not vary greatly from the rite celebrated in Hong Kong, Kwangtung, and other parts of Southeast Asia.

Part I. *K'ai T'an:* "Opening" the Altar

A. Fa Ku: The drum of the Tao. The beginning of the *P'u-tu* ritual is signaled by the beating of the "drum of the Law" or the "Taoist's drum," the traditional manner of showing that ritual is about to begin. Three long rolls of the drum are sounded announcing to the three stages of the cosmos—heaven, earth, and underworld—that a ceremony is about to begin. As the drums echo throughout the cosmos, summoning the spirits, the living, and the deceased, the temple custodians begin to light the incense and the candles at the various altars. The gongs and cymbals then join with the drum beat in a type of music known by the Cantonese as *Hsi-ch'ing.* The purpose of the *Hsi-ch'ing* music is to purify the temple of all evil influences, so that no harm or damage will be done to the community during the performance of the *P'u-tu* ritual.

B. Dance for offering incense to the Three Pure Ones. The highest Taoist spirits, the sacred trinity known as the "Three Pure Ones" *(San-ch'ing),* rule the entire cosmos from the highest three heavens. The Three Pure Ones are (1) Primordial Heavenly Worthy, the spirit of life breath and ruler of heaven; (2) *Ling-pao* Heavenly Worthy, the source of spirit and mediator of earth; and (3) *Tao-te* Heavenly Worthy, the source of vital essence and ruler of the watery yin principle from which new life is born.[48] In the ritual north of the temple of the Taoists hang scrolls depicting the Three Pure Ones, the altar dedicated to them beneath the scrolls being considered the main altar of the temple during Taoist ritual. The high priest begins the ritual by offering incense to the Three Pure Ones, and then chants a hymn to each of the deities to the accompaniment of drum, cymbals, gongs, and double-reeded flute. While chanting, he holds the ancient *shou-lu* or hand incense-burner, a wooden thurible shaped like a dragon with three sticks of incense inserted into an ornate lotus-like head. After the chant is finished, the chief cantor reads a lengthy memorial *(piao)* addressed to the Heavenly Worthies, which tells of the purpose for which the *P'u-tu* is held, the prayers of the entire community, and lists the names of all the community members who have contributed to offering the sacrifice.

When the chanting of the hymns of praise and the reading of the memorial is finished, the high priest begins to chant the traditional hymn to the three treasures, which is used by Buddhist and Taoist alike. In the Taoist interpretation of the *San-pao,* or "Three Treasures," a term obviously borrowed from Buddhism, the first of the treasures is the eternal transcendant Tao, the nameless *Wu-wei* or unmoved first mover, of which the Three Pure Ones are the immanent manifestation.[49] The second treasure is the *San-tung* or the three arcana of the Taoist Canon, that is, the Taoist version of the Buddhist scripture. The third treasure is the Heavenly Master Chang Tao-ling, the founder of religious Taoism, who first taught to the world the doctrines of the Three Pure Ones and began the movement which ultimately gave rise to present-day religious Taoism. While the three laudatory passages are being sung, the high priest performs a meditation during which he envisions or sees in his heart-mind the appearance of the Three Pure Ones. The Three Pure Ones are envisioned, that is, seen in all of their colorful robes and splendor. By bringing the Three Pure Ones into the center of the microcosm, that is, the meditative center of the high priest's body, union with the eternal Tao is thought to be effected. In the state of union with the Tao, the priest now has the authority to perform the *P'u-tu* ritual.

C. Traveling to the P'u-tu Altar. Leaving the main altar, the Taoist priests first walk to the front of the paper image of Ta-shih Yeh. With the *shou-lu* (hand-held censer) in one hand, the high priest draws secret talismans in the air with the other hand, using three sticks of incense as a brush. He then chants the mantra of the Ta-shih Yeh, causing the spirit to come into the papier maché effigy. The rite is called *k'ai-kuang,* or "opening the eyes" of the statue. At the end of the incantation, the three sticks of incense are placed in the incense pot dedicated to Ta-shih Yeh. The three priests then turn counterclockwise and face the inner part of the temple, toward the *P'u-tu* altar. The chief cantor proceeds to the opposite end of the altar and stands in front of the sacrificial offerings, by the throne or chair in which the high priest will sit. He pours the *kan-lu* liquid into the metal bowl and then holds the bowl in his left hand, meanwhile bending the middle and fourth finger under the bowl to form the lotus mudra, a symbol of purification.

While the chief cantor is performing the ablutions, the high priest begins to sing the prayer for purifying water. The cantor meanwhile dips the middle finger of his right hand into the bowl of *kan-lu* water, in a mudra which symbolizes "the protector."[50] He then sprinkles holy water in the ten directions, that is, east, south, west, north, northeast, northwest, southeast, southwest, the zenith above, and the nadir below.[51] The purification is done in preparation for the entrance of the high priest and his seating at the throne of the *P'u-tu* altar.

After the sprinkling is completed, the chief cantor holds three sticks of unlit incense in his right hand and invites the high priest to ascend the throne:

> Praise the most superior and mysterious 36 divisions
>   (of ministers, realized men, and generals of the heavens).
> From the center of Dragon-tiger mountain, descend here.
> Guide the souls to birth in ultimate happiness.
> Come forward, master, and take the precious throne.

The high priest responds:

> Make it known that my origins are not sullied,
> The six roots[52] (eyes, ears, nose, tongue, body, mind)
>   will not interfere, for I am of pure mind.
> The compassionate sovereigns of the three ages,[53]
> (Past, present, future) whom I am one with!
> Be present in your multitudes as I ascend the throne.
> Come and save all souls and hungry ghosts!

The chief cantor responds:

> Three thousand holy ones come to the feast,
> To realize the salvation of all living beings.

Strike the drum of the Tao three times,
Ascend the precious throne.
All souls and hungry ghosts, come to save them!

The musicians then play the Cantonese exorcism melody called *Ta-k'ai Men* "Open wide the gates," during which the high priest and the assistant cantor enter the area of the *P'u-tu* altar. While entering, the high priest shields his face with his sleeve, symbolizing the wiping away of the six roots of desire, keeping all evil influences away on his progress to the throne.

D. Protecting the sacred area through mudras. When the high priest has ascended the sacred throne of the *P'u-tu* altar, the chief cantor takes the three unlit sticks of incense and some paper money, and burns both items outside in the temple furnace. This is the signal for the Ta-shih Yeh to allow the tumultuous multitude of ghosts waiting outside the temple to enter. As the hungry ghosts enter, the musicians play the *Hsi-ch'ing* exorcism music and the high priest performs a series of exorcistic mudras to form a protective circle around the altar. The series of secret gestures ends with the *Chin-kuang* mudra (golden light), extending the middle finger on each hand as a final protection from the ghosts. The mudras are thus used to protect the priests and the attendants.

Part II. *Ch'ing Shen* "Inviting the Spirits"

A. Offering of Incense. The Taoists priests now begin to sing the invitational passages in the *P'u-tu* text. While the assistant priests take their seats alongside the table, the high priest remains standing, starting the invitation to all the gods. Incense sticks are lit. While inviting the gods and goddesses of the three realms by name or group, the high priest offers three sticks of incense to each after the invocation has been made. These incense sticks are then inserted into a banana tree stump placed on the altar to serve as a temporary incense holder. Upon completion, the high priest takes his seat and reads a document explaining the purpose of the *P'u-tu,* where it is being held, and what benefits he hopes will be granted by performing the service.

B. Welcoming the Wu-lao. Taking the bridge-shaped box, one of the priests then opens it and takes out the five-pointed crown. On each section are embroidered pictures of the *Wu-lao* "Five Sovereigns of the Five Directions," and two long silk ends embroidered with the character *Shou* "Longevity" are attached to each end. The *Wu-lao* are the sovereigns that protect mankind and aid the ghosts to freedom.[54] They are the five emperors of the five directions corresponding to the five primordials: that is, wood in the east, fire in the south, metal in the west, water in the north, and earth (soil) in the center.[55] Each emperor has a symbolic primordial number. Together the numbers of the emperors form a perfect *Ho-t'u* chart of the five elements as they exist in the Prior Heaven (Figure 5.2), that is, in their life-bearing order—wood gives birth to fire, fire to earth, earth to metal, metal to water, and water to wood.[56] The *Wu-lao* are:

1. *Tung-fang Ch'ing-ling Shih-lao Chiu-ch'i T'ien-Chün,* The Green Sovereign of the East, Spiritual Beginning Spirit of Nine Primordial Breaths
2. *Nan-fang Tan-ling Chen-lao San-ch'i T'ien-chün,* The Red Sovereign of the South, Spiritual Realized Spirit of the Three Primodial Breaths
3. *Chung-yang Yüan-ling Yüan-lao I-Ch'i T'ien-chün,* The Yellow Sovereign of the Center, Spiritual Primordial of One Primordial Breath
4. *Hsi-fang Hao-ling Huang-lao Ch'i-ch'i T'ien-chün,* The White Sovereign of the West, Spiritual Emperor of Seven Primordial Breaths
5. *Pei-fang Wu-ling Hsüan-lao Wu-ch'i T'ien-chün,* The Black Sovereign of the North, Spiritual Profound of Five Primordial Breaths

The heavenly *Wu-lao* could easily be confused with the earthly spirits of the five directions found in popular religion. These are commonly known as:

1. In the East *T'ai-i T'ien-tsun,* Heavenly Worthy who Protects the Soul
2. In the South *Ch'ang-sheng Ta-ti,* Emperor of Longevity who Prolongs Life
3. In the Center *Yü-huang Ta-ti,* Jade Emperor who Rules the World
4. In the West *T'ien-Huang Ta-ti,* Heavenly Emperor who is in Charge of all Spirits
5. In the North *Tz'u-wei Ta-ti,* Emperor of the Purple Heaven who Grants Life

. The five-pointed crown is also another adaptation from the Chinese Buddhists, who wear a similar crown during their *Yoga Tantra* ritual of "Relieving Burning Mouths and Distributing Food." On the Buddhist crown are embroidered Buddhas who in a similar manner represent the five directions:

1. In the East *Akṣobhya,* Immutable and Sovereign
2. In the South *Ratnasambhava,* Bliss and Glory
3. In the Center *Mahāvairocana,* Eternal and Pure
4. In the West *Amitābha,* Wisdom and Action
5. In the North *Śākyamuni,* Incarnation[57]

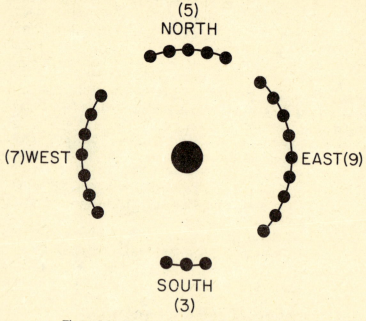

Figure 5.2   The *Ho-t'u* chart of the Prior Heavens.

Taking this five-pointed *Wu-lao* crown, the high priest then presses his middle fingers on the center pearl of the *Chin-k'uan* hat to cover it with a second crown. Then, moving his fingers along each side, he ties a knot in the back of the hat to hold it in place. Taking the tips of the silk ends, he sprinkles holy water on them and throws them behind his shoulders. Now he is the representation of *Ti-tsang,* a Buddhist Bodhisattva ecumenically used as a Taoist ruler of the underworld.[58] The high priest then is able to deliver the souls of the dead from torment. The god, *Ti-tsang,* took upon himself the duty of assisting sinners during their stay in the underworld. Therefore, he received from the Jade Emperor the title "Instructor of the regions of darkness, who travels unceasingly throughout the nether world to succour the damned."[59]

C. Meditation on the Pearl. The priests then chant prayers asking the many Heavenly Worthies and gods to aid them throughout the *P'u-tu.* Then, while the assistant priests chant invitations to the ten Kings of Hell, the high priest begs Primordial Heavenly Worthy to give the pearl on his *Chin-k'uan* hat the powers to illuminate the entire underworld.[60] The pearl is the drop of yang which grows and overcomes yin.[61] One can always see this symbol of pure yang, the flaming pearl, on temple rooftops, during dragon dances, and in religious objects and paintings. The high priest imagines hearing eight musical sounds (calabash, earthenware, hides, stone, metal, bamboo, wood, and silk strings), and envisions that the eight treasures of the immortals surround him.[62] Then he envisions jade maidens scattering flowers and fruits from heaven all over the world to the ten classes of men (mandarins, farmers, workers, liturgical officiants, musicians, warriors, guards, teachers, businessmen, and beggars), to the four types of birth[63] (birth from womb, egg, damp waters, and transformation), and to the six paths of rebirth (in heaven or hell, as a man, spirit, ghost, or animal).

The six paths of rebirth are Buddhist concepts adopted by the Taoists, though there is an important difference in the third path. Buddhists list the six paths as gods *(Deva)*, men *(Manuṣya)*, fighting demons *(Asura)*, animals *(Tiryag-yoni)*, hungry ghosts *(Preta)*, and demons *(Naraka)*.[64] The Taoists replace *Asura* fighting demons with *Shen-hsien* or immortal spirits.[65] Taoist masters teach that the path of heaven is reserved for those able to become adepts while the ordinary believers win rebirth in the blissful land of the Queen Mother of the Western Heavens, *Hsi Wang Mu*.

Part III. Releasing the Souls from Torment

Breaking Hell's Gates. Next, a circular platform shaped in an octagonal form, about two inches high and a foot in diameter, is placed on the altar in front of the high priest. On top of the octagonal box, which is in fact a mandala of hell (see Figure 5.3), are placed a pair of *Ju-i,* a gracefully curved scepter with a mushroom-like flower at the end. The *Ju-i* were once made of jade, but today they are often made of pewter or some less precious metal. The high priest chants the mantra "P'o Ti-yü chou" to break open the gates of hell.[66] This mantra is used throughout all funeral rites, and is found in the *Hsüan-chiao Li-ch'eng Chai Chiao I,* volume 264 of the Taoist Canon. The mantra is sung nine times in loud strident tones, a technique which requires much training. The chanting of the mantra signals that the Taoist funerary liturgy, *Huang-lu Chai* (Yellow Register Chai), has begun, the purpose of the rite being to effect a general passage of all souls confined in hell. The rite as described here is quite similar to Buddhist ritual.

The priest holds the *Ju-i* in his left hand between the middle finger and the thumb. With his right hand he pinches a few grains of uncooked rice between the middle finger and the thumb, and circles the *Ju-i* backward and forward twice over the mandala of hell. Then the pinch of rice is placed in one of the eight directions and the center of the octagonal box. The process is repeated nine times, until all nine gates of hell have been broken. As the grains of rice are laid in place, a mantra is chanted, which

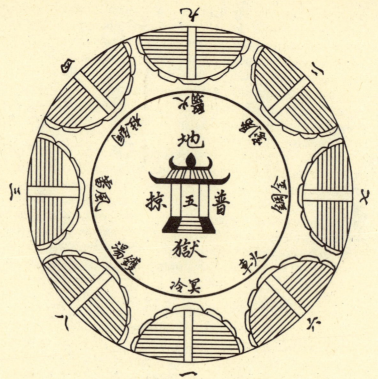

Figure 5.3   The Nine Prisons of torment in Hell, arranged after the model of the *Lo-shu,* the magic square of nine.

stops the tortures and breaks open the gate, releasing the souls therein.[67] The mantra always ends with the words *Chi-chi Ju Lü-ling,* one of the most ancient chants found in the Taoist Canon.[68] Finally, holy water is sprinkled over the entire octagonal mandala, bringing the rite to a close.

The nine hells are called a *Lo-shu,* the square chart of the posterior world of change.[69] The souls are made to pass through the various stages of a *Lo-shu* hell until they have atoned for their sins, following the course of the five elements as they destroy each other; that is, wood conquers earth, metal cuts wood, fire melts metal, and so forth.[70] The *Lo-shu* thus guides the process of change in the underworld.

After the gates have been opened, the souls are asked to fall into orderly formation, again utilizing the magic chart of the *Lo-shu,* that is the magic square of nine. In a magic square, no matter in which direction the numbers are added, the sum is always fifteen.[71] The souls are therefore asked to follow the Taoist in a dance through the nine courts of hell, making the world of torture and punishment into a place of order and blessing for a brief time. The stately ritual dance steps are called *Yü-pu,* that is, the "Steps of Yü." The demiurge Yü the Great was thought to use the magic square and its ritual dance to stop the floods in China and restore order to nature. The Taoist now uses the dance steps in a secret left-handed mudra, tracing the nine steps on the palm of the left hand, with the thumb.[72] As the souls reach the ninth court, they are taken upward to the tenth court of judgment, from whence they are permitted to come forth and attend the *P'u-tu* banquet on earth.

Part IV. Offering Incense and Preaching the Sermons of Merit

When the ghosts have been released from hell and gather before the *P'u-tu* altar in front of the temple, the Taoist high priest reads to them a lengthy series of sermons of merit, many of which are borrowed from the well-known *Yü-chia Yen-k'ou,* the Buddhist equivalent of the Taoist *P'u-tu* rite. The sermons are preceded by a brief rite in which the high priest offers incense to all the spirits of the temple, purifying and separating the inner part of the temple from the unruly orphan souls and hell spirits assembled outside. The Hungry Ghosts are admonished that they too can become *cheng* or upright spirits by performing meritorious good works for the living community, emulating the spirits in the interior of the temple. The sermons of merit and repentance are then read, three sticks of incense being offered as each sermon is begun. In the Honolulu text there are exactly twenty-seven sermons, though these can be shortened according to the time of day and desires of the people.[73]

Part V. Feeding the Ghosts

Tossing the Buns. When the sermons of merits are completed, the high priest then preaches to the ghosts on proper behavior and ways for their achieving the status of immortals. This is done for more than twenty minutes, during which time the other priests take some buns off the bun mountain. At every *Chiao* celebrated by the people of the Chung-shan district there is always a stack of sweet buns placed on the *P'u-Tu* altar. It is known as the *Wan Shou Pao Shan* "Ten Thousand Longevity-Bun Mountain." The buns, made out of flour and sugar, are predominantly white with red, yellow, and green added for artistic effect. As they are stacked to form a circular pyramid, the symbol of long life, colored designs of fruits and flowers made from the flour are stacked on the buns. Projecting out at the very top is a hand shaped from the sweet flour (see Figure 5.4). The design is of the left hand, with the thumb and last finger bent inward toward the palm while the three other fingers stand straight up. In the middle of the palm the character *Tao* is required to be written, but since there are new owners of the bakery shop where the buns come from, the bakers write the character *Fo* for Buddha instead. It is the temple committee that orders the bun mountain, so the Taoist priests have no authority over the detail of which character belongs on the hand. Also, from the people's point of view, they themselves make no distinction between *Tao* and *Fo,* for both characters are religious terms used to refer to gods.[75]

Figure 5.4   The six paths of rebirth represented on the left hand.

The hand represents the six rebirths a soul must be incarnated into. On the top three points of the three fingers, heaven's path is on the middle finger, animal's path on the index finger, and hell's path on the fourth finger. On the bottom points of the three fingers are the immortal's (spirit's) path on the middle finger, ghost's path on the index finger, and man's path on the fourth finger. Two other hands made from the sweet flour emerge out on both sides of the bun mountain, each with the thumbs bent inward. On the left hand is written *Fang Shih,* meaning to "distribute food," and on the right hand *Fen I,* to "divide clothing." These two side hands state the exact theme of a *P'u-tu,* "feeding and clothing the souls."

神之死起骸廻

Figure 5.5 *Hui-hai Ch'i-szu*, the spirit who causes souls to be reborn.

When the high priest has completed preaching, the actual period of feeding the hungry ghosts begins. The priests invoke *Hui-hai Ch'i-szu Ta-tz'u Tsun,* the "Merciful Worthy who returns souls to their bones and raises the dead." (See Figure 5.5.) The priests chant the passage of "healing medicine to relieve suffering and cure the bruises and wounds of the tortured." The Taoists bless the food offerings so that they will give nourishment and strength upon being eaten. Then the people are given a signal by one of the priests to grab the buns which are on the altar. To grab one of these small buns, especially the hands, fruits, and flowers, will insure good luck and good health for years.

A few buns that the priests have put aside are kept for feeding the ghosts. In a hole of each of three buns, a cone-shaped cup made of paper money is inserted and several raw grains of rice are then placed in the cup. During the passage of feeding the elixir of sweet dew to the ghosts to quench their thirst, the high priest takes one of the three buns in his left hand. Holding it in the lotus mudra, he sprinkles the *Kan-lu* elixir of sweet dew into the paper cone, lights the cone, and tosses it out in front of the *P'u Tu* altar. The other two buns are also held one after another in the same manner, being tossed after each passage. Three incantations over the *Kan-lu* elixir of sweet dew mystically make the dew become multitudes of quenching liquid like water, rain, and oceans.[76]

Following each toss of the bun by the high priest, the other priests throw loose buns all over the floor for the hungry ghosts to fetch. These tossed buns are not taken by the living, for they are meant especially for the ghosts, and it would be rude to take from what is thrown on the ground.

Part VI. Sending off the Ghosts and Spirits

A. Burning of Ta Shih Yeh. The *Wu-lao* crown is removed from the Taoist's head and placed back into the metal container. Then the *Pang,* a list of names of all those who had contributed to the *P'u-tu* put up for public display on the first day of the festival, is taken down by the temple committee. Folded, it is first offered to the various altars by the Taoist with three low bows. Finally it is placed and tied over the shoulders of Ta-shih Yeh. The Ta-shih Yeh is taken out and burned while the musicians again play the exorcising piece *Ta K'ai Men.* It is believed that the Ta-shih Yeh will first accompany those souls who must go back to the torments of hell and then take with him those who are able to enter heaven. Finally he presents the *Pang* to the Heavenly Worthies so that blessings can be bestowed to all who have contributed to the ritual. While the Ta-shih Yeh is leaving, the high priest pulls the silk curtains tightly closed in front of him so that the evil yin influences from those vengeful souls sent back to the torments of hell will not cause damage while the Ta-shih Yeh is leaving.

The lantern and paper shrine are also taken down and burned along with the paper bags filled with god and silver paper bullion, paper money, paper clothing, and paper colored material. These gifts are given so that life in the spirit world will be much more comfortable. Ancestors also receive offerings at this time from those wishing to send presents with the Ta-shih Yeh so that he may deliver them personally to prevent other ghosts from stealing them.

B. Throwing of Incense Sticks. While the offerings are being burnt outside, the high priest opens the curtains and commands all sprits to leave the world of the living, and go on toward their destination. A prayer of thanks to the three realms of heaven, earth, and water is chanted and all three priests stand up to bid farewell to the deities of each realm. At the end of each passage to each of the realms, incense sticks are thrown out in front of the *P'u-tu* altar. This is the last offering to the ghosts, purifying the area with tossed incense so that the ghosts are forced to enter into one of the three realms.

The priests then chant the canons of *Kung Te,* or "Merit of the P'u Tu." The incense sticks from the dragon censer are taken out and placed in the *P'u-tu* altar's incense pot, while the priests chant the last *Yüan Shih* mantra,[77] begging continual blessing from the "Primordial Breath."[78] The priests give three bows to the *P'u-tu* altar and walk back to the Three Pure One's altar. Music is once again played, and there the priests give three low bows thanking the master *Lao Tzu* for aiding in the services.[79] The awning around the *P'u-tu* altar is taken down, the ritual equipment and robes are put away, and the food offerings on the altars are taken for good luck. This concludes the *P'u Tu* ritual, and a banquet is held for the Taoist priests, musicians, and those members of the community and visitors who stayed for the entire ritual.

EDITOR'S CONCLUSION

The *P'u-tu* is a way of salvation for the many. By the intercession and mediating powers of the Taoist priests, the gates of hell are broken open and the souls of the damned are set free. The breaking open of the gates of hell is not accomplished by the Taoist alone, however. The merits of the entire community are invoked to win this great grace. The people of the community must be fasting, must prepare a great banquet, and must forgive their enemies, reintegrating all into the world of the living, before the rite is efficacious. The Taoist priests appear in the role of mandarin of the heavens, bearing the petitions of the people before the thrones of the heavenly rulers. The Taoist is a man or woman who can envision spirits and who by the use of his marvelous powers can control the forces of nature for the good of mankind. The mudras, mantras, meditations, and chants win over the spirits to man's side. But it must not be thought that the Taoist acts against nature. Rather his role is to bring men and women back into the course of nature, and to demonstrate this by the instructive beauty of his orthodox ritual. In the proper sense, the Taoist must be "one with the Tao" before his ritual is honest.

The Chinese people view the *P'u-tu* as fulfilling a social obligation. The ritual or spiritual obligations of man are but a symbol for social forces. Man, the microcosmic center of the village, stands in the same relationship to ancestor, spirit, and hungry ghost as he appears in the real order to family, friend-associate, and stranger-enemy.[80] It is redundant to point out that ancestor ritual reinforces the value of family, just as ritual to the spirits demonstrates professional or trade associations.[81] The *P'u-tu* is in the final analysis the ritual of social unity. By a banquet the lost and the hungry are brought into the community. It is indeed significant that this ancient rite is preserved in the modern city of Honolulu.

NOTES

1. The *Chung-yüan Chieh* and the rituals connected with it have been treated by Yoshioka Yoshitoyo, *Dōkyō to Bukkyō,* vol. II (Tokyo: Toshima Shobō, 1970), pp. 167–285. The concept for punishment for the soul after death as illustrated in the *P'u-tu* ritual performed on this day is Buddhist, whereas the notion of *Chung-yüan,* a celebration of the principle of earth, is more properly Taoist.

2. For an excellent study of the *P'u-tu* and bibliography of works on the Buddhist ritual *Yü-lan P'en* see Claudine Lombard-Salmon, "La Ceremonie du P'u-du," *Bulletin de L'École Française d'Extrême-Orient* 67 (1975):1–2.

3. The Chinese concept of care for ancestors and the Buddhist notion of salvation for all sentient beings, after the teaching of the Bodhisattva ideal in Mahāyāna Buddhism, are syncretistically blended in this festival of the popular religion. Many of the elements of the Taoist *P'u-tu* ritual are obvious borrowings from Buddhism. See J. J. M. De Groot, *Les Fêtes annuellement celebrées a Emoui* (Paris: Annales du Musée Guimet, 1886), vol. XII, p. 419.

4. For this and the following festival, see Derk Bodde, *Annual Customs and Festivals in Peking* (Peking: Henry Vetch, 1936).

5. Bodde, *Annual Customs and Festivals in Peking.*

6. The *Chiao* festival of cosmic renewal is often celebrated around the time of the winter solstice. With the same theme of renewal in mind, the *Lum-sai Ho-tang* temple of Honolulu celebrates a *Chiao* once every three years on the occasion of the 10/15 festival.

7. The Japanese version of the *Chung-yüan Chieh* includes the *Bon Odori,* i.e., dances performed by the community in honor of the deceased.

8. The *Ching* canons of merit and the *Ch'an* litanies of repentance are also of Buddhist inspiration. The ecumenical adaptation by the Taoist of Buddhist forms of worship was not wholly uncritical, however. Professor Shioiri Ryodo writes of the peculiarly Chinese-Taoist tone of the *Ch'an-hui* (Litanies of Repentance) used by the Buddhists in his "The process of adapting the *Ch'an-hui* in

Chinese Buddhist Ritual," *Indogaku Bukkyōgaku Kenkyū* [Journal of Indian and Buddhist Studies] 11, no. 2 (1962): 731–736.

9. The *Fang Shui-teng* or "ritual for floating the lanterns" is not now celebrated by the Chinese community of Honolulu, although the Japanese community still performs a similar lantern ceremony at the time of the *Bon Odori* festival. Cf. note 10.

10. The rituals celebrated in connection with the 7/15 and the lengthier rites of the *Chiao* festival of renewal are listed immediately below and in Michael Saso's *Taoism and the Rite of Cosmic Renewal* (Pullman: Washington State University Press, 1972), chap. 4.

11. The virgin deity Ma-tsu, a girl belonging to the Lin clan of Fukien according to pious legend, is almost universally worshipped along the coastline of southeast China. Devotion to Ma-tsu is especially strong in the city of Peikang, Taiwan. The Lin clan of Honolulu maintains the colorful temple on River Street in her honor.

12. See Michael Saso, *Taoism and the Rite of Cosmic Renewal,* pp. 65–83 for *Chiao* ritual.

13. The meditations of union actually comprise a series of refining meditative rituals, for which see Michael Saso, *Taoism and the Rite of Cosmic Renewal,* pp. 65–83, and "Buddhist and Taoist Notions of Transcendence," the first chapter of the present work.

14. Taoist Canon *(TT)* 217, *Hsüan-tu Ta-hsien Yü-shan Ching-hung Yi;* chap. 60 of the lengthy *Ling-pao Ling-chiao Chi-tu Chin-shu.* The text was collated by Ning Ch'uan-chen (1101–1181) and edited by Lin Ling-chen (1239–1302).

15. See *Yü-chia Chi-yao Yen-k'ou Shih-shih Yi,* Taishō Tripiṭaka, vol. 21, 473–484, #1320.

16. See Michael Saso, *Taoism and the Rite of Cosmic Renewal,* p. 86 for the five great orders of south China.

17. *P'u-tu* text, manuscript ritual manual used by Taoists of Honolulu, p. 23.

18. The concept of the *Lo-shu* or the magic square of nine is central to the ritual of orthodox Taoism. The *Lo-shu* is used in a slightly different fashion than the commonly known chart found in geomancy. It is used as a symbol for the visible world of change, specifically the nine central provinces of China, and by derivation for the nine hells directly beneath China. The term itself was quite popular during the Han dynasty, being conceived of as the nine squares of prognostication seen on a turtle's back. Cf. Yasui Kozan, *I-sho* [A treatise on the Wei Apocrypha] (Tokyo: Meitoku Press, 1969).

19. Thus sin is seen to be social rather than personal guilt. The punishments of Taoist hell are meted out for sins against society, for ritual impurity, or for actions which cause calamity in nature.

20. See *Tao-chiao Yüan-liu* [Taoist novice's manual] (Taipei: Wen-hsüeh Press, 1976), pp. 137–139.

21. The courts are numbered one to nine after the model of the *Lo-shu* (see Saso: 1972, p. 59; and illustration p. 112 below), i.e., number 5 is in the center, number 1 in the north, and number 9 in the south.

22. The nine stages of Taoist hell are described in many Taoist works, and are to be found in popular temple manuals. Cf. Wolfram Eberhard, *Guilt and Sin in Traditional China* (Berkeley: University of California Press, 1967), pp. 106–116 et passim.

23. The tenth court of hell contains no punishments, but rather is the route of escape, that is, the number of completion which ends the cycle of change or

punishment and leads to the land of permanent and unchanging life, *ch'ang-sheng*. The Taoists account for the unacceptable notion of transmigration by administering a potion of forgetfulness.

24.   See Eberhard, *Guilt and Sin in Traditional China,* pp. 106–116 for details of the hells.

25.   Orthodox Taoism is defined by the Taoists themselves as a ritual tradition which derives from the Taoist Canon, descends from antiquity, and includes the meditations of union with Tao as a part of the rite.

26.   The terminology used here follows the popular Chung-shan tradition; for a more appropriate Taoist usage, see *Tao-chiao Yüan-liu* (Taipei, 1976), p. 4.

27.   *Tao-chiao Yüan-liu,* p. 3.

28.   *P'u-tu* ritual manual manuscript used by the Taoists of Honolulu, appendix II. The hat adorns the statues of Kṣitigarbha seen in Buddhist temples, but is given the title *P'i-lu Mao* in the Taoist text.

29.   The Taoist thus plays the role of Ti-tsang Wang, the Bodhisattva who descends into hell to find his suffering mother and becomes the patron who helps release souls from hell in the popular Chinese imagination. But the Taoist wears his own proper gold crown under the hat of Kṣitigarbha, thus maintaining his own identity, disguised as a Buddhist in the underworld.

30.   *Tao-chiao Yüan-liu,* pp. 34–35.

31.   *Tao-chiao Yüan-liu,* p. 34.

32.   The "fish-tail" hat is commonly worn by the Taoists of the popular *Cheng-i* sect of southeastern China, with the exception of Fukien and Taiwan, where the gold crown alone is more common.

33.   See Saso, *Taoism and the Rite of Cosmic Renewal,* p. 65.

34.   Social integration is thus symbolized by the table which joins the outside impure world with the purified altar of the *P'u-tu.* There are three stages to be distinguished here: (1) the inner sacred altar to the Three Pure Ones: (2) the *Yü-huang Tien* or the altar dedicated to the spirits of the popular religion to the south; (3) the third stage, when the *Yü-huang Tien* with its incense pot is connected to the external world where the orphan souls are waiting. The *Yü-huang Tien* now becomes the intermediary altar of the north, and the orphan souls are seen to be in the south, or rather to the south of the second stage.

35.   The influence of Buddhism has been strongly felt in Honolulu in recent years, thus changing the quantity and style of meat offerings. The traditional offerings are raw meat for the hungry orphan souls before the ritual; cooked food for the living and the freed souls after the *P'u-tu;* and pure foods such as incense and wine for the heavenly spirits.

36.   The taboo on killing animals is of Chinese and not Buddhist origin. Meat is not supposed to be taken or an animal slain for the three days preceding the *P'u-tu,* and for a week or longer before the *Chiao* festival of renewal. Once the *P'u-tu* has ended, the requirement of abstinence from meat is lifted and life returns to normal.

37.   The *Ju-i* were often sent as gifts from the rulers of Southeast Asia to the Chinese emperors during the Ming and Ch'ing dynasties. The Word *Ju-i* is homonymous for a prayer that all good things and blessings are given to the recipient of the gift.

38.   Ling-pao T'ien-tsun, the second of the Taoist Trinity, is described more fully in note 48.

39.   Kuan-yin Buddha, or the Bodhisattva Avalokiteśvara, was conceived of as a male deity in India, and still bears a moustache in the earliest Chinese and Japanese statues made of him. But the idea of the Bodhisattva of mercy and compas-

sion so caught the imagination of the Chinese that the deity metamorphosed into a female deity, and was canonized in the hierarchy of Taoist spirits. The *Kan-lu* vase of purifying water will be used by the Taoist at the end of the *P'u-tu* to douse the fires of hell.

40.   The silk curtain marks the boundary between the ritually pure area of the Taoist and the contaminated area where the hungry ghosts attend the banquet.

41.   A third metamorphosis of Kuan-yin Buddha, in the violent or martial aspect of Ta-shih Yeh, is also seen depicted in tantric or *Chen-yen* art in Chinese and Japanese Buddhist temples.

42.   The Ta-shih Yeh is seen throughout the Chinese communities of Taiwan and Southeast Asia in his role of protecting the community during the *P'u-tu;* thus the common name "Lord of the *P'u-tu*" is often given him.

43.   The hungry orphan souls become the patron spirits of the outcasts of society. Thus gamblers, prostitutes, and beggars usually worship at shrines dedicated to the *Ku-hun* or orphan souls of the community.

44.   The taboo is against menstruating women only, that is, other women are admitted to the ritual area on an equal basis with men. Technically, the rule of abstinence, celibacy during the time of ritual, and a purifying bath before entering the sacred area should be required of women and men, but are forgotten in modern-day Honolulu. Inauspicious birth-years for a particular day are calculated on the Chinese almanac *(T'ung-shu).*

45.   *P'u-tu* manual, p. 7.

46.   See note 34.

47.   The majority of the Honolulu Chinese are from Chung-shan district in Kwangtung province, with a smaller number of Hakka and Lung-tu (the latter speaking a language closer to Fukienese) Chinese ethnic groups. Since there are only three Taoists in present-day Honolulu, all of the groups must use the Chung-shan text for ritual purposes. No matter which vernacular is used, however, the texts of the orthodox Taoist tradition usually conform to the Taoist Canon.

48.   The Three Pure Ones are considered to be manifestations of the One transcendant eternal Tao. Thus the Tao of the *Wu-wei* (transcendant act) gives birth to the One, Primordial Heavenly Worthy, lord of primordial breath in man. The One gives birth to the Two, *ling-pao* Heavenly Worthy, lord of spirit in man. The Two give birth to the Three, *Tao-te* Heavenly Worthy, lord of vital essence in man. The three are thought to dwell in the head, chest, and belly, respectively, within man. The last *Tao-te* Heavenly Worthy is *Lao-tzu.*

49.   Cf. note 48. The *San-pao* or "three treasures" are not to be confused with the *San-ch'ing,* the Three Pure Ones.

50.   Noted by V. P. Burkhardt, *Chinese Creeds and Customs,* vol. I (Hong Kong: South China Morning Post, 1958), p. 38.

51.   The ten directions *(shih-fang)* are a Taoist adaptation of a Buddhist concept. See William Soothill and Lewis Hodous, *A Dictionary of Chinese Buddhist terms* (London: Kegan Paul & Co., 1937), p. 50.

52.   Soothill and Hodous, *A Dictionary of Chinese Buddhist Terms,* p. 57.

53.   Soothill and Hodous, *A Dictionary of Chinese Buddhist Terms,* p. 57.

54.   Cf. *TT* 291, *Huang-lu Wu-lao Tao-mang Yi,* pp. 1–4.

55.   Michael Saso, *Taoism and the Rite of Cosmic Renewal,* p. 53.

56.   Michael Saso, *Taoism and the Rite of Cosmic Renewal,* p. 54: *P'u-tu* manual, p. 48.

57.   See M. W. De Visser, *Ancient Buddhism in Japan,* vol. I (Leiden: E. J. Brill, 1935), p. 111.

58.   M. W. De Visser, *The Bodhisattva Ti-tsang (Jizō) in China and Japan* (Berlin: Oesterheld and Co., 1914), p. 25.

59.   Henri Maspero, "The Mythology of Ancient China," in *Asiatic Mythology,* ed. J. Hackin (London: Gèorgè Harrap & Co., 1932), p. 375.

60.   *P'u-tu* manual, p. 26.

61.   The red pearl is a common art motif in popular Chinese painting. It symbolizes the red pill of immortality, the possession of which causes the roots of life to be kept burning within the microcosm. The dragon chases after the red flaming pearl during the dragon dance on 1/15, and the same red pearl is seen atop all temples of the Chinese popular religion.

62.   *P'u-tu* manual, p. 41.

63.   See Soothill and Hodous, *A Dictionary of Chinese Buddhist Terms,* p. 178.

64.   See "The Triple World," in *The Kyōgyō Shinshō* (Kyoto: Shinshu Otaniho, 1973), p. 351.

65.   *TT* 291, chap. 4, p. 16.

66.   *P'u-tu* manual, p. 48.

67.   *P'u-tu* manual, p. 48. The Buddhist ritual at this point builds a 37-stage mandala, in the same fashion, from grains of rice.

68.   *P'u-tu* manual, pp. 52–57.

69.   Michael Saso, *Taoism and the Rite of Cosmic Renewal,* p. 58.

70.   Schuyler Camann, "The Magic Square of Three in Old Chinese Philosophy and Religion," *History of Religions,* 1, no. 1 (Summer 1961): 57.

71.   Michael Saso, *Taoism and the Rite of Cosmic Renewal,* p. 59.

72.   Michael Saso, *Taoism and the Rite of Cosmic Renewal,* p. 59.

73.   *P'u-tu* manual, pp. 100–101.

74.   *P'u-tu* manual, pp. 116–117.

75.   Holmes Welch, "The Chang T'ien-shih and Taoism in China," *Journal of Oriental Studies* 4 (1957–1958):207.

76.   *P'u-tu* manual, p. 175.

77.   *P'u-tu* manual, p. 177.

78.   *TT* 308, chap. 4, pp. 10–11.

79.   *P'u-tu* manual, p. 196.

80.   Michael Saso, "Religion in Modern Taiwan," in *Asian Religions,* ed. Carlo Caldorado (The Hague: Mouton Publishing Co., forthcoming), manuscript p. 12.

81.   Michael Saso, "Religion in Modern Taiwan," p. 36.

Bibliography of Taoist Studies

DONNA AU AND SHARON ROWE

Alexander, G. G. *Lao-tzse, the Great Thinker.* With a translation of his thoughts on Nature and the Manifestations of God. London: Kegan Paul, Trench, Truebner and Co., 1885.

Anonymous. *Konkordanz zum Lao-tzu.* Munich: Publikationen der Fachschaft Sinologie München, 1968.

Anonymous. *Li Chi.* Kio-hsüeh Chi-pen Ts'ung Shu. Taipei: Shang-wu Press, 1969.

Balasz, Etienne. "La crise sociale et la philosophie politique à la fin des Han." *T'oung-pao* 39 (1949): 83–131.

_____. "Entre révolte nihiliste et évasion mystique, les courants intellectuels en Chine au 3e siècle de notre ère." *Asiatische Studien* 2 (1948): 27–55.

_____. *Chinese Civilization and Bureaucracy: Variations on a Theme.* Edited by A. F. Wright. Translated by H. M. Wright. New Haven: Yale University Press, 1964.

Barnes, W. H. "Possible References to Chinese Alchemy in the 4th or 3d Centuries B.C." *China Journal of Science and Arts* 23 (1953): 75–79.

Baumann, C. "Reflections Prompted by Lao-tse: A Psychological Approach." *Bulletin de la Société Suisse des amis de l'Extrême-Orient* 23 (1946): 49–62.

Beky, Gellert. *Die Welt des Tao.* Freiburg: Verlag Karl Alber, 1972.

Belpaire, Bruno. "Note sur un traité taoiste." *Muséon* 59 (1946): 655–659.

Benton, Richard P. "Tennyson and Lao Tzu." *Philosophy East and West* 12 (1962): 233–240.

Bertuccioli, G. "Il taoisme nella Cina contemporanea in Cina." *Cina* 2 (1957): 66–77.

Biroen, H. "Taoismus: Praktische Systeme der Wandlung und Sublimation." *Yoga, Zeitschrift für Yoga-Synthese und Vedanta* 7 (1960): 27–31.

Bodde, Derk. "The New Identification of Lao Tzu Proposed by Professor Dubs." *Journal of the American Oriental Society* 62 (1942): 8–13.

_____. "Further Remarks on the Identification of Lao Tzu." *Journal of the American Oriental Society* 64 (1944): 24–27.

_____. "Two New Translations of Lao-tzu." *Journal of the American Oriental Society* 74 (1954): 211–217.

_____. "Lieh-tzu and the Doves: A Problem of Dating." *Asia Major* n.s. 7 (1959): 25–31.

_____. *Festivals in Classical China*. Princeton: Princeton University Press, 1975.

Boodberg, Peter A. "Philological Notes on Chapter One of the Lao Tzu." *Harvard Journal of Asiatic Studies* 20 (1957): 598–618.

Borel, Henri. *Wu-wei Lao-tse, ein Wegweiser*. Munich: Saturn, 1948.

Bowes, B. K. "Confucian and Taoist Elements in Haiku." *Transactions and Proceedings of the Japan Society* n.s. 16 (1955): 19–23.

Bucke, Richard Maurice. "Vom komischen Bewusstsein: Li-R = Laotse." *Yoga, Zeitschrift für Yoga-Synthese und Vedanta* 5 (1958): 284–288.

Bungartz, Lothar. *Der Gedanke des 'Nicht-Handelns' bei Chuang-tse*. Ein Beitrag zu den Staatsphilosophischen Spekulationen des chinesischen Altertums. Cologne: Thèse, 1956.

Chan Hok-lam. "Liu Pin-chung (1216–1274), a Buddhist-Taoist Statesman in the Court of Khubilai Khan." *T'oung-pao* 53 (1967): 98–146.

Chan Wing-tsit. "Taoism." In: *Encyclopaedia Britannica*. 14th ed. Chicago: William Benton Company, 1960.

Chang I-t'iao (Amos Ih Tiao). *Existence of Intangible Content in Architectonic Form Based upon the Practicality of Lao-tzu's Philosophy*. Princeton: Princeton University Press, 1960.

Chang Chung-yüan. "The Concept of Tao in Chinese Culture." *Review of Religion* 17 (1953): 115–132.

_____. "Tao and the Sympathy of All Things." *Erano Jahrbuch* 24 (1955): 407–432.

_____. "Creativity as Process in Taoism." *Erano Jahrbuch* 25 (1956): 391–415.

_____. "Introduction to Taoist Yoga." *Review of Religion* 20 (1956): 131–148.

_____. "The Meaning of Tao." *Atti del XII Congresso internazionale di filosofia* 10 (1958): 33–40.

_____. *Creativity and Taoism: A Study of Chinese Philosophy, Art, and Poetry*. New York: Julian Press, 1963.

_____. "Purification and Taoism." *Proceedings of the XIth International Congress of the International Association for the History of Religions* 2 (1968): 139–140.

_____. "Tao as Inner Experience." *Zeitschrift für Religions und Geitesgeschichte* 10 (1958): 33–40.

Chao Yün-ts'ung and Davis, Tenny L. "Four Hundred Word Chin Tan of Chang Po-tuan." *Proceedings of the American Academy of Arts and Sciences* 73 (1940): 371–377.

Chen Chung-hwan. "What does Lao-tzu mean by the term 'Tao'?" *Hua-hsüeh Pao* 4 (1964): 150–161.

Ch'en, Kenneth K. D. "Buddhist-Taoist Mixtures in the Pa-shih hua-t'u." *Harvard Journal of Asiatic Studies* 1 (1957): 1–12.

_____. "Neo-Taoism and the Prajñā School during the Wei and Chin Dynasties." *Chinese Culture* 1 (1957): 33–46.

_____. *Buddhism in China: An Historical Survey.* Princeton: Princeton University Press, 1964.

Ch'en Kuo-fu. *Tao Tsang Yüan Liu K'ao.* 2 volumes. Peking: Chung Hua Press, 1963.

Ch'en Kuo-fu and Davis, Tenny L. "Inner Chapters of Pao-p'u-tzu." *Proceedings of the American Academy of Arts and Sciences* 74 (1941).

Chmielewski, Janusz. "Z problematyki wezesnego taoizmu." *Rocznik orientalistyczny* 25 (1961): 14–30.

Chou Hsiang-kuang. "Taoismus und Yoga." *Vivos voco* 35 (1962): 156–158.

Chuang-tzu. *The Classic (or Scripture) of Purity and Rest.* Translated from the Chinese by C. Spurgon Medhurst. Chicago: n.p., n.d.

_____. *The Divine Classic of Nan-hua; Being the Works of Chuang Tsze, the Taoist Philosopher.* With an excursus and copious annotations in English and Chinese by Fredric Henry Balfour. Shanghai: Kelly and Walsh, 1881.

_____. "The Writings of Kwang-sze." In: *The Texts of Taoism.* Translated by James Legge. Sacred Books of the East, volume 40. Oxford: The Clarendon Press, 1891.

_____. *The Musings of a Chinese Mystic: Selections from the Philosophy of Chuang Tzŭ.* With an introduction by Lionel Giles. London: J. Murray, 1906.

_____. *Das reich regieren.* Jena: E. Diederichs, 1919.

_____. *Chuang Tzu, Mystic, Moralist and Social Reformer.* Translated from the Chinese by Herbert A. Giles. London: B. Quaritch, 1926.

_____. *Die weisheit des Dschuang-dse in deutschenlehrgedichten.* Peking: Pekinger-verlag, 1926.

_____. *Dichtung und weisheit.* Aus dem chinesischen Urtext übersetzt von Hans O. H. Stange. Leipzig: Insel-verlag, 1936.

_____. *Discorsi e parabole.* Milano: Fratelli Bocca, 1943.

_____. *Acque d'autonno.* Con introduction a cura di Mario Novaro. 4d accrescuita e corretta. Bari: G. Laterza, 1949.

_____. *Reden und gleichnisse des Tschuang-tse.* Deutche Auswahl von Martin Burber. Zurich: Manesse, 1951.

_____. *Das wahre Buch vom sudlichen Blütenland von Dschuang Dsi.* Aus dem Chinesischen verdeutscht und erlaütert von Richard Wilhelm. Dusseldorf: E. Diederich, 1951.

_____. *Nan-hua-czên-king.* Prawdziwa ksiega poludniowego kwiatu. Przel.

Witold Jablonski, Janusz Chmielewski, Olgierd Wojtasiewicz. Warsaw: Panstwowe Wydawn Naukowe, 1953.

_____. *Sjaelen og sommerfuglen*. Ved Søren Egerod. Copenhagen: Thaning and Appel, 1955.

_____. *Chuangtse . . .* Translated by Lin Yutang. Taipei: World Book Co., 1957.

_____. *Il libro di Ciung-tse, la sezione interna*. Tradotta da F. Houang Kiatcheng. Milano: Istituto cultural Halo-einese, 1958.

_____. *The Sayings of Chuang Chou*. A new translation by James R. Ware. New York: New American Library, 1963.

_____. *Ȧkthetens urkung*. Tell svensk vers och med inledning av Åke Ohlmarks. Stockholm: FIBs lyrikklubb, 1964.

_____. *The Basic Writings of Chuang-tse*. Translated by Burton Watson. New York: Columbia University Press, 1964.

_____. *Chuang-tzu*. A new selected translation with an exposition of the philosophy of Kuo Hsiang by Yu-lan Fung. New York: Paragon, 1964.

_____. *The Complete Works of Chuang Tzu*. Translated by Burton Watson. New York: Columbia University Press, 1968.

_____. *L'oeuvre complete de Tchouang-tseu*. Traduction, préface et notes de Liou Kia-hway. Paris: Gallimard, 1969.

Cold, Eberhard. *Königtum und Adel nach dem Lao Tse's Tao Te King*. Mit den Aussprüchen des Herkleitos Epheisos. Kronshagen bei Kiel: Selbstverlag, 1957.

Creel, H. G. *Chinese Thought from Confucius to Mao Tse-tung*. Chicago: University of Chicago Press, 1953.

_____. "On Two Aspects in Early Taoism." *Zinbun-kagaku-kenkyuusyo Silver Jubilee Volume* (1954): 43–53.

_____. *La pensée chinoise de Confucius à Mao Tse-toung*. Traduction de Jean-François Leclerc. Paris: Payot, 1955.

_____. "What is Taoism?" *Journal of the American Oriental Society* 76 (1956): 139–152.

_____. "On the Origin of Wu-wei." *K'ao-ku Jen-lei Hsüeh-kan* 25–26 (1965): 105–138.

_____. "The Greatest Clod: A Taoist Conception of the Universe." In: *Studies in Chinese Humanities*. Edited by Chow Tse-tsung. Madison: University of Wisconsin Press, 1968.

Davis, Tenny L. "A Fifteenth Century Chinese Encyclopedia of Alchemy." *Proceedings of the American Academy of Arts and Sciences* 73 (1940): 391–399.

Davis, Tenny L. and Chao Yün-ts'ung. "The Secret Papers in the Jade Box of Ch'ing-hua." *Proceedings of the American Academy of Arts and Sciences* 73 (1940): 385–389.

_____. "Three Alchemical Poems by Chang Po-tuan." *Proceedings of the American Academy of Arts and Sciences* 73 (1940): 377–379.

Davis, Tenny L. And Ch'en Kuo-fu. "Shang Yang-tzu: Taoist Writer and Commentator on Alchemy." *Harvard Journal of Asiatic Studies* 7 (1942–1943): 126–129.

Demiéville, Paul. "Explication du premier chapitre de Tchouang-tseu." *Annuaire du Collège de France* 48 (1946): 143–144.

_____. "Tchouang-tsue et ses interprétations dans l'exégèse chinoise." *Annuaire du Collège de France* 46 (1946): 140–143.

_____. "Études sur la formation du vocabulaire philosophique chinois." *Annuaire du Collège de France* 47 (1947): 150–156.

_____. "Explication du deuxième chapitre de Tchouang-tseu." *Annuaire de Collège du France* 48 (1948): 160–162.

_____. "Le miroir spirituel." *Sinologica* 1 (1948): 112–137.

_____. "Le commentaire du 'Tchouang-tseu' par Kouo Siang." *Actes du XXXIe Congrès des Orientalistes* (1949): 271–272.

_____. "Enigmes taoistes." *Zinbun-kagaku-kenkyuusyo Silver Jubilee Volume* (1954): 54–60.

Desai, Santosh. "Taoism: Its Essential Principles and Reflection in Poetry and Painting." *Chinese Culture* 7 (1966): 54–64.

Dessefy, M. "Voies idéologiques de la science ancienne et médiévale (Lao-tsé et Aristote)." *Actes du VIIe Congrès International d'histoire des Sciences,* August 1953.

Diez, E. "Dauistische Unsterbliche." *Sinica* 16 (1941): 48.

Dschi, Hiän-lin. "Lieh-tzu and Buddhist Sutras." *Studia Serica* 9 (1950): 18–21.

Dubs, Homer H. "Taoism." In: *China.* Edited by Harley Farnsworth MacNair. Berkeley: University of California Press, 1946.

_____. "The Date and Circumstances of the Philosopher, Lao-dz." *Journal of the American Oriental Society* 61 (1941): 215–221.

_____. "The Identification of the Lao-tse: A Reply to Professor Bodde." *Journal of the American Oriental Society* 62 (1942): 300–304.

_____. "The Beginnings of Alchemy." *Isis* 38 (1948): 63–86.

_____. "The Origin of Alchemy." *Ambix* 9 (1961): 23–36.

_____. "A Note to Erke's Paper." *Asian Major* 3 (1953): 162.

Duyvendak, J. J. L. "The Philosophy of Wu-wei." *Asiatische Studien* 1 (1947): 81–102.

_____. "The Dreams of Emperor Hsüan-tsung." *Indian Antiquary* (1947): 102–108.

_____. "Le taoisme sous les T'ang." *Actes du XXXIe Congrès des Orientalistes* (1948): 272.

_____. "A Chinese 'Divina Commedia'." *T'oung-pao* 41 (1952): 255–316.

_____. "La philosophie du non-agir." *Conferenze* (1952): 25–47.

Eberhard, Wolfram. *Guilt and Sin in Traditional China.* Berkeley: University of California Press, 1967.

Eckhardt, André. "Der Goettesbegriff bei Laotse." *Philosophisches Jahrbuch der Görres-Gesellschaft* 58, 2 (1948): 88–99; 58, 3 (1948): 211–218.

_____. "Die Ethischen grundbegriffe bei Laotse." *Philosophisches Jahrbuch der Görres-Gesellschaft* 59 (1949): 200–207.

_____. "El Concepto de Tao en Laotse." *Notas y estudios de filosofia* 2 (1951): 131–142.

_____. *Lao-tse's Gedankenwelt: Nach dem Tao-te-king.* Frankfurt: Kommentar, 1957.

_____. *Lao-tse: Unvergängliche Weisheit.* Munich: Reinhardt, 1957.

_____. "Laotse und die Philosophie des Ostens." *Universitas* 12 (1957): 355–362.

Egerod, Søren. "Meng Tsi's and Chuang Tsi's Parting Words." *Acta Orientalia Academiae Scientiarum Hungarica* 2–3 (1960): 112–120.

Eichorn, Werner. "Die dauistische Spekulation im zweiten Kapital des Dschuang Dsi." *Sinica* 17 (1942): 140–162.

_____. "Descriptions of the Rebellion of the Sun En and Earlier Taoist Rebellions." *Mitteilungen des Instituts für Orientforschung* 2 (1954): 325–352.

_____. "Nachträglichen Bemerkungen zum Aufstand des Sun En." *Mitteilungen des Instituts für Orientforschung* 2 (1954): 463–476.

_____. "Einige Bemerkungen zum Aufstand des Chang Chio und zum Staate des Chang Lu." *Mitteilungen des Instituts für Orientforschung* 3 (1955): 291–321.

_____. "Bemerkung zur Einführung des Zölibats für Taoisten." *Rivista degle Studi Orientali* 30 (1955): 297–301.

_____. "Eine Erzählung aus dem Wen-chien hou lu." *Oriens Extremus* 2 (1955): 167–174.

_____. "T'ai-p'ing und T'ai-p'ing Religion." *Mitteilungen des Instituts für Orientforschung* 5 (1957): 113–140.

_____. "Taoism." In: *Concise Encyclopedia of Living Faiths.* Edited by R. C. Zaehner. New York: Hawthorn Books, 1959.

_____. *Beitrag zur rechtlichen Stellung des Buddhismus und Taoismus im Sung Staat.* Übersetzung der Sektion "Taoismus und Buddhismus" aus dem Ch'ing-yüan t'iao-fa shih-lei, mit original text in faksimile. Monographies du T'oung-pao 7. Leiden: E. J. Brill, 1968.

Engler, Friedrich. "Laotse, sein Leben und Seine Persönlichkeit." *Zeitschrift für praktische Philosophie* 12 (1963): 14–17.

Erdberg Consten, Eleanor von. "A Statue of Lao-tzu in the Po-yün-kuan." *Monumenta Serica* 7 (1942): 235–241.

Erkes, Eduard. "Spuren einer kosmogonischen Mythe bei Laotse." *Artibus Asiae* 8 (1940): 16–38.

_____. "Die taoistische Meditation und ihre Bedeutung für das chinesische Geitesleben." *Psyche* 2–3 (1948–1949): 371–379.

_____. *Ho-shang-kung's Commentary on Lao-tze.* Translated and annotated by Eduard Erkes. Ascona, Switzerland: Artibus Asiae, 1950.

_____. "Ein Märchenmotiv bei Laotse." *Sinologica* 3 (1953): 100–105.

_____. Ssu erh pu wang." *Asia Major* 3 (1953): 156–161.

_____. "Der Bedeutungswandel einiger philosophischer Begriffe im Taoismus." *Deutsche Zeitschrift für Philosophie* 1 (1953): 327–331.

_____. "A Note on Dubs' Note in Asia Major 3, 2." *Asia Major* 4 (1954): 149–150.

Ernst, E. "Confucius, Laotse en Mo-ti als wegbereiders voor Christus." *Kult* 14 (1947): 329–349.

Etiembel, René. *Connaissons-nous la Chine?* Paris: Gallimard, 1964.

————. "En relisant Lao-tseu." *La Nouvelle Revue Française* 171 (1967): 457–476.

Feideler, Frank. *Hua-shu, das Buch des Verwandelns.* Darstellung der Lehre und Übersetzung des Textes. Ein Beitrag zum Verständnis chinesischer Philosophie. Erlangen: E. Schmitt und M. Meyer, 1968.

Filliozat, Jean. "Taoisme et Yoga." *Dân Viêt Nam* 3 (1947–1949): 113–120.

Forke, A. "Waley's Tao-te-king." *Zeitschrift Deutschen Morgenländischen Gesellschaft* 95 (1940): 36–45.

Fraccari, Gerando. "Eraclitto e Laotse. Naturalismo Greco e naturalismo cinese." *Atti del XII Congresso Internal di Philosofia* 10 (1960): 55–61.

Fukui, Kōjun. *Dōkyō no Kisō teki Kenkyū.* Tokyo: Shoseki Bunbutsu Ryūtsū, 1960.

————. *Fundamental Problems Regarding the Schools of Religious Taoism.* Tokyo: Maruzen, 1959.

Fukunaga, M. " 'No-mind' in Chuang-tzu and Ch'an Buddhism." *Zinbunkagaku-kenkyu-syo* 12 (1969): 9–45.

Fung Yu-lan. *A History of Chinese Philosophy.* Volume 1. Translated by Derk Bodde. Peking: Henri Vetch, 1934.

————. "The Rise of Neo-Confucianism and Its Borrowings from Buddhism and Taoism." Translated by Derk Bodde. *Harvard Journal of Asiatic Studies* 7 (1942): 89–125.

————. *The Spirit of Chinese Philosophy.* Translated by E. R. Hughes. London: Kegan Paul, 1947.

————. *A History of Chinese Philosophy.* Volume 2. Princeton: Princeton University Press, 1952–1953.

————. "Confucianism and Taoism." In: *History of Philosophy; Eastern and Western.* 2 volumes. London: Sarvepalli-Padhakrishan, 1952.

————. *A Short History of Chinese Philosophy.* Edited by Derk Bodde. New York: Macmillan, 1948; Macmillan Paperbacks, 1960.

————. *Précis d'histoire de la philosophie chinoise.* D'après le texte anglais. Edité par Derk Bodde, traduction du Guillaume Dunstheimer, préface de Paul Demiéville. Paris: Payot, 1952.

Gauchet, L. "Le Tou-jen King des Taoistes, son texte primitif et sa da probables." *Bulletin de l'Université l'Aurore* 2 (1941): 511–534.

————. "A Travers le Canon Taoique: quelques synonymes du Tao." *Bulletin de l'Université l'Aurore* 3 (1942): 303–319.

————. "Contribution a l'étude du Taoisme." *Bulletin de l'Université l'Aurore* 9 (1948): 1–38.

————. "Un livre taoique, le 'Cheng-chen-king' sur la génération des ésprits dans l'homme." *Bulletin de l'Université l'Aurore* 10 (1949): 63–72.

Giles, Lionel. "Tao-te Ching: Its Practical Philosophy." *Aryan Path* 11 (1940); 399–342.

_____. *A Gallery of Chinese Immortals*. Selected Biographies translated from Chinese sources by Lionel Giles. London: J. Murray, 1948.

Graf, Olaf. *Tao und Jen: Sein und Sollen im sungchinesischen Monismus*. Wiesbaden: Harrassowitz, 1970.

Graham, A. C. "The Dialogue between Yang Ju and Chyn-tzyy." *Bulletin of the School of Oriental and African Studies* 2 (1959): 291–299.

_____. " 'Being' in Western Philosophy Compared with shih-fei and yu-wu in Chinese Philosophy." *Asia Major* 7 (1959): 79–112.

_____. *The Book of Lieh-tzu*. New York: Grove Press, 1960.

_____. "The Date and Composition of Lieh-tzuu." *Asia Major* 8 (1960–1961): 139–198.

Granet, Marcel. *La Pensée chinoise*. Paris: L'évolution de l'humanité, 1934.

_____. *La Religion des Chinois*. Paris: Gauthiers-Villars, 1922.

_____. "Remarques sur le taoisme ancien." *Asia Major* 2 (1925): 146–151.

Grava, Arnolds. "Tao: An Age-old Concept in Its Modern Perspective." *Philosophy East and West* 13 (1963): 235–250.

Grenier, J. *L'esprit du Tao*. Collection "Homo Sapiens." Paris: Flammarion, 1957.

Griffith, Gwilyn Oswald. *Interpreters of Reality: A Comment on Heraclitus, Lao-tse and the Christian Faith*. London: Lutterworth Press, 1946.

de Groot, J. J. M. *The Religious Systems of China*. 6 vols. Leiden: E. J. Brill, 1892–1910.

_____. *Les Fêtes annuellement célébrées à Emoui (Amoy)*. Paris: Annales du Musée Guimet, 1886.

_____. "On the Origin of the Taoist church." *Transactions of the 3rd International Congress for the History of Religions*. I, Oxford, 1908: 138.

Gulik, R. H. van. *Sexual Life in Ancient China*. Leiden: E. J. Brill, 1961.

Hahn, L. C. C. "De denkwereld van Lao Tzu." *Dialog* 1 (1960–1961): 183–207.

Hail, William James. "Taoism." In: *Living Schools of Religion*. Edited by V. Ferm. New York: Philosophical Library, 1948.

Han Tai-dong. "A Study of 'Daw Der Jing': Structural Analysis of Lao Tzu's Thought form." *Tung-fang Hsüeh-chih* 6 (1963): 47–75.

Heiler, Friedrich. *Weltabkehr und Weltrückkehr ausserchristlicher Mystike*. Volume 1. Munich: E. Reinhart, 1941.

Heinisch, Erich. "Der Zensor, Tao und Amtsauftrag." *Zeitschrift Deutschen Morgenländischen Gesellschaft,* 104 (1954): 412–431.

Held, Hedwig. *Dau und Kosmos*. Wein: Reneotype, 1953.

Herbert, Edward. *A Taoist Notebook*. London: Wisdom of the East Series, 1955.

Hodous, L. "Taoism." In: *The Great Religions of the World*. Princeton: Princeton University Press, 1947.

Ho Ping-yü and Needham, Joseph. "Elixir Poisoning in Mediaeval China." *Janus* 48 (1959): 221–251.

Holzmann, Ferdinand. *Kleines Laotse Brevier*. Zur Stärkung und Erleuchtung des Herzens in der Bedrängnis des Tages zusammenegestellt aus dem Taote-king. Heidelberg: F. Holzmann, 1948.

Holzman, Donald. *La vie et la pensée de Hi K'ang*. Leiden: E. J. Brill, 1957.

_____. "Les Sept Sages de la Forêt des Bambous et la société de leur temps." *T'oung-pao* 44 (1965): 317–346.

_____. "Une conception chinoise du héroes." *Diogène* 36 (1961): 37–55.

Hsiao, Paul. "Laotse und die Technik." *Die katholischen Missionen* 75 (1956): 72–74.

Hsiung Pin-ming. "Non-quietest Laotse." *Cina* 8 (1963): 39–41.

Hsu Tsao. "Chuang Tse: Chapter XXXIII, the Outline of Main Schools of Thought of Nowadays." Translated by Hsu Tsao. *East and West* 7 (1962): 8–11.

Hummel, Siegbert. *Zum ontologischen Problem des Dauismus (Taoismus)*. Üntersuchungen as Lau Dsi. Kapitel 1 und 42. Leipzig: O. Harrassowitz, 1948.

Hu Shih. "The Concept of Immortality in Chinese Thought." *Harvard Divinity School Bulletin* (1946): 23–43.

Hughes, Ernest E. *Chinese Philosophy in Classical Times*. London: Everyman Library, 1942.

Hung, William. "A Bibliographical Controversy at the T'ang Court A. D. 719." *Harvard Journal of Asiatic Studies* 20 (1957): 74–134.

Hundhausen, Vincenz. *Lau Dse: Das Tao als Weltgestz und Vorb*. Peking: Pekinger Verlag, 1948.

Hurvitz, Leon. "A Recent Japanese Study of Lao-tze (Kimura Eiichi's Rōshi no Shin-kenkyū)." *Monumenta Serica* 20 (1961): 311–367.

Ikeda Toshio. *Taiwan no Katei Seikatsu (Family Life in Taiwan)*. Taihoku: Toto Shoseki, 1944.

Jaspers, Karl. *Laotse die grossen Philosophen*. Munich: R. Piper, 1957.

Kaltenmark, Max. "Taoisme." In: *Aspects de la Chine*. Volume 1. Paris: Publications de Musée Guimet, Bibliothèque de Diffusion, 1959.

_____. "Lao-tseu." In: *Dictionaire Biographiques des Auteurs*. Volume 2. Paris: Laffont-Bompiami, 1964.

_____. "Deux Philosophes Chinois, Siun-tseu et Tchouang-tseu." In: *Philosophes Célèbres*. Paris: Mazenod, 1957.

_____. *La Mystique et les Mystiques*. Paris: Desclées de Brower, 1965.

_____. *Lao Tseu et la taoisme*. Paris: Editions du Seuil, 1965.

_____. *Lao Tzu and Taoism*. Translated from the French by Roger Greaves. Stanford, Calif.: Stanford University Press, 1969.

_____. "Le Lie-sien Tchouan." In: *Biographies légendaires des immortels taoistes de l'antiquité*. Peking: University of Paris, Publications du Centre d'études sinologiques de Pékin, 1953.

_____. "Au Sujet du Ling-pao Tou-jen king." *Ecole pratique des hautes études* Sc. R. Annuaire (1960–1961): 81–82.

_____. "Au Sujet du Ling-pao Wou-fou king." *Ecole pratique des hautes études* Sc. R. Annuaire (1961–1962): 53–54; (1962–1963): 50; (1963–1964): 54.

_____. "Au Sujet du Houang-t'ing king." *Ecole pratique des hautes études* Sc. R. Annuaire (1967–1968): 80–81.

_____. "Au Sujet du Tcheou-yi Ts'an-t'oung-k'i." *Ecole pratique des hautes études* Sc. R. Annuaire (1964–1965): 67.

_____. "Hygiène et Mystique en Chine."·*Bulletin de la Société d'Acuponcture* 33 (1959): 21–30.

_____. "L'alchimie en Chine." *Bulletin de la Société d'Acuponcture* 37 (1960).

_____. "Les commentaires du Tao-tö-king." *Ecole pratique des hautes études* Sc. R. Annuaire (1958–1959): 64; (1959–1960): 54.

_____. " 'Ling-pao': note sur un terme du taoisme religieux." *Mélanges Publiés par l'Institut des Hautes Etudes Chinoises* 2 (1960): 559–588.

_____. "Notes à Propos du Kao-mei." *Ecole pratique des hautes études* Sc. R. Annuaire (1966–1967): 5–34.

_____. "Le Maitre Spirituel dans la Chine Ancienne." *Hermes* 4 (1967): 219–225.

_____. "Lao-tseu dans la religion taoiste." *Ecole pratique des hautes études* Sc. R. Annuaire (1958–1959): 63–64.

_____. *La philosophie chinoise.* Paris: Presses Universitaires de France, 1972.

_____. "Au Sujet du T'ai-p'ing king." *Ecole pratique des hautes études* Sc. R. Annuaire (1968–1969): 92–93.

_____. "Religion et Politique dans la Chines des Ts'in et des Han." *Diogène* 34 (1961): 18–46.

_____. "Recherches sur l'histoire du taoisme religieux." *Ecole pratique des hautes études* Sc. R. Annuaire (1959–1960): 53–54.

Kamata Shigeo. *Chūgoku Bukkyō Shisō shi Kenkyū* [A study of Chinese Buddhist thought]. Tokyo: Shunjū Sha, 1968.

Kao, George, ed. *Chinese Wit and Humor.* Introduction by Lin Yu-tang. New York: Coward-McCann, 1946.

Karlgren, Bernhard. *Religion: Kina Antiken.* Stockholm: Swensk bokförlag, 1964.

Kataoka Iwao. *Taiwan Fūzoku, Meishin no Bu* [Taiwan customs: section on superstitions]. Taiwan: Taiwan-go Kenkyū kai, 1912.

_____. *Taiwan Fūzoku-shi* [A book of Taiwanese customs]. Taihoku: Taiwan Nichi-nichi Shinposha, 192–.

Kent, George W. "The Yin-sheng Opposition in Chapter Two of the Lao Tzu." *Journal of the American Oriental Society* 87 (1967): 296–297.

Kimura, Eiichi. "A New Study on Lao Tzu." *Philosophical Studies of Japan* 1 (1959): 85–104.

_____. "The New Confucianism and Taoism in China and Japan from the Fourth to the Thirteenth Centuries A.D." *Cahiers d'histoire Mondiales* 5 (1959–1960): 801–829.

Koyanagi Shigeta. *Rō-Sō no Shisō to Dōkyō* [The thought of Lao-tzu and Chuang-tzu and Taoism]. Tokyo: Morikita Shoten, 1942.

_____. *Tao Chiao Kai Shuo.* Translated by Ch'en Pin-ho. Shanghai: Shang-wu Press, 1926.

Kraft, Eva. "Zum Huai-nan-tzu . . . Einführung, Übersetzung (kapitel 1 und 2) und Interpretation." *Monumenta Serica* 16 (1957): 191–286; (1958): 128–207.

_____. "Eine Bemerkungen zur Philosophie des Huai-nan-tze." *Transactions of the International Conference of Orientalists in Japan* 1 (1956): 103–104.

Kramers, R. P. "Die Lao Tzu's Discussionen in der Chinesischen Volksrepublik." *Asiatische Studien* 22 (1968): 31–67.

Kubo Noritada. *Dōkyō Shisō no Hensen* [Changes in Taoist thought]. Tokyo: Seikai-shi no Kenkyū, Yamakawa Shuppansha, 1965.

_____. *Junyōkyū no Hekiga ni Mieru Ō Chō-yō Den* [Wang Chung-yang as seen in the drawings on the walls of Ts'un-yang Kung]. Tokyo: Tokyo Daigaku, 1964.

_____. *Zenshinkyō no Seiritsu* [The founding of the Ch'üan-chen sect]. Tokyo: Tokyo Daigaku, 1966.

_____. "The Transmission of Taoism to Japan, with Particular Reference to the San-shih." *Proceedings of the 9th International Congress for the History of Religions* (1958): 335–337.

Kwee Swan Liat. *De betekenis van Lao Tse's denken voor onze tijd.* Grote filosofien. Amsterdam: Wereld Bibliotheek, 1959.

Lai Chih-te. *Lai Chu I-Ching T'u Chieh (Ming).* Taipei: I-chün Press, reprint, 1969.

Lanczkowski, Günther. "Neutestamentliche Parallelen zu Lao-tse's Tao-teking." *Gott und di Götter* (1958): 7–15.

Lao Tzu. *Le livre des récompenses et des peines.* Traduit du Chinois avec des éclaircissemens par J. P. Rémusat. Paris: A. A. Renouard, 1816.

_____. *Premier livre du Tao-te-king de Lao-tseu.* Translated by Jean Pierre Guillaum Pauther. n.p., 1838.

_____. *Lao Tseu Tao-te king, le livre de la voie et de la vertu,* Composé dans le VIe siècle avent l'ère chrétienne par le philosophe Lao Tseu; traduit en français, et publié avec le texte chinois et un commentaire perpétual, par Stanislas Julien. Paris: Imprimerie royale, 1842.

_____. *The Speculation on Metaphysics, Polity and Morality of the "Old Philosopher", Lao Tsze.* Translated from the Chinese with an introduction by John Chalmers. London: Trübner and Co., 1868.

_____. *Lao-tse Tao-te-king.* Der Weg zur Tugend; aus dem Chinesischen übersetzt und erhlärt von Reinhold von Plaenckner. Leipzig: F. A. Brockhaus, 1870.

_____. "Tao te Ching." In: *Texts of Taoism.* Translated by James Legge. Sacred Books of the East, volume 39. Edited by F. Max Müller. London: Oxford University Press, 1891.

_____. *The Book of the Path of Virtue; or a Version of the Tao-teh-king of Lao Tze.* With an introduction and essay on the Tao as presented in the writings of Chuang-tze, the apostle of Lao Tze, by Walter G. Old. Madras: Theosophical Society, 1894.

_____. *Le Tao de Lao-tseu.* Traduit du chinois par Matgioi (pseud. Albert de Pouvourville). Paris: Librairie de l'Art indépendence, 1894.

_____. *The Tao teh king.* Literally translated with notes by Thomas W. Kingsmill. Shanghai: n.p., 1899.

————. *Le livre de la voie et la ligne-droite de Laotsé*. Paris: Edition de la Revue blanche, 1902.

————. *The Book of the Simplest Way of Laotze*. A new translation from the text of the Tao-teh-king; with introduction and comments by Walter G. Old.

————. *The Tao-teh king*. A translation of the Chinese classic by E. H. Parker. London: Luzac, 1905.

————. *The Tao-teh-king*. A short study in comparative religion by C. Spurgeon Medhurst. Chicago: Theosophical Book Concern, 1905.

————. *Lau-tseu*. Traduit par Jules Besse. Paris: E. Leroux, 1909.

————. *Lao-tsze's Buch vom höchsten Wesen und vom Löchsten Gut (Tao-te-king)*. Aus dem Chinesischen übersetzt, mit Einleitung vom Julius Grill. Tubingen: J. C. B. Mohr, 1910.

————. *Die Bahn und der rechte Weg des Laotse*. Der Chinesischen übersetzt Schrift nachgedact, von Alexander Ular. Leipzig: Insel-verlag, 1917.

————. *Menschen/werde wesentlich! Lao-tse Sprüche*. Deutsch von Klabund (pseud. Alfred Henschke). Berlin: F. Heyder, 1921.

————. *Laotse (Tao-teh-king)*. Translated from the Chinese by Shuten Inouye, with critical and exegetical notes, comparing various renderings in Chinese, Japanese and English, including a new English version by the translator. Tokyo: Daitokaku, 1928.

————. *Laotse Tao teh king*. Vom Geist und seiner Tugend; übertragung von H. Federmann. Munich: O. Beck, 1921.

————. *Bóken em veginn Jakob Jóh Smáriog Yngvi Johannesson ritadi ef-tirmalann*. Reykjavek: Gudm. Gamalielsson, 1921.

————. *Laotse*. Der Anschuss an das Gesetz, oder der grosse Anschluss Versuch einer Wiedergabe des Tao-te-king, von Carl Dallago. Innsbruch: Brenner, 1921.

————. *Betrachtungen über das Tao-teh-king*. Der Weg, die Wahrheit und das Licht. Deutsche Ausgabe nach der englischen Überstetzung aus dem Chinesischen des Lao-tze. Bearbeitet von Franz Hartmann M. D. Leipzig: n.p., 1922.

————. *Tao te King*. Deutsch von F. Fiedler. Herausgegeben von Gustav Wynehen. Hannover: P. Steegemann, 1922.

————. *Lao-tzu, Tao teh king*. A tentative translation from the Chinese by Isabella Mears. London: Theosophical Publishing House, 1922.

————. *Das Buch des Alten vom Sinn und Leben*. Aus dem Chinesischen verdeutscht und erläutert von Richard Wilhelm. Jena: Eugene Wiedirichs, 1923.

————. *Laotse Wollen ohne Wahl*. Die grund Weisheit des Tao-te-king in freilt um Schöpfung vergegenwärtigt von Elizabeth Hahn. Rudolstadt: Greifen-verlag, 1924.

————. *The Simplest Way of Lao Tsze*. An analysis of the Tao-teh Canon with commentaries by the editors of the Shrine of the Wisdom. London: Shrine of Wisdom, 1924.

_____. *Tao te king.* Oversat af Victor Dantzer. Copenhagen: Aage Marcus, 1924.

_____. *Laò-Tse's Taò-te King.* Aus dem Chinesischen ins Deutsch übersetzt, eingeleitet und commentirt von Victor von Straup. Leipzig: Verlag der "Asia Major," 1924.

_____. *Tao . . . a Rendering into English Verse of the Tao-teh Ching of Lao Tsze.* With foreword by Charles Henry MacKintosh. Chicago: Theosophical Press, 1926.

_____. *The Philosophy of Lao Tze.* Translated by Wu-wu-tze. Chengtu: n.p., 1926.

_____. *Tao te-king.* Herausgegeben und erläutert von J. G. Weiss. Leipzig: P. Reclam, 1927.

_____. *The Teachings of the Old Boy.* An account of the teachings of Lao Tzu together with the Tao te King, translated by Thomas Robert Edward McInnes. London: J. M. Dent, 1927.

_____. *La regola celeste di Lao-tse (Tao-tê Ching).* Prima traduziona integrale italiana dal testo cinese, con introduction trascrizione e commento a cura de Alberto Castellani. Florence: G. C. Sansoni, 1927.

_____. *Lao-tzu.* Die Bahn des All und der Weg des Lebens. Munich: F. Bruckmann A. G., 1934.

_____. *Laotzu's Tao and Wu-wei.* A new translation by Bhikshu Wai-Tao and Dwight Goddard. Interpretative essays by Henri Borel. Outline of Taoist philosophy and religion by Dr. Kiang Kang-Hu. 2d edition, revised and enlarged. Santa Barbara, California: Dwight Goddard, 1935.

_____. *Tao teh king (The Way of Peace) of Lao Tzu 600 B.C.* As restated by A. L. Kitselman II. Palo Alto: The School of Simplicity, 1936.

_____. *Tao teh Ching.* Translated and annotated by Hu Tse-ling. Chengtu: Canadian Mission Press, 1936.

_____. *Laò-tze's Tao teh king, the Bible of Taoism.* English version by Sum Mung Au-Young. With an introduction by Merton S. Yewdale. New York: March and Greenwood, 1938.

_____. "Laotzu's The Tao and Its Virtue." Translated and annotated by John C. H. Wu. *T'ien-hsia Monthly* 9 (1939): 401–423.

_____. *The Simplest Way (by) Lao-tze (the 'Old Boy').* A new translation of the Tao-te-king with introduction and commentary by Walter G. Old. Philadelphia: Davis McKay Co., 1939.

_____. *Dau dö jing.* Des alten Meisters Kanon vom Weltgisetz und seinem Wirken. Neuübertragung von Franz Esser. Peking: Verlag der Pekinger Pappelinsel, 1941.

_____. *Lao-Tseu, Le livre de la voie et de la vertu.* Paris: J. Haumont, 1942.

_____. *Acht Kapital des Tao-tê-king von K. Wulff.* Herausgegeben von Victor Dantzer. Copenhagen: E. Munksgaard, 1942.

_____. *Lao tse, The Book of Tao (The Tao Teh Ching).* In: *The Wisdom of India and China.* Edited by Lin Yutang. New York: Random House, 1942.

_____. *The Way of Life According to Lao Tzu's Tao-teh-king.* An American version by Witter Bynner. New York: John Day Co., 1944.

————. *Le Doctrinal de Lao Tseu.* Traduit par Stanislas Julien. Collection des Petites Oeuvres. Paris: J. Haumont, 1944.

————. *Tao Teh King.* Vertaald door W. B. Vreugdehil. Amsterdam: In eigen beheer, 1945.

————. *The Sayings of Lao Tzu.* Translated from the Chinese with an introduction by Lionel Giles. London: J. Murray, 1945.

————. *Tao te king von Lao-tse.* Die Weisheit des Östens. Nach der übertragung von O. Sumitomo. Zurich: Scientia, 1945.

————. *The Way of Acceptance.* A new version of Lao Tse's Tao-te Ching. London: A. Dahers, 1946.

————. *Führung und Kraft aus der Ewigkeit (Dau-dö-jing).* Aus dem chinesischen Urtext übertragen von Erwin Rouselle. Wiesbaden: Insel-verlag, 1946.

————. *Tao Te King.* Das Buch des Alten vom Weltgrund und der Weltweise. Aus dem chinesischen Ürtext, neu übertragen und gedeitet von Dr. Haymo Kremsmayer. Salzburg: Jgonta-verlag, 1947.

————. *Tao-te-king.* Vertaling uit het Chinesischen voorword, inleiding en toelichtung van E. J. Welz. Baussum: F. G. Kroonder, 1947.

————. *Libro del sendero y de la linea recta.* Unica version castellana y prologo de Edmundo Montagne. Buenos Aires: Editorial Kier, 1947.

————. *Das verborgene Jeiwel Laotse's Verküngung.* Ausdentung und Nachdichtung von Sprüchen aus dem Tao-te King des chinesischen Weisen und Mystikers Lao-tse, vom Josef Tiefenbacher. Stuttgart: Schuler, 1948.

————. *The Tao Teh of Laotse.* A new version of the Chinese classic with comments and annotations by Frederick B. Thomas. Oakland, Calif.: n.p., 1948.

————. *Tao te Ching.* A new translation by Ch'u Ta-kao. London: Buddhist Society, 1948.

————. *The Works of Lao Tzu, Truth and Nature, Popularly Known as Daw-Der-Jing by Lao Dan.* Appended with Chinese texts and the oldest commentaries, editions and translation with an introduction by Cheng Lin. Shanghai: World Book Co., 1949.

————. *La voie et sa vertu.* Texte Chinois presenté traduit par Houang-Kia Tcheng et Pierre Leyris. Paris: Editions du Seuil, 1949.

————. *The Great Synderesis, being a translation of the Tao-te Ching.* Attributed by tradition to Li Erh (Lao-tse). Translated by Poynton Orde. Adelaide, Australia: Hassel Press, 1949.

————. *The Way and Its Power.* A study of the Tao-te Ching and its place in Chinese thought by Arthur Waley. London: G. Allen and Unwin, 1949.

————. *Tao-te-king.* Textgestaltung und Einführung vom Rudolf Backofen. Thielle: Franchauser, 1949.

————. *Laotzu.* Das Buch von der Grossen Weisheit. Deutsch von Andre Eckardt. Frankfurt: A. Lutzeyer, 1950.

————. *Tao te king.* Aus dem Chinesischen übersetzt und kommentvert von Victor von Strauss. Bearbeitung und Einleitung von W. Y. Tonn. Zurich: Maness-verlag, 1950.

_____. *Lao-tseu, Tao-te-king.* Le livre du Tao et de sa vertu. Traduction nouvelle suivie d'aperçus sur les enseignments de Lao Tseu. Lyon: P. Derain, 1951.

_____. *La sabiduría de Laotsé.* Edited by Lin Yutang. Buenos Aires: Editions Sudamericana, 1951.

_____. *So spricht Laotse.* Tao te king übertragen von Walt Jerven. Munich: O. W. Barth, 1952.

_____. *Tao-te King.* Alteste und Lehrer als Führer zum Wege Gottes und zum echten Leben. Aus dem chinesischen Ürtext neu übersetzt und gedeutet von Edwin Müller. Mit einer Auslegung "Der Tempel des Tao" hrsg. von Gottfried Ginter. Buhl-Baden: Verlag Conkordia, 1952.

_____. *Lao-tseu.* Par Evrad de Rouvre. Paris: Vrille, 1952.

_____. *Tao tö king.* Le livre de la voie et de la vertu. Texte chinois établi et traduit avec des notes critiques et une introduction par J. J. L. Duyvendak. Paris: Librairie d'Amérique et d'Orient, 1953.

_____. *Lao Tzu, Tao-teh King.* Translated by D. S. Nivison. New York: R. Frederich Under, 1953.

_____. *Bogeu om alt eller intet (Lao-tse Tao Teh King).* Pa'dansk ved Ole Kulerich Svendsen. Copenhagen: Thaning of Appel, 1953.

_____. *Tao-te Ching: The Book of the Way and Its Virtue.* Translated from the Chinese and annotated by J. J. L. Duyvendak. London: J. Murray, 1954.

_____. *The Canon of Reason and Virtue . . . Being Lao Tse's Tao-teh-king.* Chinese and English [translation] by Paul Carus. La Salle, Ill.: Open Court Publishing Co., 1954.

_____. *Lao Tzu: The Way of Life of the Tao Te Ching.* A new translation by Raymond B. Blakney. New York: New American Library, 1955.

_____. *Der Chinesische Philosoph Laudse und Seine Lehre.* Von Jang Chingschun. Übersetzt von G. Kahlenbach. Berlin: Deutscher Verlag der Wissenschafter, 1955.

_____. *Le Tao Te King de Lao Tseu.* Par Paula Reuss. Angers: Au Masque d'Or, 1955.

_____. *Tau Teh Tsing.* In geleid en vert. door J. A. Blok. Deventer: N. Klwer, 1956.

_____. *Tao-te king.* Deutsche Übersetzung von G. Coudenhove. Frankfurt: Fischer, 1956.

_____. *Tao-te king.* Tradizione de Chin Hsiung Wu e di Rosanna Pilone. Introduzione di L. Magrine. Milano: Istituto Culturale Italo-Chinese, 1956.

_____. *The Wisdom of Laotse.* Translated and edited with introduction and notes by Lin Yutang. London: M. Joseph, 1958.

_____. *Tao-tö-king.* Par Jean Herbert. Paris: Club des Libraires, 1958.

_____. *Tao Teh King.* Interpreted as Nature and Intelligence. Edited by Archie Bahm. New York: F. Unger Publishing Co., 1958.

_____. *Dao due Kinh.* By Nghien Taon. Saigon: Département de l'Education Nationale du Vietnam, 1959.

_____. *Tao Teh Ching.* Chinese text with English translation by John C. H.

Wu. Edited by Paul K. Shih. Asian Institute Translations, no. 1. New York: St. Johns University Press, 1961.

————. *La gnosis taoista del Tao te Ching.* Analisis y traduccion por Carmelo Elordey. Burgos: Ona, Facultad de Teologia S. J., 1961.

————. *Lao Tse: Tao-teh-king.* Weg-Weisung zur Wirlkechkeit hrsg. und erläutert von Karl Otto Schmidt. Phullingen: Baum-verlag, 1961.

————. *Das Kleinod des Lao-tse; eine mystische Erzählung.* Rothenburg of der Charles Waldemar. Tauber: Hegereiter-verlag, 1958.

————. *Tao Te King ou la Jonction Supreme.* Perception et présent par St. Remy. Avec une calligraphie nippone du début du 19e siècle. Anvers: Librairie des Arts, 1962.

————. *The Book of Tao.* Translated by Frank J. MacHovec. Mt. Vernon, N.Y.: Pauper Press, 1962.

————. *Tao te king.* Traité sur le principe et l'art de la vie des vieux maîtres de la Chine. Introduction, glose, commentaires et notes par Jacques Lionett. Paris: Adrien Maisonneuve, 1962.

————. *Tao-te Ching.* Translated with an introduction by D. C. Lau. Baltimore: Penguin Books, 1963.

————. *Tao-te-king.* Par Armel Guerne. Paris: Club français du livre, 1963.

————. *The Way of Lao Tzu.* Translated with introductory essays, commentaries and notes by Chan Wing-tsit. Indianapolis: Bobbs-Merrill, 1963.

————. *Lao tzu: Die Ordnungspekulationen im Tao-te-ching.* Vom Peter Joachim Opitz. Munich: List, 1967.

————. *Tao-te-king.* Das heilige Buch vom Weg und der Tugend. Übersetzung, Einleitung und Anmerkungen von Günther Debon. Stuttgart: P. Reclam, 1961.

————. *Tao-tö king.* Traduit du chinois par Kia-hway Liou. Préface de René Etiemble. Paris: Gallimard, 1969.

————. *Tao-te Ching.* Kuo-shüeh Chi-pen Ts'ung Shu. Taipei: Chang-wu Press, 1969.

————. *The Great Art of Laotse.* A new English version translated from Chinese by A. R. Home of Laotse's 81 meditations on the way of power *(Tao teh Ching).* Exeter: Newbard, 1972.

Legge, James. *The Religions of China: Confucianism and Taoism described and compared with Christianity.* London: Trübner, 1880.

Lermer. "Laotse: Ein Geistgezeugter nach der Ordnung des Melchisedek." *Das edle Leben* 8 (1959): 42–45.

Levy, Howard S. "The Bifurcation of the Yellow Turbans in Later Han." *Oriens* 13–14 (1960–1961): 251–255.

————. "Yellow Turban Religion and Rebellion at the End of the Han." *Journal of the American Oriental Society* 76 (1956): 214–227.

Li Ch'iao-ping. *Chemical Arts of Old China.* With a foreword by Tenny L. Davis. Easton, Pa.: Journal of Chemical Education, 1948.

Li Chih-ch'ang. *The Travels of an Alchemist: The Journey of the Taoist Ch'ang-ch'un, from China to the Hindukush at the Summons of Chingiz Khan.*

Translated with an introduction by Arthur Waley. London: G. Routledge and Sons, 1931.

Li Tche-houa P. and J. "La vie légendaire de Tchoang-tse." *Arts et Lettres* 1 (1946): 113–120.

Liebenthal, Walter. "The Immortality of the Soul in Chinese Thought." *Monumenta Nipponica* 8 (1952): 327–397.

_____. "Chinese Buddhism during the 4th and 5th Centuries." *Monumenta Nipponica* 11 (1955): 44–83.

Lieh-tzu. *Taoist Teachings from the Book of Lieh Tzü*. Translated from the Chinese, with introduction and notes, by Lionel Giles. 2d ed. London: J. Murray, 1959.

_____. *Le vrai classique du vie parfait par Lie tseu*. Traduit du chinois par Bededykt Grynpas. Paris: Gallimard, 1961.

_____. *ĨAn Chzhu, Leĩszy, Chzhuanĩszy, 4–6 B.C. do n.e.; ateisty, materialisty, dialektiki drevnego Kitaĩa*. Vstup. stat'ĩa perevod i kommentarii L. D. Pozdneevoĩ. Moscow: Glav. red. vostochnoĩ lit-ry, 1967.

_____. *Das wahre Buch vom quellenden Urgrund*. Die Lehren d. Philosophen Liä Yükou u. Yang Dschu. Von Liä Dsï. Aus d. Chinesischen übertragen und erläutert von Richard Wilhelm. Dusseldorf: Diederichs, 1968.

Lin Tung-chi. "The Taoist in Every Chinese." *T'ien-hsia Monthly* 11 (1940–1941): 211–225.

Lin Yutang. "Lao Tse Speaks to Us Today." *Asia* 42 (1942): 618–621.

_____. *The Wisdom of China*. London: Michael Joseph, 1944.

_____. "A Note on Lao-tse." *Eastern World* 3–4 (1949): 18–19.

_____. "The Wisdom of Lao-tse." *Aryan Path* 20 (1949): 2–5.

Link, Arthur E. "Shyh Daw-an's Preface to Sangharakṣa's Yogācārabhūmi-sūtra and the Problem of Buddho-taoist Terminology in Early Chinese Buddhism." *Journal of the American Oriental Society* 77 (1957): 1–14.

Liou Kia-hway. "Le judgement paradoxal chez Tchouang-tseu." In: *L'ésprit synthetique de la Chine*. Paris: Presses Universitaires de France, 1961.

Liu An. *Huai Nan Hung Lieh Chi Chieh* [An annotated edition of the Huai-nan-tzu]. Kuo-hsüeh Chi-pen Ts'ung Shu. Taipei: Shang-wu Press, 1969.

Liu Chih-wan. *Taipei-shih Sung-shen Ch'i An Chien Chiao Chi Tien* [The *Chiao* ritual celebrated in Sung Shan, Taipei]. Monograph no. 14. Nankang, Taipei: Academia Sinica, 1967.

_____. *Essays on Chinese Folk Belief and Folk Cults*. Monograph no. 22. Nankang, Taipei: Academia Sinica, 1974.

Liu P'ei-yüan (pseud. Liu I-ming). *I-tao Hsin-fa Chen-chuan* [A Taoist interpretation of the *I-ching*]. Taipei: Freedom Press, 1962.

Liu Ts'un-yan. *Buddhist and Taoist Influences on Chinese Novels*. Wiesbaden: Harrassowitz, 1962.

_____. "Lu Hsi-hsing: A Confucian Scholar, Taoist Priest and Buddhist Devotee of the Sixteenth Century." *Asiatische Studien* 18–19 (1965): 115–142.

———. "Lin Chao-en, the Master of the Three Teachings." *T'oung-pao* 53 (1967): 253–278.

———. "Lu Hsi-hsing and His Commentaries on the Ts'an t'ung ch'i." *Ch'inghua Hsüeh Pao* 7 (1968): 71–98.

———. "Taoist Self-Cultivation in Ming Thought." In: *Self and Society in Ming Thought.* Edited by William T. de Bary. New York: Columbia University Press, 1970.

Luk, Charles (Lu K'uan-yü). *The Secrets of Chinese Meditation.* London: Rider, 1964.

Lüth, Paul E. H. "Weltgeheimnis und Weltegefühl bei Lao Tse. Schule der Freiheit." *Uchtdorf im Pommern* 9 (1941–42): 306–312.

———. *Der seidene Mond.* Die Legenden von Lao Tse und Li T'ai-po. Wiesbaden: Limes, 1947.

Maclaghan, P. J. "Taoism." In: *Encyclopedia of Religion and Ethics.* Edited by James Hastings. Edinburgh, 1958.

Mahidihassan, S. "Chinese Origin of Alchemy." *United Asia* 5 (1953): 241–244.

———. "Alchemy is of Chinese Origin." *Orient* 4 (1954): 39–42.

———. "The Chinese Origin of Three Cognate Words: Chemistry, elixir, and genii." *Journal of the University of Bombay* 20 (1951): 107–131.

Marin, Juan. *China: Lao-tsze, Confucio, Buda.* Madrid: Espasa Calpe, 1945.

———. *Triptico Chino: Confucio, Lao-tsze, Sakiamuni.* Madellin: Universidad de Antiloqia, n.d.

———. *Lao Tsze o el universo magico.* Buenos Aires: Editorial Claridad, 1952.

Maspero, Henri. "Les religions chinoises." In: *Mélanges posthumes sur les religions et l'histoire de la Chine.* Volume 1. Paris: Publications du Musée Guimet, 1950.

———. "Le Taoisme." In: *Mélanges posthumes sur les religions et l'histoire de la Chine.* Volume 2. Paris: Publications du Musée Guimet, 1950.

———. "Les Procédés de Nourrir le Principe Vital dans la Religion Taoiste Ancienne." *Journal Asiatique* 229 (1937): 177–252.

———. "Les dieux taoistes, comment on communique avec eux." *Tōhō Jhukyō* (1963): 26–40.

———. "L'église taoique au temps des Six Dynasties." *Journal Asiatique* (1940): 305.

———. "L'école taoiste." In: *La Chine Antique.* Paris: de Boccard, 1927.

Masuda Fukutarō. *Taiwan Hontō-Jin no Shūkyō.* [The religion of the people of the island of Taiwan]. Tokyo: Meiji Shotoku Kinen Gakkai, 1935.

———. *Taiwan no Shūkyō.* [The religions of Taiwan]. Tokyo: Yōken-dō, 1939.

———. *Chūgoku no Zokushin to Hōshisō.* [China's popular beliefs and legalistic mentality]. Tokyo: Sanwa Shobo. 1966.

Maurer, Herrymon. *The Old Fellow.* New York: John Day, 1943.

Meurs, Van. "Lau-tze's Wijsbegeerte in een nieuw kleed." *Studia Catholica* 19 (1943): 227–242.

———. "De Vreesgedachte bij Lau-tze." *Studia Catholica* 19 (1943): 276–290.

———. "De Godskennis van Lau-tze." *Studia Catholica* 20 (1944): 63–90.

———. "Het Tao-begrip van Lau-tze." *Studia Catholica* 30 (1944); 189–190.

Morgan, Evan. *Tao, the Great Luminant; Essays from Huai-nan Tze*. London: Kegan Paul, 1933.

Mortier, F. "Du sens primitif de l'antique et célèbre figure divinatoire des taoistes chinois et japonais (Sien T'ien)." *Bulletin de la société d'anthropologie de Bruxelles* 65 (1948): 150–160.

_____. "Le taoisme et ses variations doctrinales." *Bulletin de la société d'anthropologie de Bruxelles* 65 (1954): 161–166.

Mote, Frederick W. "Confucian Eremitism in the Yüan Period." In: *The Confucian Persuasion*. Edited by A. F. Wright. Stanford: Stanford University Press, 1960.

Munro, Donald J. *The Conception of Man in Early China*. Stanford: Stanford University Press, 1969.

Murakami Yoshimi. " 'Nature' in Lao-Chuang Thought and 'No-mind' in Ch'an Buddhism." *Annual Studies of Kwansei Gakuin University* 14 (1965): 15–31.

_____. *Chūgoku no Sennin, Hōbokushi* [A Chinese immortal, Pao-p'u-tzu]. Kyoto: Heiraku-ji, 1956.

Natsume Ikken. "Various Phases of Revelation in Taoism." *Tenri Journal of Religion* 1 (1955): 53–65.

Needham, Joseph. *Science and Civilisation in China*. 5 Volumes. Cambridge: Cambridge University Press, 1952–1974.

Needham, Joseph and Ho Ping-yü. "Theories of Categories in Early Mediaeval Chinese Alchemy." *Journal of the Warburg and Courtauld Institute* 22 (1959): 173–210.

_____. "The Laboratory Equipment of the Early Mediaeval Chinese Alchemists." *Ambix* 7 (1959): 57–112.

Needham, Joseph, Ts'ao T'ien-ch'in and Ho Ping-yü. "An Early Mediaeval Chinese Alchemical Text in Aqueous Solutions." *Ambix* 7 (1959): 173–210.

Ōbuchi Ninji. *Dōkyō-shi no Kenkyū* [Research on the history of Taoism]. Okayama: Okayama Daigaku, 1964.

Osgood, Cornelius. *Village Life in Old China: A Community Study of Kao Yao Yünnan*. New York: Ronald Press, 1963.

Otto, J. H. F. "Das Dau in der Chinesischen Heilkunst." Festschrift für J. H. Schultz. *Anthropologie* 62 (1954): 1–10.

Peroni, B. *Laotse e il Taoismo*. Milano: Garzanti, 1949.

Petrov, A. "Yan Chzu-vol'nodumets drevnogo Kitaya." *Sovetskoe vos kovedenie* 1 (1940): 174–211.

Pokora, Timoteus. "On the Origin of the Notions T'ai-p'ing and Ta-t'un in Chinese Philosophy." *Archiv Orientalni* 29 (1961): 448–454.

_____. "An Important Crossroad of the Chinese Thought." *Archiv Orientalni* 29 (1961): 64–79.

Porkert, Manfred. *The Theoretical Foundation of Chinese Medicine*. Cambridge: Massachusetts Institute of Technology Press, 1963.

_____. "Üntersuchengen einiger philosophisch-wissenschaftlicher Grundbegriffe und Beiziehungen im Chinesischen." *Zeitschrift Deutschen Morgenländischen Gesellschaft* 110 (1961): 422–452.

Pourourville, Albert de (pseud. Matgioi). *La voie rationnelle.* Paris: Editions traditionnelles, 1940.

Pyun, Y. T. "Tidbits from Laotzu and Chuangtzu." *Asian Studies* 6 (1963): 423–433.

Reichelt, Karl Ludwig. *Taoism: Religion in Chinese Garment.* Translated and edited by Joseph Tetlie. London: Butterworth Press, 1951.

Rinaker Ten Broek, Janet and Yiu Tung. "A Taoist Inscription of the Yüan Dynasty, the Tao-chiao Pei." *T'oung-pao* 40 (1950): 60–122.

Robertson, Leo C. "The Concept of Tao According to Lao-tzu and Chuang-tzu." *Atti del Congresso Internazionale di Filosofia* 10 (1960): 197–203.

Rogers, Millard. "A Taoist Figure Dated 607 A.D." *Artibus Asiae* 20 (1957): 45–49.

Roi, J. and Ou Yun-joei. "Le Taoisme et les Plantes d'Immortalité." *Bulletin de l'Université l'Aurore* 2 (1941): 534–546.

Rouselle, Erwin. "Lau-dsi gang durch die Seele, Geschichte und Welt." *Eranos Jahrbuch* 3 (1935): 179–205.

———. "Lau-dsi und sein Buch." *Sinica* 16 (1941): 120–129.

Ruyer, R. "Dieu-personne et Dieu Tao." *Revue de metaphysique et de morale* 52 (1947): 141–157.

Saitschich, Robert. *Schöpfer Lebenswerte von Lao-tse bis Jesus.* Zurich: Rascher, 1945.

Saso, Michael R. *Taoism and the Rite of Cosmic Renewal.* Pullman: Washington State University Press, 1972.

———. *Taiwan Feasts and Customs.* Hsinchu, Taiwan: Fu Jen University Language School Press, 1967 (2d ed.); 1969 (3d ed.).

———. "The Chinese New Year Festival." *Journal of the China Society* 5 (1965): 37–52.

———. "Taiwanese Feasts and Customs." *Monumenta Nipponica* Monograph Series 25 (1966): 74–104.

———. "The Taoist Who Did Not Die." *Afrasian* (1969): 1–6.

———. "The Taoist Tradition in Taiwan." *China Quarterly* (1970): 83–101.

———. "On Ritual Meditation in Orthodox Taoism." *Journal of the China Society* 8 (1971): 1–19.

———. "Classification of Taoist Orders According to the Documents of the 61st Generation Heavenly Master." *Bulletin of the Institute of Ethnology* 30 (1972): 69–79.

———. "On the Meditative Use of the Yellow Court Canon." *Journal of the China Society* 9 (1974): 1–20.

———. "Mao Shan, Long Shan and Lung-hu Shan: A Study of Rivalry in Taiwan." *Bulletin of the Institute of Ethnology* 33 (1974): 119–141.

———. "Methodology in the Study of Religious Taoism." In: *Publications of the 1974 AAR Conference on Asian Studies.* Missoula, Montana: University of Montana Press, 1974.

———. "Orthodoxy and Heterodoxy in Taoist Ritual." In: *Religion and Ritual* in Chinese Society. Edited by Arthur Wolf. Stanford: Stanford University Press, 1974.

_____. *Chuang-lin Hsü Tao-tsang: An Encyclopedia of Taoist Ritual.* 25 volumes. Taipei: Ch'eng-wen Press, 1975.

_____. *Seitō Dōkyō no Denju Kyōkai (On the Ordination of an Orthodox Taoist Priest).* Translated by Nariko Saso. Kyoto: Tōhō Shūkyō, 1975.

_____. *The Teachings of Master Chuang.* New Haven: Yale University Press, 1977.

Scaligero, Massimo. "Tao and Grail, the Search of Earthly Immortality." *Philosophy East and West* 8 (1957): 67–72.

Schafter, E. H. "Notes on Mica in Mediaeval China." *T'oung-pao* 43 (1954–1955): 265–286.

_____. "Orpiment and Realgar in Chinese Technology and Tradition." *Journal of the American Oriental Society* 75 (1955): 73–89.

Schipper, Kristofer Marinus. *L'empereur Wou des Han dans la Légend Taoiste, Han Wou-Ti Nei Tchouan.* Paris: Ecole Française d'Extrême-Orient, 1965.

_____. "Remarks on the Functions of 'Inspector of Merits' (in Taoist ecclesiastical organization with a description of the ordination ceremony in Taiwan Cheng-I Taoism)." *Communication to the 2d International Conference of Taoist Studies.* Tateshina, Japan, 1972. Manuscript.

_____. "Priest and Liturgy: the Live Tradition of Chinese Religion." A lecture delivered at Cambridge University, 1967.

_____. "Taoism: The Liturgical Tradition." *Communication to the 1st International Conference of Taoist Studies.* Villa Serbellion, Bellagio, 1968. Manuscript.

_____. "Le Wu-yue Tchent-hing-t'ou et son Culte." *Etudes Taoistes* (1967): 114–162.

_____. *Le Fen-teng: Rituelle Taoiste.* Publications de l'Ecole Française d'Extrême-Orient 103 (1975).

Scuckij, J. "Ein Dauist im Chinesischen Buddhismus, aus dem Russischen." Übersetzt von W. A. Unkrieg. *Sinica* 15 (1940): 114–129.

Seidel, Anna K. *La Divinisation de Lao-tseu dans le Taoisme des Han.* Paris: Publications de l'Ecole Français d'Extrême-Orient, 1969.

_____. "Chang San-feng, a Taoist Immortal of the Ming Dynasty." In: *Self and Society in Ming Thought.* Edited by William T. de Bary. New York: Columbia University Press, 1970.

_____. "Die Mythologie des Taoismus." In: *Wörterbuch der Mythologie.* Herausgegeben von H. W. Haussig. Stuttgart: Ernst Klett, 1967.

_____. "The Image of the Perfect Ruler in Early Taoist Messianism: Lao-tzu and Li-hung." *History of Religion* 9 (1969): 216–247.

Shien Gi-ming. "Nothingness in the Philosophy of Lao-tzu." *Philosophy East and West* 1 (1951): 58–63.

Shih, J. *The Tao: Its Essence, Its Dynamism and Its Fitness as a Vehicle of Christian Revelation.* Rome: Universitas Gregoriana, 1966.

Shih, Vincent Y. C. *The Taiping Ideology: Its Sources, Interpretation and Influences.* Seattle: University of Washington Press, 1967.

――――. "Some Chinese Rebel Ideologies." *T'oung-pao* 44 (1956): 150–226.

Shiu, Maurice Poy. *The Eight Immortals of the Religion of Taoism in Chinese Mythology.* Illustrated by Thomas Shiu. Chicago: Overseas Art Shop, 1941.

Sin, R. G. H. *The Tao of Science: An Essay on Western Knowledge and Eastern Wisdom.* Cambridge: Massachusetts Institute of Technology, 1957.

Sivin, Nathan. "On the Pao-p'u-tzu, Nei-p'ien and the Life of Ko Hung." *Isis* 60 (1969): 388–391.

――――. *Chinese Alchemy: Preliminary Studies.* Foreword by I. Bernard Cohen. Harvard Monographs in the History of Science. Cambridge, Mass.: Harvard University Press, 1968.

Smith, D. Howard. *Chinese Religions.* London: Weidenfeld and Nicolson, 1968.

Soothill, William Edward. *The Three Religions of China: A Study of Confucianism, Buddhism and Taoism.* London: Oxford University Press, 1923.

――――. *Les Trois Religions de la Chine: Confucianisme, Bouddhisme, Taoisme.* Traduit par G. Lepage. Paris: Payot, 1946.

Soymie, Michel. "Le Lo-Feou Chan, étude de géographie religieuse." *Bulletin de l'Ecole Française d'Extrême-Orient* 48 (1956): 1–139.

Soymie, Michel and Yoshioka Yoshitoyo, eds. *Dōkyō Kenkyū* [Studies in Taoism]. 4 volumes. Tokyo, 1967–1971.

Spalding, K. J. *Three Chinese Thinkers (Chuang-tzu, Mo-tzu, Hsün-tzu).* Nanking: National Central Library, 1947.

Spencer, Sidney. *Mysticism in World Religions.* London: Penguin Books, 1963.

Spooner, Roy C. "Chinese Alchemy." *Journal of the West China Border Research Society* 12 (1940): 82–102.

Spooner, Roy C. and Wang C. H. "The Divine Nine Turn Tan Sha Method, a Chinese Alchemical Recipe." *Isis* 38 (1947–48): 235–242.

Stapleton, E. H. "The Antiquity of Alchemy." *Archives Internationales d'Histoire des Sciences* 30 (1951): 35–38.

――――. "The Antiquity of Alchemy." *Ambix* 5 (1953): 1–43.

Stein, R. A. "Jardins en Miniature d'Extrême-Orient, Le Monde en Petit." *Bulletin de l'Ecole Français d'Extrême-Orient* 42 (1943): 1–104.

――――. "Architecture et Pensée Religieuse en Extrême-Orient." *Arts Asiatiques* 4 (1957): 163–186.

――――. "Les Religions de la Chine." In: *Encyclopédie Française.* Volume 19: "Philosophie et Religion." Paris, 1957.

――――. "L'Habitat, le Monde et le Corps Humain en Extrême-Orient et en Haute-Asie." *Journal Asiatique* 245 (1957): 37–74.

――――. "Remarques sur les Mouvements du Taoisme Politico-Religieux au IIe siècle ap. J. C." *T'oung-pao* 50 (1963): 1–78.

――――. "Au Sujet du Tchen-kao." *Ecole Pratique des Hautes Etudes* Sc. R. Annuaire (1963–1964): 51–52; (1964–1965): 63–64.

_____. "Textes Taoistes Relatifs à la Transmission des Livres Révéles." *Annuaire du Collège de France* 68 (1967–1968): 453–457.

_____. "Aspects de la Foi Jurée en Chine." *Annuaire du Collège du France* 67 (1966–1967): 411–415.

Steininger, Hans. *Hauch-und Körperseele und der Dämon bei Kuan-Yin-Tze; Üntersuchungen zur Chinesischen Psychologie und Ontologie.* Leipzig: Harrassowitz, 1953.

_____. "Der Heilige Herrscher-sein Tao und sein praktische Tun (Kuan Yin Tze Traktat)." *Sino-Japonica* (1956): 170–177.

Stejn, V. M. *Daosskaja utopija v̇ Kitae* [Taoist utopia in China]. Moscow: Vestnik istorii mirovoj kultury, 1960.

Stern, A. L. "Remarks on Two Chapters of Laotse's Tao Teh Ching." *Syntheses* 1 (1950–1951): 59–65.

Strickmann, M. "On the Alchemy of Thao Hung-Ching." *Contribution to the 2d International Conference of Taoist Studies.* Revised. Tateshina, Japan, 1972. Unpublished.

_____. "Taoism in the Lettered Society of the Six Dynasties." *Contribution to the 2d International Conference of Taoist Studies.* Tateshina, Japan, 1972. Unpublished.

Sun Siao-fang. "Chuang-tzu's Theory of Truth." *Philosophy East and West* 2 (1953): 137–146.

Sung Yin-tzu and Shih Ho-yang. *Huang T'ing Wai Ching . . . (T'ai-shang Huang T'ing Ching Chu), Li Ming-Ch'e P'ing* [The Yellow Court Canon, Supplement with comm.]. Peking: Pai-yüan Shan Fang, 1794.

Suzuki Seiichirō. *Kan-kon-sō-sai to Nenjū Gyōji* [Weddings, funerals and annual festivals of Taiwan]. Taihoku: Taiwan Nichi-nichi Shinpōsha, 1934.

Takeuchi Sadayoshi. *Taiwan.* Taipei: Taiwan Kankō Kai, 1913.

Tang Yung-t'ung. "Wang Pi's New Interpretation of the I-Ching and Lun-yü." Translated by Walter Liebenthal. *Harvard Journal of Asiatic Studies* 10 (1947): 124–161.

Tchen, M. "Il mundo e l'uomo nella concezione taoistica." *Il pensiero missionario* 15 (1943): 16–23.

Thiel, Joseph. "Der Streit der Buddhisten und Taoisten zur Mongolenziet." *Monumenta Serica* 20 (1961): 1–81.

Thompson, Laurence G. *Chinese Religion: An Introduction.* Belmont, Calif.: Dickenson Publishing Co., 1963.

Tien, Tsung. "The Eight Immortals." *Orient* 31 (1952): 50–52.

Ting Nai-tung. "Laotzu's Critique of Language." *ETC: A Review of General Semantics* 19 (1962–1963): 5–38.

Tolstoy, L. *Izrecheniya kitaiskovo mudretsa Laotze* [The sayings of the Chinese sage Lao-tzu]. Selected by Tolstoy, with an essay by I. Goburnow Posadov, "About the Sage Lao-tzu" and an essay by Tolstoy, "On the Essence of Lao-tzu's Teachings." Moscow: Posrednik, 1910.

Tolstoy, L. and Konishi. *Lao-si Tao-te King ili Pisanie o Nravstvenno ti, ped* redaksiej L. N. Tolstogo perevod s kitajskogo D. Konnissi primetchnaja S. N. Durylina. Moscow: Tolstoi-Konishi Masutarō Kyōyaku Rōshi, Roshiya gemban fukusie, 1913.

Toivo, Koshikallio. *Salaisuuksien Tie* [The way of the secrets]. Helsinki: n.p., 1950.

Tomita Kojiro and Chü A. Kaiming. "Portraits of Wu Ch'üan-chih (1269–1350), Taoist Pope in Yüan Dynasty." *Bulletin of the Museum of Fine Arts* 44 (1946): 88–95.

Tomonobu A. Imamichi. "Das Seinsproblem in der Philosophie des Ostasiatischen Altertums. Konfutse und Tschuang Tschou." *Jahrbuch für Psychologie und Psychotherapie* 6 (1958): 54–64.

Tradier, Georg. "Die Lehre Lao-tse's." *Vivos voco* 34 (1961): 465–466.

Tscharner, E. H. von. "La pensée 'metaphysique' et éthique de Lao-tse." *Scientia* 72 (1942): 29–36.

———. "Laotse Sprüche über den Krieg." *Asiatische Studien* 1 (1947): 6–9.

———, ed. and trans. "Fragment einer Lao-tse Übersetzung." *Asiatische Studien* 8 (1954): 8–20.

———. "Laotse und das innere Licht." *Die weisse Fahne* 28 (1955): 68–71.

Tseng Ching-lai. *Taiwan Shūkyō to Meishin Rōshū* [Taiwanese religion and rigid superstitions]. Taihoku: Taiwan Shukyo Kai, 1938.

Vandier-Nicholas, Nicole. "Pensée chinoise et taoisme." *Asiatische Studien* 4 (1950): 64–89.

———. *Le taoisme.* Paris: Presses Universitaires de France, 1965.

———. *Three Ways of Thought in Ancient China.* London: G. Allen and Unwin, 1939.

———. *Trois Courants de la Pensée Chinoise Antique.* Traduction de G. Deniker. Paris: Payot, 1949.

———. *Lebensweisheit in Alten China.* Berechtigte Übersetzung von Eva-Franziska Meister Weidner. Hamburg: von Schröder, 1947.

Wallacker, Benjamin E. *The Huai-nan-tzu.* Book 11: *Behavior, Culture, and Cosmos.* American Oriental Series. New Haven, Conn.: American Oriental Society, 1962.

Walshe, W. Gilber. "Chinese Mysticism." In: *Encyclopaedia of Religion and Ethics.* Edited by James Hasting. Volume 9, pages 87–89. New York: C. Scribner's Sons, 1957.

Ware, James R., trans. *Alchemy, Medicine and Religion in the China of A.D. 320: The Nei-p'ien of Ko Hung (Pao-p'u-tzu).* Cambridge, Mass.: MIT Press, 1966.

———. "The Wei Shu and the Sui Shu on Taoism." *Journal of the American Oriental Society* 53 (1933): 215–250; (1934): 290–294.

Watson, Burton. "Metaphysics and Government in the Lao Tzu: Selections from the Lao Tzu (Tao-te Ching)." In: *Sources of Chinese Tradition.* Compiled by William Theodore de Bary, Wing-tsit Chan, and Burton Watson. New York: Columbia University Press, 1960.

Watts, Alan Wilson. *The Way of Zen.* New York: Pantheon Books, 1957.

_____. "La Philosophie du Tao." In: *Le Booddhisme Zen*. Traduit de l'Anglais par P. Berlot. Paris: Payot, 1960.

Weber, Max. "Taoism." In: *The Religion of China: Confucianism and Taoism*. Translated and edited by Hans H. Gerth. New York: Free Press, 1951.

Wei Wu Wei. *All Else is Bondage: Nonvolitional Living Tao*. Hong Kong: Hong Kong University Press, 1964.

Welch, Holmes. "The Chang T'ien Shih and Taoism in China." *Journal of Oriental Studies* 4 (1957–1958): 188–212.

_____. "Syncretism in Early Taoism." In: *Papers on China*. Cambridge, Mass.: Harvard University Press, 1956.

_____. *The Parting of the Way, Lao Tzu and the Taoist Movement*. Boston: Beacon Press, 1957.

_____. "Bellagio Conference on Taoist Studies." *History of Religions* 9 (1969–1970): 107–136.

Wen Tao-tzu. *Tao Hua Lu*. Taipei: Chen Shan Mei Press, 1966.

Weöres, Tökei and Sandor, Ferenc. *Lao-ce: As Ut es Ereny Könyve*. Budapest: Europa Könyvkaido, 1958.

Wilhelm, Richard. "Eine Chou Inschrift über Atemtechnik." *Monumenta Serica* 13 (1948): 385–388.

_____. *Das Geheimnis der Goldene Blüte, ein Chinesisches Lebensbuch (T'ai-i-chin-hua Tsung-chih)*. Übersetzt und erläutert von Richard Wilhelm, mit einem europäischen Kommentar von C. G. Jung. Zurich: Rascher, 1957.

Wilhelm, Hellmut. "The Fisherman without Bait." *Asiatische Studien* 18–19 (1965): 90–104.

Wilson, William Jerome. "The Background of Chinese Alchemy." *Ciba Symposia* 2 (1940): 595–599.

_____. "Leading Ideas of Early Chinese Alchemy." *Ciba Symposia* 2 (1940): 600–604.

_____. "Biographies of Early Chinese Alchemists." *Ciba Symposia* 2 (1940): 605–609.

_____. "Later Developments of Chinese Alchemy." *Ciba Symposia* 2 (1940): 610–617.

_____. "Relation of Chinese Alchemy to That of Other Countries." *Ciba Symposia* 2 (1940): 618–619.

_____. "Alchemy in China." *Ciba Symposia* 2 (1940): 623–624.

Wu Chi-yü. *Pen Tsi King (Livre du Terme Origine)*. Ouvrage Taoiste inédit du VIIe siècle. Manuscrits rétrouvés à Touen-houang reproduits en facsimiles. Paris: Mission Paul Pelliot, 1960.

Wu, John C. H. "The Wisdom of Chuang Tzu: A New Appraisal." *International Philosophical Quarterly* 3 (1963): 5–36.

Yang, C. K. *Religion in Chinese Society*. Berkeley: University of California Press, 1961.

Yang, Richard F. S. "A Study of the Origin of the Legends of the Eight Immortals." *Oriens Extremus* 5 (1958): 1–22.

Yewdale, M. S. "The Wisdom of Tao." *Aryan Path* 21 (1950): 365–368.

Yoshioka Yoshitoyo. *Dōkyō no kenkyū* [Studies on Taoism]. Tokyo: Hōzōkan, 1952.

———. *Dōkyō Kyōten Shiron*. [A treatise on the history of Taoist documents]. Tokyo: Taisho Daigaku, 1955.

———. *Dōkyō to Bukkyō* [Taoism and Buddhism]. Volume 1. Tokyo: Nihon Gakujutsu shinkōsha, 1959. Volume 2. Tokyo: Toshima shobo, 1970.

———. *Eisei e no negai: Dōkyō* [The quest for immortality: Taoism]. Sekai no shukyō, Volume 9. Kyoto: Tankōsha, 1970.

Yü Ying-shih. "Life and Immortality in the Mind of Han China." *Harvard Journal of Asiatic Studies* 25 (1964–1965): 80–122.

———. *View of Life and Death in Later Han China, A.D. 25–220*. Cambridge, Mass.: Harvard University Press, 1962.

Zen, J. "Le Chapitre 33 du Tchoang-tse, avec texte critique établi par Tsong Tai." *Bulletin de l'Université l'Aurore* 3 (1949): 104–136.

Zenker, E. V. "Der Taoismus des Frühzeit: Die alt-und gemein chinesische Weltanschauung." *Philosophisch-historische Klasse* 222 (1943): 1–56.

Zia, Rosina C. "The Conception of 'Sage' in Lao-tze and Chuang-tze as Distinguished from Confucianism." *Chung Chi Journal* 5 (1966): 150–157.

Zürcher, E. *The Buddhist Conquest of China*. Leiden: E. J. Brill, 1959.

EDITOR'S NOTE

This bibliography is a good starting point for those beginning Taoist studies. It attempts to build on the earlier work of Soymié and Litsch (which, unfortunately, is now hard to find) by adding many new titles in Western languages, by including a few works by major Japanese scholars in the field, and by arranging the works alphabetically by author rather than topically. However, those seeking further references will benefit by consulting:

Doub, William. *Dōkyō kenkyū bunken mokuroku (Nihon)* [A bibliography of Taoist studies in Japan]. Colorado, 1972. Photocopied.

Kubo Noritada. *Dōkyō Shi* [A history of religious Taoism]. Tokyo: Yamazawa, 1977.

Ronbun Mokuroku [An index of articles], pages 419–439. Tokyo: Kokusho Kankōkai, 1976.

Soymié, Michel. "Bibliographie du Taoisme: Etudes dans les langues occidentales, seconde partie." In: Yoshioka Yoshityo and Michel Soymié, editors, *Dōkyō Kenkyū*. Volume 4, pages 290–225. Tokyo: Henkyōsha, 1971.

Soymié, Michel and Litsch, F. "Bibliographie du Taoisme: Etudes dans les langues occidentales, premiere partie." In: Yoshioka Yoshitoyo and Michel Soymié, editors, *Dōkyō Kenkyū*. Volume 3, pages 318–247. Tokyo: Toshima Shobo, 1968.

Thompson, Laurence G. *Studies of Chinese Religion: A Comprehensive and Classified Bibliography of Publications in English, French, and German through 1970*. Encino, Calif.: Dickenson, 1976.

Index of Romanizations and Corresponding Chinese Characters

hsien kuang ming 急急如律令唵吽
吒唎現光明

Chi-lu t'an-ch'ing yüan-k'o 給籙壇靖
元科

Chi shou kuei i san pao 稽首皈依三寶

Chi-tsang 吉藏

Ch'i 氣、契、炁

Ch'i-sheng 啟聖

Chia-i 甲乙

Chia-ju-k'ung 假入空

Chiang-kung 絳宮

Chiang-t'ai 絳台

Chiao 醮

Chieh-t'ou chu shen 解脫諸神

Ch'ien 乾

Chih 治

Chih Ch'ien 支謙

Chih-feng 執縛

Chih-hui-fo 智慧佛

Chih-i 智顗

Ch'ih-fa 勅法

Ch'ih-fu 勅符

Ch'ih-tzu 赤子

Chin-kang 金剛

Chin-k'uan 金冠

Chin-kuang 金光

Chin-kuang wang 秦廣王

Chin-t'an 禁壇

Ching 精、經、景

Ching-shen 景神

Ching-tai 清泰

Ching-t'u 淨土

Ching-t'u lun 淨土論

Ching-ying Hui-yüan 淨影慧遠

Ch'ing-ching 清淨

Ch'ing-shen 請神

Ch'ing nien chieh 青年節

Ch'ing-wei 清微

Chiu-k'u t'ien-tsun 救苦天尊

Chiu yü yu men 九獄幽門

Chou 周，咒

Chou-i ts'an-t'ung ch'i 周易參通契

Chou wen-wang wu wan kua 周文王
(之)五碗卦

Ch'ou en chiao 求恩醮

Ch'u chiang wang 楚江王

Chu chieh hsiao ti yü 鋸解小地獄

Chu-i t'ung-t'i 諸義同體

Chu-jung 祝融

Chu-wei-mo-ch'i-ching 注維摩詰經

Ch'u-kuan 出官

Ch'u-shih erh chen 觸事而眞

Chuan lun wang 轉輪王

Chuang-ch'en teng-yün 莊陳登雲

Chuang-lin hsü tao-tsung 莊林續道藏

Chuang-lin tao-tsang 莊林道藏

Chuang-tzu 莊子

Chuang-tzu nei-p'ien 莊子內篇

Chü-mang 句芒

Ch'ü-hsiang 取相

Ch'ü Yüan 屈原

Chūgoku bukkyō shisōshi kenkyū
中國佛教思想史研究

Chūgoku Jōdokyōrishi
中國淨土教理史

Chüan-hsü 顓頊

Ch'üan sheng 權聖

Chung 忠

Chung-kuo min-chien hsin-yang lun
chi 中國民間信仰論集

Chung shan 中山

Chung yang p'u ling ti yü 中央普掠
地獄

Chung yang yüan ling yüan lao i ch'i
t'ien chün 中央元靈元老一炁天君

Chung-yüan chieh 中元節

Dai-Nihon zoku-zōkyō [ZZK] 大日本
續藏經

Dōkyō to Bukkyō 道教と佛教

Erh-ti 二諦

Erh-ti i-shih yüan-ch'i fa-chieh 二諦
一實緣起法界

Fa-ch'ang 法場

Fa-chieh 法界

Fa-hsiang 法相

Fa-hsing ching-t'u tse pu-lun ch'ing
cho 法性淨土則不論清濁

Fa-hsing fa-shen 法性法身

Fa-hsing shih-li 法性實理

Fa-hsing-t'u 法性土
Fa-hsing wu-sheng 法性無生
Fa-hua ching 法華經
Fa-hui 法會
Fa-ku 發鼓
Fa-lu 發爐
Fa-shen 法身
Fan-fu 凡夫
Fan-sheng erh-t'u 凡聖二土
Fan-sheng t'ung-chu t'u 凡聖同居土
Fan-sheng t'ung-wang 凡聖通往
Fang 方
Fang-pien fa-shen 方便法身
Fang-pien yu-yu t'u 方便有餘土
Fang shih 放食
Fang Shui-teng 放水燈
Fen-i 分衣
Fo 佛
Fo-ch'a 佛剎
Fo-kuo 佛國
Fo-pao-shen 佛報身
Fo-ti-ching lun 佛地經論
Fo-t'u 佛土
Fo wu-ting suo-ying wu erh hsien 佛無
定所應物而現
Fu 符
Fu-chiang 副講
Fu-hsi 伏羲

Han 漢
Heng shan 衡山
Ho-ch'ang 鶴氅
Ho-t'u 河圖
Hou-t'ien 後天
Hsi-ch'ing 喜慶
Hsi fang chin kang ti yü 西方金剛
地獄
Hsi fang hao ling huang lao ch'i ch'i
t'ien chün 西方皓靈皇老七炁天君
Hsi-fang yao-chüeh 西方要決
Hsi nan fang t'u ko ti yü 西南方屠割
地獄
Hsi pei fang huo ch'e ti yü 西北方火車
地獄
Hsi wang mu 西王母
Hsia-yüan chieh 下元節

Hsiang 相
Hsiang-ching-t'u 相淨土
Hsiang-t'u 相土
Hsiang wu-hsiang 相無相
Hsiao 孝
Hsien-shih tsung 顯實宗
Hsien-shu 仙術
Hsien-tsai 現在
Hsin 心、信
Hsin-chai 心齋
Hsin-hsing 信行
Hsin-yin ching 心印經
Hsü 盧
Hsü chen-jen 許真人
Hsü-hui 許遜
Hsü-mi 許謐
Hsüan 玄
Hsüan chiao li ch'eng chai chiao i 玄教
立成齋醮儀
Hsüan-ming 玄冥
Hsüan t'ien shang ti 玄天上帝
Hsüan-tsang 玄奘
Hua 化
Hua mu lan 花木蘭
Hua shan 華山
Hua-shen 化身
Hua-t'u 化土
Hua-yang k'uan 華陽冠
Huai-nan 淮南(子)
Huai-nan-tzu 淮南子
Huang 皇
Huang-ch'üeh 黃闕
Huang hua kang 黃花崗
Huang-lu chai 黃籙齋
Huang-ti 黃帝
Huang-ti nei ching su wen 黃帝內經
素文
Huang-t'ing ching 黃庭經
Huang-t'ing nei-ching 黃庭內經
Huang-t'ing wai-ching 黃庭外經
Huang-t'ing wai-ching chu 黃庭外經諸
Hui hai ch'i szu ta tz'u tsun 廻骸起死
大慈尊
Hui-tsung 徽宗
Hui-t'u 穢土
Hui-yüan 慧遠

Hun 魂
Hun-tun 混沌
Hung-p'ao 紅袍
Hupei (province) 湖北

I 義，疑
I-chieh hao-ta 一切好大
I-fa-chü 一法句
I-hsiang 依相
I-hsiang ch'eng hsiang 一向乘相
I-shih-ti 一實諦
Indogaku bukkyōgaku kenkyū 印學
　佛教學研究

Jan-ching 染淨
Jan erh-ti tao li fei wu yüan ch'iu 然二
　諦道理非無緣求
Jen 仁
Jen-kuei 壬癸
Jen-wang p'an-jo ching 仁王般若經
Ju-chia-kuan 入假觀
Ju-i 如意
Ju-ju-fo 如如佛

K'ai-kuang 開光
K'ai-t'an 開壇
Kamata Shigeo 鎌田茂雄
Kan-lu 甘露
K'an 坎
Kao-shang yü-huang 高上玉皇
Ken 艮
Keng-hsin 庚辛
Keng tao chi 庚道集
Kiangsi (province) 江西
Ko hung 葛洪
Ko-tsao shan 閤皂山
K'o-i 科儀
K'ou-chüeh 口訣
Ku-ch'ang 孤塲
Ku-hun 孤魂
Ku-wei shu 古微書
Kuan-p'u-hsien-ching 觀普賢經
Kuan-shih-yin p'u-sa shou-chi ching
　觀世音菩薩授紀經
Kuan-wu-liang-shou ching 觀無量
　壽經

Kuan-wu-liang-shou ching i-shu 觀無
　量壽經義疏
Kuan-yin 觀音
Kuang 廣
Kuang-lüeh 廣略
Kuei 鬼
Kuei-jen 貴人
Kuei-men 鬼門
Kuei-wang 鬼王
K'un 坤
K'un-lun (mountain) 崑崙山
Kung-te 功德
Kung-te-fo 功德佛
K'ung 空
K'ung chia erh kuan 空假二觀
K'ung-chien 空見
Kwangtung 廣東
Kyōgyō shinshō 教行信證

Lao shu yao hsiao ti yu 老鼠鹹小地獄
Lao-tzu 老子
Lau-chün 老君
Li 理、離、李、哩
Li-ch'u chi-chen 立處即眞
Li sui wu-sheng 理雖無生
Li-tai san-pao-chi 歷代三寶記
Lieh-ying-shen 劣應身
Lien ch'i hua shen 煉氣化身
Lien ching hua ch'i 煉精化氣
Lin 林
Lin Ju-mei 林汝梅
Lin Ling-su 林靈素
Ling-pao 靈寶
Ling-pao five talismans 靈寶五符
Ling-pao ling-chiao chi-tu chin shu 靈寶
　領教濟度金書
Ling-pao t'ien-tsun 靈寶天尊
Liu an 劉安
Liu Chih-wan 劉枝万
Liu-ken 六根
Lo shu 洛書
Lu 籙
Lu Hsiu-ching 陸修靜
Lu-shan 廬山
Lu-shan Hui-yüan 廬山慧遠
Lü shan 閭山

Lüeh 略

Lüeh-ju 略入

Lum sai ho tang 林西河堂

Lung-hu shan 龍虎山

Mahāvairocana (see Ta jih fo)

Mantras (see Chou)

Mao shan 茅山

Mao shan shang-ch'ing 茅山上清

Mao shan shih-yeh 茅山師爺

Meng-p'o 孟婆

Meng-wei 盟威

Mu-yü 木魚

Ming 明

Ming t'ang 明堂

Ming-t'ung chi 冥通記

Mu-yü 木魚

Mudras (see Shou yin)

Muo-wang 魔王

Nan-chi ch'ang-sheng ta-ti 南極長生 大帝

Nan fang huo i ti yü 南方火翳地獄

Nan fang tan ling chen lao san ch'i t'ien chün 南方丹靈眞老三炁天君

Nanking 南京

Nao-t'an 鬧垓

Nao-t'ien 鬧天

Nei-ching 內經

Nei-kuan 內觀

Nei-tan 內丹

Ni-huan (or Ni-wan) 泥丸

O-mi-t'o-ching shu 阿彌陀經疏

O-mi-t'o-fo 阿彌陀佛

O-mi-t'o-fo-ching 阿彌陀佛經

O-mi-t'o ku-yin-sheng-wang t'o-lo-ni ching 阿彌陀鼓音聲王陀羅尼經

Pa-kua 八卦

Pa yen hsiao ti yü 拔眼小地獄

Pai-ho hsien-jen 白鶴仙人

Pai wai-yin 拜外陰

P'an-chiao 判教

Pang 榜

Pao 報

Pao fan chieh yin t'ien tsun 寶方接引 天尊

Pao-hua-fo 報化佛

Pao-hua-shen 報化身

Pao-p'u-tzu 抱朴子

Pao p'u-tzu nei-p'ien 抱朴子內篇

Pao-shen 報身

Pao sheng fo 寶生佛

Pao-t'u 報土

Pao-ying chih t'u 報應之土

Pao-ying t'u 報應土

P'ao-fa 跑法

Pei-chi 北極

Pei fang ming leng ti yü 北方冥冷地獄

Pei fang wu ling hsüan lao wu ch'i t'ien chün 北方五靈玄老五炁天君

Pei-ti 北帝

Pen 本

Pen-hsing ching 本行經 (本行集經)

Pen-ming 本命

P'eng-tsu 彭祖

P'i-lu Mao 毘盧帽

Piao 表

Pien ch'eng wang 卞城王

P'in 牝

Ping-ting 丙丁

P'ing teng wang 平等王

P'o 魄

P'o-sang yin-kuo 破喪因果

P'o ti-yü chou 破地獄咒

Preta (see Ku hun)

Pu-hao t'u 不好土

Pu-k'ung tsang 不空藏

Pu-ming wu fan-nao 不名無煩惱

P'u-tu 普度

P'u-tu kung 普度公

Ratnasambhava (see Pao-sheng-fo)

Śākyamuni (see Shih-chia-fo)

San chiao 三焦

San-ch'ing 三清

San-kuan 三觀

San-kuan-i 三觀義

San-lun 三論

San-nai 三奶

San-pao 三寶
San-shen san-t'u 三身三土
San-shih 三世
San-tung 三洞
Satō Tetsuei 佐藤哲英
Seng-chao 僧肇
Seng-jui 僧叡
Shang 上
Shang-yüan chieh 上元節
Shang-ch'ing 上清
Shanghai 上海
Shang-pei sheng 上輩生
Shao-hao 少昊
Shen 神
Shen-hsiao 神霄
Shen-hsien 神仙
Shen-nung 神農
Shen-tsou wen-chuang 伸奏文狀
Sheng 生
Sheng lieh 勝劣
Sheng-miao 勝妙
Sheng wu-sheng 生無生
Shensi (province) 陝西
Shih 事
Shih-chi 史記
Shih-chia fo 釋迦佛
Shih-ching-t'u 事淨土
Shih-fang 十方
Shih-hsiang 實相
Shih-hsiang li-fa 實相理法
Shih-pao-t'u 實報土
Shih-pao wu-chang-ai-t'u 實報無障礙土
Shih-sheng 實聖
Shih-shih yao-t'ai 施食瑤臺
Shih-ti-ching 十地經
Shih-ti-ching-lun 十地經論
Shinnyo ichiri 眞如一理
Shinshu seiten 眞宗聖典
Shou 壽
Shou-i 守一
Shou-lu 手爐
Shou-shan ko ts'ung-shu 守山閣叢書
Shou-yin 手印
Shu 疏
Shun-ching 沌淨

Ssu-chiao 四教
Ssu-ma 司馬
Su 俗
Su-ch'i 宿啟
Sui 隋
Sui-T'ang 隋唐
Sung 宋
Sung shan 嵩山
Sung ti wang 宋帝王
Szechuan 四川
Szu-ch'i 死氣
Szu-sheng 四生

T (see Taishō Shinshū daizōkyō)
TT (see Tao-tsang)
Ta-ch'eng i-chang 大乘義章
Ta-ch'eng t'ung-hsing ching 大乘同性經
Ta-chih-tu-lun 大智度論
Ta-chung yeh 大眾爺
Ta-fang-teng ching 大方等經
Ta jih fo 大日佛
Ta-k'ai men 大開門
Ta-shih 大師
Ta-shih yeh 大士爺
T'a-shou-yung 他受用
T'ai-chi 太極
T'ai ch'ing shih pi chi 太清石壁記
T'ai-hsi 胎息
T'ai-hsi ching 胎息經
T'ai-i 太一
T'ai-i t'ien-tsun 太乙天尊
T'ai-pao 太保
T'ai-p'ing 太平
T'ai p'ing ching 太平經
T'ai p'ing yü lan 太平御覽
T'ai-shan wang 泰山王
T'ai-shang ch'ih-wen tung-shen san-lu 太上赤文洞神三籙
T'ai-shih 胎食
Taishō Shinshū dai-zōkyō 大正新脩大藏經
Tan-t'ien 丹田
T'an 壇
T'an-luan 曇鸞
T'ang 唐

Tao 道
Tao-ch'ang 道場
Tao-ch'o 道綽
T'ao Hung-ching 陶弘景
Tao-p'ao 道袍
Tao-sheng 道生
Tao-te 道德
Tao-te ching 道德經
Tao-te t'ien-tsun 道德天尊
Tao tsang 道藏
Tao-tsang yüan-liu k'ao 道藏源流考
Te-i 得一
Tendai daishi no kenkyū 天台大師の研究
Teng-chen yin-chüeh 登真隱訣
Teng-kao chu 燈篙竹
Ti 帝
Ti-tsang 地藏
Ti-tsang wang 地藏王
T'i 體
T'i fei ch'eng huai 體非成壞
T'i-shen 替身
T'i-yung 體用
T'ien-hou 天后
T'ien-huang ta-ti 天皇大帝
T'ien-kung 天公
T'ien-t'ai 天台
T'ien-t'ai Chih-i 天台智顗
Tin-hau 天后
Tou-mu hsing-chün 斗母星君
Tōyō bunka kenkyū jo 東洋文化研究所
Ts'an-t'ung chi 參通契
Tsao-ch'ao 早期
Tso-wang 坐忘
Ts'un-szu 存思
Tsung-pieh 總別
Ts'ung-chen ch'ui pao-kuo 從真垂報國
Ts'ung-k'ung ju-chia kuan 從空入假觀
Tu-chiang 都講
Tu-jen 度人
Tu-jen ching 度人經
Tu ti wang 都帝王
Tung fang 東方, 洞房

Tung fang ch'ing ling shih lao chiu ch'i t'ien chün 東方青靈始老九炁天君
Tung fang feng lei ti yü 東方風雷地獄
Tung nan fang t'ung chu ti yü 東南方銅柱地獄
Tung pei fang hu t'ang ti yü 東北方鑊湯地獄
T'ung-shu 通書
Tung wang kung 東王公
T'ung-shih i-chien 同視異見
Tzu-shou-yung 自受用
Tzu-su 緇素
Tzu-wei ta-ti 紫微大帝
Tzu-yu (press) 自由出版社

Wai-ching 外經
Wai-tan 外丹
Wan-ch'ao 晚朝
Wan shou pao shan 萬壽包山
Wang-sheng lun-chu 往生論註
Wei Hua-ts'un 魏華存
Wei-lai 未來
Wei-mo-ching lüeh-shu 維摩經略疏
Wei-mo-ching wen-shu 維摩經文疏
Wu 無
Wu-ch'ang meng-chiang 五昌猛將
Wu-ch'ao 午朝
Wu-chi 戊己
Wu-chiao 沃焦
Wu-fang 無方
Wu-hsiang 無相
Wu-hsiang-t'u 無相土
Wu-hsin 無心
Wu kuan wang 五官王
Wu-lao 五老
Wu-liang 無量
Wu-lei yüan-shuai 五雷元帥
Wu-liang-i-ching 無量義經
Wu-liang-shou-ching 無量壽經
Wu-liang-shou-ching i-shu 無量壽經義疏
Wu-liang-shou-fo 無量壽佛
Wu-lou hsiang shih-hsiang hsiang 無漏相實相相
Wu-nien 無念

Wu-shang-i-ching 無上依經
Wu-shang pi-yao 無上秘要
Wu-sheng 無生
Wu-tang shan 武當山
Wu-ti 五帝
Wu-tso 無作
Wu-t'u 無土
Wu-wei 無爲

Ya 鴨、壓
Yang 陽
Yang hsi 楊羲
Yang kuang 陽光
Yen lo wang 閻羅王
Yin 陰
Yin-yang 陰陽
Ying 應
Ying-hua-fo 應化佛
Ying-shen 應身
Ying-tao 營道
Ying-t'u 應土
Yu 有
Yu chi 于吉
Yu-hsi shen-t'ung 遊戲神通

Yu-wei 有爲
Yu-wei chih tao 有爲之道
Yü 禹
Yü-chia Chi-yao Yen-kou Shih-shih I
    瑜伽集要焰口施食儀
Yü-huang 玉皇
Yü-huang ta-ti 玉皇大帝
Yü-huang tien 玉皇殿
Yü-lan 盂蘭
Yü-lan p'en ching 盂蘭盆經
Yü shan 玉山
Yü-wei k'uan 魚尾冠
Yü-ying-shou-chung tz'u-fo-shou-
    ch'ang 於應壽中此佛壽長
Yü-yüan 郁元
Yüan-shih chou (mantra) 元始咒
Yüan-shih t'ien-tsun 元始天尊
Yüan-shih wu-liang tu-jen miao-ching
    元始無量人妙經
Yüan-ying-t'u 圓應土
Yüeh-ling 月令
Yung 用

Zen 禪
ZZK (see Dai-Nihon zoku-zōkyō)

Index

Michael Saso earned degrees in Chinese studies from Yale (M.A.) and London (Ph.D.). He has taught at Fu Jen University (Taiwan), Sophia University, and the University of London, and is presently an associate professor of religion at the University of Hawaii. Among his publications are *Taoism and the Rite of Cosmic Renewal* (1972), *Chuang-lin Hsü Tao-tsang* [An encyclopedia of Taoist ritual] (1975), and *The Teachings of Taoist Master Chuang* (forthcoming).

David W. Chappell is a graduate of McGill (B.D.) and Yale (Ph.D.) and is presently an assistant professor of religion at the University of Hawaii. His research is in the area of Chinese Buddhism and includes such forthcoming publications as *T'ien-t'ai Buddhism: An Outline of Its Fourfold Teachings* and articles on the Fourth Ch'an Patriarch Tao-hsin (580–651) and on the Pure Land Patriarch Tao-ch'o (562–645) in the *Berkeley Buddhist Studies Series*.